Great American Post Offices

Great American Post Offices

JAMES H. BRUNS

Preservation Press

John Wiley & Sons, Inc.

NEW YORK CHICHESTER WEINHEIM BRISBANE SINGAPORE TORONTO

A cooperative publication with the National Trust for Historic Preservation, Washington, D.C., chartered by Congress in 1949 to encourage the preservation of sites, buildings, and communities significant in American history and culture.

This text is printed on acid-free paper.

Published by John Wiley & Sons, Inc.

Designed by Brian Noyes

LIBRARY OF CONGRESS CATALOGING-IN-PUBLICATION DATA

Bruns, James H.

Great American post offices / James H. Bruns
p. cm.
Includes bibliographical references and index.
ISBN 0-471-14388-X (pbk. : acid-free paper)
1. Post office buildings — United States — Pictorial works. 2. Post office buildings — United States — Directories. 3. Postal service — United States — History. I. Title.
NA4451.B78 1997 97-7457
725'.16'0973—dc21

Printed in the United States of America

10 9 8 7 6 5 4 3 2 1

There are simply too many postmasters who have furnished helpful information, photographs, and advice to acknowledge each one of them individually.

As a way of expressing the author's appreciation, this book is dedicated to America's postmasters, past and present.

CONTENTS

ACKNOWLEDGMENTS

IT WOULD HAVE BEEN IMPOSSIBLE to assemble all of the vignettes about the individual post offices that are presented here without the generous support and cooperation of the members of the National League of Postmasters and the National Association of Postmasters of the United States. Both organizations assisted in gathering the many stories and illustrations used in this book.

Individual thanks also go to Victoria Ballard and Amy Kaufman, research assistants for this project, and Meg Ausman, the historian of the United States Postal Service.

The author also is grateful to John Sorenson, Federal Preservation Officer, and William Loewenthal, Real Estate Specialist, of the Postal Service's Facilities office for their assistance in reviewing the manuscript and recommending much needed revisions.

Several special people and friends also reviewed portions of this work prior to publication, including Dr. John Weimer and Seymour Stiss.

A number of professional architects and engineers provided assistance in conjunction with this project, including James E. Moody and Glen Hopkins.

The following individuals from state historical preservation offices, historical societies and other public and private organizations provided significant information, photographs or guidance: Kathy A. Bailey, Charles Bennett, Jan Claves, Pat Duncan, Jim Gaynes, David Hedrick, Larry Hestdorfer, Jane Hightower, Katherine M. Jourdan, Maralyn Perry, Joe Pois, Doris Rich, Andrew Shick, Susan Shultz, Peggy Sinclair, and Brenda Williams.

Special thanks must also be given to present and past employees of the United States Postal Service, including: Jim Ahlgren, George E. Allen, Jimmie L. Bonner, Walter L. Borla, Felice Broglio, Lovenia Broussard, Scott Budny, Karl Camertsfelder, Joseph Cohen, Joyce Colin, Vincent Coreel, Willis Cox, Wayne L. Gibson, Ernest Gonzales, Deb Graham, Bob Hammervold, Rochelle Henderson, Charles Hightower, Susan K. Jones, Larry Jordan, Michael Kay, Dave Kolander, Dorthy A. Larson, Dan McCarty, Harris McCraw, Jr., Michael Miles, Ed Moore, Thomas C. Nucifore, Lenore Peterson, Nancy Ros, George T. Rowe, Theresa Scott, Valerie A. Thomas, Bob Uisnovckas, Carol Weiss, David W. Wild, Robert E. Winters, Shirley Wooster, and Ellen M. Young.

I should also acknowledge the key role played by Linda DeWitt in getting this project started in the first place, back in 1991.

TOP: *For much of the nation's history, the village post office served as the hub of the community and has represented the federal presence in small-town America.*

INTRODUCTION

American Post Offices

HIS BOOK BEGAN AS A SERIES OF anecdotal accounts, odd "would you believe" kinds of stories about post offices and postmasters. When it came time to look at actual buildings though, to see if they were still standing, I was dumbfounded by the void. Far too many of these buildings were gone: They'd been razed in the name of progress, fallen victim to tornadoes or floods, or been casualties of arson or of accidental fires.

Hopefully, though, enough of the original manuscript's storytelling quality remains to give this book about buildings a human side. I believe that this is an essential ingredient for a book about post offices, because they are principally human places.

In this respect, it should come as no surprise that many of the structures depicted in this book are less than "great" by architectural standards. This stems in part from the fact that before the mid-1800s the government did not really own many post office buildings—outside of the capital in Washington, D.C. The first marble building in Washington, was the General Post Office, designed by Robert Mills and constructed in the late 1830s.

There were few "great" federal buildings before the 1850s. By the late 19th century, however, the government began constructing post offices, usually as part of a building that housed various

PRECEDING PAGE, BOTTOM:

A rendering of Robert Mills's General Post Office, a building that housed the Washington, D.C., post office, as well as Post Office Department headquarters. This building until recently was still in use, although it no longer is associated with the postal system.

federal agencies. These buildings were restricted to larger communities, and these mixed-use offices were often grander than was necessary, but such an appearance was part of the nation's emerging image.

Smaller post offices, on the other hand, mirrored the growth of the communities they served. Hanover, New Jersey, is typical of countless other small towns; a series of buildings have housed its postal facilities. Its first post office was opened in the late 1700s in a private home. It moved into a general store in the mid-1800s. The community did not finally receive its own separate federally-owned post office building there until 1950.

Something else should also be kept in mind. This book is not only about buildings, it's also about the customers and communities served by the postal system. In this respect, the "greatness" of the buildings depicted here is derived from a combination of form and function.

MAIL HAS HELPED SHAPE THE CHARACTER AND WILL OF this nation's people. Perhaps Postmaster General John Wanamaker said it best in 1889: "The Post Office is the visible form of the Federal Government to every community and to every citizen. Its hand is the only one that touches the local life, the social interests, and business concern of every neighborhood." Because Americans from all walks of life, from all corners of the country, and from diverse ancestry receive mail, they share a common experience. We do not, however, all share the same-style post office. This book portrays post offices, not merely as a pictorial guide to architectural styles, but also as intrinsically social centers of the community.

The nation's postal system is the largest civilian employer of Native Americans, African-Americans, Hispanic-Americans, and Asian-Americans, as it has been for generations. For the elderly, it delivers loving missives from scattered friends and family, along with well-earned Social Security and retirement checks. For those raised on farms or in the country's rural hamlets, it brings merchandise from around the nation and the world directly to their doorstep.

Indeed, it does not matter where one lives, whether in an affluent suburb or the "inner city," whether in northern Alaska or at the bottom of the Grand Canyon, everyone receives mail!

Since the 1850s, the postal service has also provided a variety of public services that have little to do with mail delivery. It has distributed over a million pounds of free vegetable and flower seeds at Congress's request, gathered hog surveys and weather forecasting information, distributed tax forms, assisted in draft and Selective Service registrations, distributed food stamps, sold savings bonds and federal duck stamps to waterfowl hunters, and furnished flags for the burial of veterans.

To fulfill all these missions, the postal service has always needed buildings. Article I of the Constitution vested the federal government with the power "to establish post offices...." This was an essential mandate, for, as George Washington predicted, the postal service would be the principal means by which the people of the United States would be bound together in loyalty to the government. But, to make that dream a reality, the government had to create post offices. With the exception, perhaps, of local places of worship and schools, the local post office has frequently been among the largest buildings and generally the most important cultural structure in a town.

The general store and post office at College Hill, Mississippi, was the center of community life. Now undergoing restoration, this old post office is located across the street from the town's only place of worship, a Presbyterian Church where novelist William Faulkner was married.

SECTION I

History of the Postal Service

SOUTH
EAST

Post Offices Across a Young Nation

TAVERN AT THE END of Boston's Long Wharf served as America's first post office. This was a convenient point where ship masters could drop off and pick up overseas correspondence, which represented the bulk of colonial America's mail. The drop site was designated by the General Court of Massachusetts in 1639, which decreed:

> That Richard Fairbanks, his house in Boston, is the place appointed for all letters which are brought from beyond the seas, or are to be sent thither, to be left with him; and he is to take care that they are to be delivered or sent according to the directions; and he is allowed for every letter a penny, and he must answer all miscarriages through his own neglect in this kind.

Not much is known about the architectural details of Fairbank's Tavern. The only surviving description is from a deed of the property when it was sold in 1652. The property was described as a "dwelling house, garden and yard."

Similarly, New York City's first post office, opened in 1642, was in a coffeehouse. Coffeehouses were seen as a temperate alternative to taverns. New York's post office continued to be housed in a succession of coffeehouses, the last of which was the Merchant's Coffeehouse, located at Wall and Water Streets, from 1737 to 1804. These popular gathering places were ideal for letters to await the coming of their owners. They were described as "the headquarters of life and action, the pulsating heart of excitement, enterprise, and patriotism."

Postal business was relegated to a small portion of such places, if it was given any space at all. Architectural form was not the least bit important; and, judging from the comments of the time, function was not all that crucial either.

Over a century later, Charlestown, South Carolina, had much the same type of arrangement. Its post office was kept "in a room in the most frequented coffee-house in the most publick part of the town." The delivery system at this time in America's history was simple. Mail was either tossed onto a spare table, where it lay until claimed, or was dumped into a common basket or box that everyone could paw through whether they were expecting a letter or not. Another common practice was to tack a letter onto a board in a conspicuous space in the hope that

PRECEDING PAGE:

The interior of the post office at New York City was depicted elsewhere in this book as a tidy and orderly place in 1845. Operations had become chaotic by 1875, however, as depicted in this illustration.

Merchant's Coffeehouse, New York City, the city's post office from 1737 to 1804.

it would be noticed by the intended recipient, who had to pay the postage. The idea was for the addressee to collect his or her own letters, but more often than not, well-intentioned friends, family members, or strangers were willing to pay the postage in the expectation of being reimbursed later, and often carted off letters for the addressee.

Under these makeshift circumstances letters were frequently miscarried. Henry Callister, an exasperated Maryland resident, writing in 1761 to a friend, observed, "I know not by whom this will be handed you; it waits for the first traveler of good aspect." Callister had many bad experiences with the mails. The previous year he advised a friend:

> I have been mortified these two days by notice given me of a letter being seen at Georgetown [about nine miles from his home] directed to me with the postage marked on it. I sent to enquire about it yesterday, and find it was delivered to someone to be left at a certain place for me; I sent thither; but no letter was to be found. So that it is not likely I shall hear from you till you write again.

Occasionally, acquaintances and well meaning strangers carried mail containing money or bills of exchange, but not everyone was so kindly disposed. As the *Maryland Gazette* reported in 1753, this practice had its darker side:

> For want of due Care of such letters, in which the same are enclosed, no settled Post-Houses being appointed for the Reception of them, many times sundry evil-minded Persons find Occasion clandestinely to take such Letters out of the Public Houses, where they are generally left, and break open and conceal the same, to the great Detriment of sundry of the Inhabitants, Merchants, and Traders.

Jonas Green, the publisher of the *Gazette,* had first-hand experience of this type of theft, having lost about two hundred subscribers' payments.

One way around the thievery was to hire a private carrier. Colonial Americans frequently banded together to form cooperatives to employ mounted messengers, for which a fixed fee was charged. According to the summary of the 1764 *Moravian Diaries of Travels Through Virginia,* published in 1915, "Private messengers might always be sent, and were made much use of." Demand for this type of service was sufficient enough for riders to advertise. One Maryland rider was prepared to serve "as reasonably as any one" for those with an "occasion to send a Messenger to any Distant Part of this, or to any of the Neighboring Governments."

Architecturally, postal repositories had changed little by the 1790s. Joseph Habersham, who served as U.S. Postmaster General from 1795 to 1801, claimed that "There is scarcely a village ... of any consequence but is accommodated with the mail." The truth of the matter, however, was that there were only about 200 post offices nationwide. Post offices in the late 18th century continued to be located in taverns, coffeehouses, hotels, or other public places, with little space devoted to postal affairs. The post office at Woodbridge, New Jersey, for example, which opened on July 31, 1792, was known as Cross Keys Tavern. The proprietor, John Manning, hosted George Washington on the night of April 22, 1789, during his inaugural journey to New York. Years later, during the American Civil War, Samuel Moore's Tavern likewise served as Woodbridge's post office.

Private messengers were often the surest way of ensuring delivery of mail.

The postmasters' private homes also were used as post offices in some areas. The post office at Falmouth, Massachusetts, was run like one giant open house. "Every person who looks for a letter or a news paper freely enters [the postmaster's] home, be it post day or not; he cannot afford to set apart a room in his house as an office; he is continually disturb'd in his family," noted one passerby in 1773. The nuisance was so great that the postmaster freely admitted that he was more than willing to give up the job, if anyone else wanted it. The reason for this was far more than just personal, it was economic. Postal business was often conducted as an unprofitable sideline.

Early on, however, newspaper publishers realized how to make their association with the postal system pay. Many publishers were themselves postmasters, and for good reason. Being a postmaster was an ideal way of killing off the competition. Benjamin Franklin learned all about this firsthand. Franklin, the publisher of the *Pennsylvania Gazette,* and his rival, Andrew Bradford, publisher of the *Mercury,* went head-to-head over advertising in the 1730s. Bradford had the advantage, because as postmaster of Philadelphia he used his influence to exclude the *Gazette* from the mails. Bradford reasoned that the lack of visibility would prompt potential advertisers to conclude that Franklin's paper lacked the kind of circulation they desired, prompting them to advertise instead with him. But Franklin got around Bradford's ploy by bribing post riders to carry his newspaper. The need for such deviousness left a lasting impression on Franklin, however, who later replaced Bradford as postmaster. "I thought so meanly of the practice that when I afterwards came into his situation I took care never to imitate it," he said.

Another sentiment in late colonial days, expressed in countless newspapers, including the Newport, Rhode Island, *Mercury,* was that the Crown's post had to be replaced. "The grand design of establishing a new American post office, seems now to engage the attentions of all ranks. In our present situation, it is ... important and indispensable."

There was a need for something better, and Baltimore newspaper publisher William Goddard had an alternative. When Goddard's newspaper was denied use of the Crown's post because of his patriotic leanings, he created an alternative postal system, one that was well received. The *Connecticut Journal* of May 27, 1774, detailed the popularity of this rival post by announcing that "we have the pleasure of assuring the public that the subscription for establishing a new and constitutional post office was opened in this town last evening and has already met with great encouragement from many of the respectable inhabitants of this place." As this *Connecticut Journal* account reveals, Goddard's system had its limits. It was based upon subscriptions, only serving those of certain wealth. The subscribers were to have a hand in selecting the postmasters and would share the profits, if there were any.

Goddard also pressed the Continental Congress for permission to establish his "Constitutional Post" throughout the colonies. His two-and-one-half page petition, now in the collection of the National Postal Museum, was presented to the Continental Congress in 1774. It advocated that the Congress "establish an American Post Office" founded on Constitutional principles. This plan, in a modified form, ultimately helped lay the foundation for the United States postal system.

Goddard's scheme dramatized the urgent need to replace the Crown's post with one that could be trusted. Royal representatives had the authority to open mail, and they frequently used this privilege to snoop through the mails. As loyal subjects of the King, they felt compelled to ferret out disloyalty to England. Noted the *Mercury* on May 2, 1774, "a set of officers, ministerial indeed, in their creation, direction, and dependance, are maintained in the colonies, into whose hands all the social, commercial and political intelligence of the Continent is necessarily committed; which at this time every one must consider as dangerous in the extreme."

Rebellious Americans realized that they needed to replace the British system with one of their own. One of the greatest attributes of William Goddard's plan was its intent to preserve the sanctity of the mail. He promised that the mails "shall be under lock and key, and liable to the inspection of no person but the respective postmasters to whom directed, who shall be under oath for the faithful discharge of the trust reposed in them." The principle of the sanctity of the mail would become one of the strictest cornerstones of the American system that ultimately was created.

Another of the triumphs of the American Revolution was the recognition of the vital importance that books, magazines, and newspapers held to a republic. That was so apparent that the writers of the Constitution insisted upon both a postal system and a free press. The Congress went even further in 1792 with the enactment of the Post Office Act, which among other things called for the expansion of post roads, the sanctity of the mails, and the inclusion of general publications. In effect, the Act subsidized the press. It established cheap newspaper rates that remained in effect for decades. In the 1840s newspapers over 1,900 square inches in size could travel 100 miles for slightly more than two cents. Magazines and pamphlets were charged slightly more; but much less than the rate applied to a single letter composed of one piece of paper. Letter postage was twice that charged for periodicals.

The price break was an incentive to the distribution of news. It was a small price to pay for national unity. The rush of migration along and over the Allegheny Mountains was unsettling to government officials, who feared that without a functional free press, the frontier population might soon lose all sense of loyalty to the new Republic. This was a frightening thought to the nation's early leaders. In his first annual address in 1790, George Washington focused on the need to bind the nation together through the mails. His view was that "facilitating the intercourse between the distant parts of our country by a due attention to the post office and post roads" was imperative. A year later, in his opening address to the first session of the Second Congress, Washington again repeated the need to greatly expand service in the expectation of "diffusing a knowledge of the laws and proceedings of the Government, especially to some of the important points in the western and northern parts of the Union."

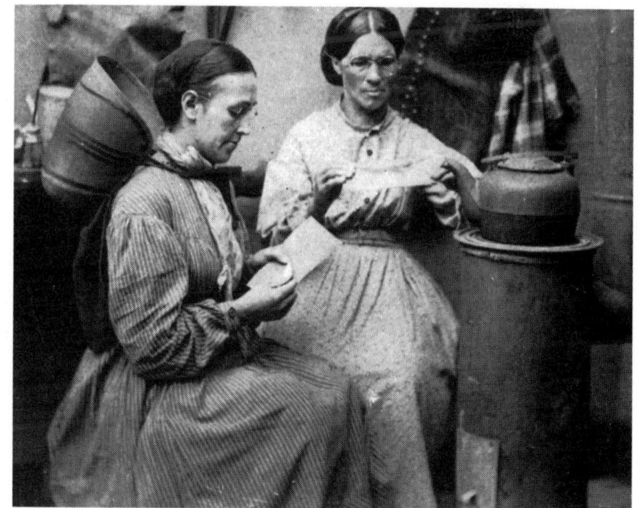

The ability to send and receive correspondence was considered a cornerstone of democracy.

This sentiment was echoed by Postmaster General Charles Pickering who, in 1793, stated that without a postal system "our fellow citizens in the remote portions of the Union ... will not only be embarrassed in their correspondence, but remain destitute of every necessary information. Their great distance from the seat of government and principal commercial towns subject [many Americans] to peculiar difficulties in their correspondence."

The view of Congress at the time was that "the establishment of the Post Office is agreed to be for no other purpose than the conveyance of information into every part of the Union." This pronouncement relieved the postal service of the burden of being a money-making proposition. Profits did not matter; service was more important.

Repeated attempts to make newspapers and periodicals pay more were vigorously opposed. Such publications were seen as "the strongest

This view of the post office at Roosevelt, Arizona, illustrates the connection between transportation and the mails.

bulwark of free government." Attempts to curb their exchange were envisioned as an "unconstitutional means of stopping in any degree the sources of that information which distinguishes America from the people of all other countries."

Statesmen, such as John C. Calhoun, fully appreciated this. His view in 1817 was that "The mail and the press ... are the nerves of the body politic. By them the slightest impression made on the most remote parts is communicated to the whole system." Further, writing in 1909 for the *Annual Report of the American Historical Association,* Cornell professor Julian P. Bretz noted that "everywhere the posts went newspapers sprang into existence, and by the time of the second war with Great Britain [the War of 1812], 33 had appeared in Kentucky and 31 in Ohio, while elsewhere the development was proportionate to the extent of settlement."

Postal Service Expands with the Nation

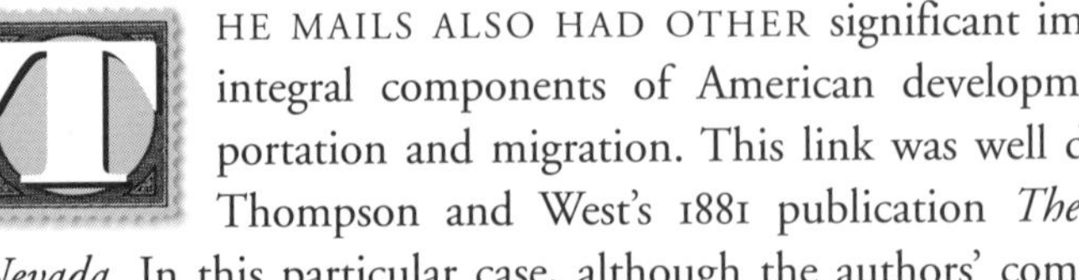

THE MAILS ALSO HAD OTHER significant impacts upon integral components of American development—transportation and migration. This link was well described in Thompson and West's 1881 publication *The History of Nevada.* In this particular case, although the authors' comments were specific to Nevada, with slight variation they just as easily could have applied to any other place in the Union. The writers observed that:

> The mails and express lines have borne an important part [in the growth of this country], penetrating the wilderness they have followed close upon the footsteps of the prospector, rendering aid and comfort in the development of the country. Wherever the miners made a camp the stage was quick to go. In the excitement of new discoveries of mines a rush of people would follow, a stage line would be put on, a mail route petitioned for, and post-office established. The National Government was generous in granting subsidies or

letting contracts for carrying the mail, and thus aided materially in maintaining [stagecoach] lines where the income was small and the necessity for such accommodations to important enterprise was great.

The railroads also contributed to the spread of people and the mail. Many communities, such as Cheyenne, Wyoming, in 1867, located the first post office in a tent. This particular railroad "tent town" grew from two settlers to a thriving community within six months, and daily mail began to arrive by train after November 1867, ensuring the prompt distribution of the latest news to an ever-expanding population.

The Post Office and the Press

BECAUSE OF CHEAPER POSTAGE RATES, newspapers constituted the bulk of the mail, thereby creating a profound impact upon the methods used to move the mail throughout our nation's history. Riders on horseback were unable to haul the quantities of newspapers entering the mail stream. Coaches, steamboats, and trains had to be used instead, and this reliance had a corresponding ripple effect upon the creation of post offices along road, rail, and inland-water mail routes.

The mails also furnished newspaper publishers with a wealth of newsworthy material. According to Hugh Finlay, the Crown's "Surveyor of Post Roads on the Continent of North America," a New London, Connecticut, printer "extracts all advice from newspapers, which requires considerable time; the New London paper is afterwards printed containing the extracts." In this case the publisher paid extra to have other newspapers carried by private couriers so he could have them 12 to 14 days ahead of the mail. This enabled him to scoop his competition.

Cheyenne, Wyoming's first post office was in a tent.

Newspapers, which were seen as exerting a patriotic nationalizing influence on the population, were often delayed because of being read and reread in transit. More often than not, it was the postmasters, who were also newspaper publishers, who did the reading, thereby creating the closest thing to a news service that early newspaper publishers could afford. Any delay of mail meant a

Oklahoma City's first post office amounted to little more than a pile of logs.

delay in timely reporting the news. The editor of the Frankfort, Kentucky, *Palladium* advised his readers on March 13, 1800 that, because nothing of importance arrived in the previous day's mail, he was publishing George Washington's will.

Occasionally the personal or political views of early newspaper printers collided with those of their community, threatening to literally bring the roof down on the post office. That certainly was the case in Baltimore, although in this instance the publisher was not a postmaster. By the beginning of the 19th century, Baltimore was the nation's third largest city. During the War of 1812, Federalist opposition to the war and Republican enthusiasm for it collided. In Baltimore, a Republican stronghold, the populace demolished the offices of the city's Federalist newspaper. The publisher succeeded in having subsequent editions printed elsewhere and shipped to Baltimore by mail, which further enraged the citizenry. Residents promptly turned on the post office, threatening to tear that building down also. Only hasty intervention by the militia saved the post office from the wrath of the angry mob.

Fortunately, this was not a common occurrence. On the contrary, the dissemination of news was essential to a republic, especially one with a growing frontier population. As a westerner, Andrew Jackson knew that all too well. In his first annual message, in 1829, Jackson described the mission of the postal service as being "to the body politic what the veins and arteries are to the natural body—conveying rapidly and regularly, to the remotest part of the system, correct information of the operations of the government. Through its agency, we have secured to ourselves the fullest enjoyment of the blessings of a free press."

Indeed, as the November 1843 issue of *Hunt's Merchants' Magazine* observed, "The publication of cheap papers containing the latest information in a familiar form, whatever objections may be urged against the quality of the matter contained in some of them, has been of immense influence in increasing the number of readers, and consequently the demand for reading matter."

Not everyone agreed with such sentiments, especially in light of the fact that newspapers had been carried either for free or at a greatly reduced rate of postage entirely disproportionate to the expense. In 1838, Postmaster General Amos Kendall complained that "the weight of letters is only three per cent that of newspapers, while the postage is ten times as much." Two years later, the complaint was that "printed matter constitutes ninety-five per cent of the whole mails, while it pays about twelve per cent of the gross revenue."

By 1848, the view was echoed again in the Postmaster General's *Annual Report:* "The postage on newspapers fails to pay their cost by one third of the postage, and is in the nature of a tax on letters for the benefit of the service that forced anxious editors to print less than first-rate newspapers."

There were other problems too. For more than 30 years before the Civil War, antislavery advocates were testing the bounds of the freedom of the press. Copies of the *Emancipator,* the *Liberator,* the *Observer,* and the *Evangelist* were being sent to the South by mail, making many Southerners extremely uneasy. The memories of the slave rebellion led by Nat Turner in 1831 were freshly aroused every time such literature arrived. Each issue provoked new fears of another revolt. Southern postmasters were caught in the middle of a conflict they were powerless to resolve. If they refused to deliver antislavery material they faced federal penalties; however, if they delivered it, they faced the wrath of local residents.

In 1835, the postmaster of Charleston, South Carolina, Alfred Huger, wrote to Postmaster General Amos Kendall for permission to reject antislavery publications. Huger feared that a mob might sack the post office at any moment, which they ultimately did. Irate residents forcibly removed the "incendiary publications" from the post office and burned them in the streets. Now Kendall was in the middle, and he took a politician's way out. He told Huger that he had "no legal authority to

The post office at Charleston, South Carolina, was ransacked in 1835 because of its abolitionist mail.

exclude newspapers from the mail, nor prohibit their carriage or delivery on account of their character or tendency, real or supposed." But, Kendall wrote, "I am not prepared to direct you to forward or deliver the papers of which you speak." Instead, he left everything up to Huger.

The simple fact was that real news was not always easy to come by. Sometimes it had to be borrowed. Taking news from another paper was an acceptable practice that continued well into the 19th century. In 1851 a Baltimore paper noted "The Southern mail has arrived, but the papers contain no news of importance." A decade and a half later another newspaper observed, "The mails by the *Asia* ... arrived at a late hour last night. There is nothing striking in the news. It is too late to make our usual extracts."

Even when it was difficult to gather other forms of reliable intelligence, information continued to be extracted during the Civil War. The April 7, 1862 issue of the *New York World* announced, "We have received from our correspondent at Nashville late copies (of six) Southern papers." As usual, segments of articles were copied verbatim, however, publishers had to be selective in the information they used, avoiding articles that might be considered pro-Southern. Newspapers publishing questionable material, or those that were clearly sympathetic to the South, risked swift retribution, as the publishers of the *Missouri Standard* discovered. The publisher was convicted in 1862 in military court on charges of publishing information for the benefit of the enemy and inviting rebellion. The conviction carried a mandatory expulsion order from the state for the duration of the war. His printing equipment was also confiscated and ordered sold for the benefit of the government.

Despite such risks, some newspaper publishers continued to freely exchange the news from one newspaper to another by mail during the war years without penalty, and readership rose. By 1875, five million newspapers reportedly were distributed daily by mail, roughly equal to two a week for every literate American.

For all their reliance upon the mails, printer/postmasters typically were stingy about providing space for conducting post office business. That was true from the colonial period to the late 19th century. In colonial Providence, Rhode Island, the post office was in John Carter's printing office. In the journal of his inspection tour of the colonial post office made in 1773-1774, Hugh Finlay noted that Carter did not actually devote any floor space to the post office as such, but did pledge to keep incoming letters under lock and key until the recipients came to call.

Such early printer/postmasters also had to deal with another postal problem, that of collecting postage. Before the second half of the 19th century mail could be sent either prepaid or collect. This allowed countless fees to go uncollected when mail was simply refused. Not wishing to get stuck with unwanted mail, some postmasters tried to lay down the law. The publisher of the *Continent of the North-west Territory*, who was also the postmaster of Cincinnati from 1794 to 1795, advised his patrons, "those who have a right to calculate on receiving letters and papers at this office in the future, must come prepared with cash in hand, or no letters or papers."

A Growing Need for Postal Facilities

LIKE TAVERNS, COFFEEHOUSES, and print shops, churches also served as early post offices. New York City's Post Office was once a church. Although beloved as a place of worship, it was hated as a post office. One old-time postal patron described it as "the dingy and gloomy old post office."

Dedicated in 1732, the Middle Dutch Church on Nassau Street had a rich history. During the American Revolution, British troops stripped its interior to house captured American patriots. When it was no longer needed as a prison, it served as a riding stable for British cavalry. The congregation got the building back after the British evacuated the city. By the 1840s, the church was put up for sale. The original asking price was $350,000, far too much for the Post Office Department, which did not really want the property anyway. Under pressure to buy the building, the postal service reluctantly said it was willing to pay $300,000, but no more. To make up the difference, local merchants hastily passed the hat for the rest.

When the second-hand post office was opened local residents were invited "to view the interior arrangement of the establishment," but the inquisitive crowds were shocked to see that not much had changed. Despite $80,000 worth of renovations, the pulpit and religious ornamentations were still in place. Even worse, the original occupants were still there too! The vaults underneath and around the church were left as they had been for 112 years—occupied! The buried human remains were finally moved; but, according to one account, "for a long time the spectacle was presented of coffins and mailbags, of carts and extemporized hearses, jostling each other while engaged in their allotted work."

The building received a steady stream of scorn, including this 19th century commentary: "There was nothing in the world so unsuited as [this] building for such a purpose.... The extravagance and folly of the federal government in buying property erected for a church, and attempting to alter it to accommodate a post office ... finds an illustration, but not an exceptional one, in this

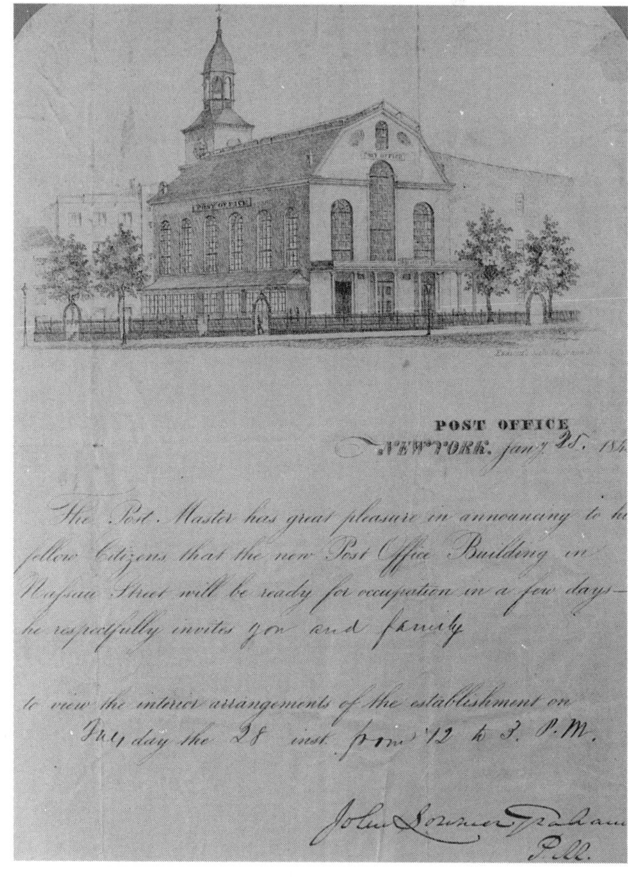

POST OFFICE
NEW-YORK. Jany 25. 184

The Post Master has great pleasure in announcing to his fellow Citizens that the new Post Office Building in Nassau Street will be ready for occupation in a few days— he respectfully invites you and family

to view the interior arrangements of the establishment on Tuesday the 28 inst. from 12 to 3. P.M.

John Lorimer Graham
P.M.

New York City's post office occupied an old Dutch Reform Church in 1845. It was extremely impractical and a city-wide joke. This invitation was issued to prominent citizens to inspect the "new" post office.

Local residents hated their second-hand post office, which never was as nice as shown here. It was always crowded and service was poor.

'high old Dutch Church post office.'" It was also said of the building that its "inconvenience, the necessarily miserable arrangement, the total unfitness of the place—inherently so by the original design of the building—has been a source of constant discomfort." These conditions were tolerated for approximately three decades.

Others accused "the old Dutch church in Nassau-street" of being the black hole for the metropolis' mail, and they had conducted experiments to prove their assertions. One publication did test mailings to see how long it took for mail to get to its destination; 14 letters were mailed in various parts of the city, between Central Park and the Battery, to an address in Cortlandt Street, roughly five minutes' walk from the post office. The letters took about 16 hours to get there, which by modern standards is fast! The bottom line at the time was that "once [letters] lodged [in the post office], the possibility of further delays are ample and varied."

New York City residents were quick to compare their flawed service to that of England. Residents of London enjoyed a vast contrast, there, city delivery service worked. A transplanted New Yorker, John Oxenford, voiced his opinion in *The London Times*, saying the "Suffering the inconvenience of [New York's] system, or rather no system, two or three times, I execrated the internal postal arrangements of New York in no measured terms, and loudly extolled the frequent 'deliveries' of London. ... the merchants and bankers perfectly sympathized with my execration, and envied the Londoner with his complete postal system."

American magazines also hammered away at the way we were "barbarously behind other nations." "In contrast with [London's] perfect institution, is it needful to describe the derangements, the difficulties, the methods of incommoding the public, which annoy our [largest] metropolis?" asked one popular periodical. "In this vast, enormously increasing, double or triple city, one of the things which most strikes a stranger with surprise and disappointment, and a well-informed citizen with shame, is the miserable deficiency of its postal accommodation."

Thankfully, by the mid-1870s, New York City had a new post office, a massive Second Empire building designed by Alfred Mullett. In vacating the old Dutch Reform church, city postal clerks and letter carriers sang "Auld Lang Syne" previous to the last day of service, and then on August 28, 1875, the clerks left the building in a formal procession, led by fifes, drums and flag bearers. The clerks each carried some of the old furnishing, such as chairs and stools, with them to the new building.

New York City's old post office was far from uncommon. Many of the nation's early postal facilities were mediocre. The post office in Salem, Massachusetts, was described as "a small mean-looking place" by a visitor in the early 1770s. Even after the Revolution, the postal system actually owned few buildings. Federal ownership would come much later and even then, those buildings were largely acquired secondhand. Postal service headquarters, for example, was housed in a converted hotel. During this nation's formative years, almost any building would do.

Between 1728 and 1882, the Philadelphia post office was located in about 20 different places, including, in the 1830s, the Merchant's Exchange. Such sites quickly fell in and out of favor. In 1863, Philadelphia's post office was considered "one of the most extensive and completely-appointed establishments of the kind in the country," but, by 1882, it was described as "wholly inadequate." In the cycle of fickle public opinion, its replacement was said to be "with the exception of the Chicago post-office ... the largest and most complete building of its kind in the Country," but that view would not last for very long!

Philadelphia's Merchant's Exchange served as the city's main post office before the American Civil War.

Fires contributed greatly to the turnover in post offices. No city was immune. On December 16, 1836, a fire broke out in the rear of the New York post office, then housed in the Merchant's Exchange on Wall Street. The blaze raged for 15 hours, consuming about 50 acres of the city's business district. Luckily, no mail was lost. Postal workers, along with some conscripted soldiers from Governor's Island, hastily evacuated the mail before the building was consumed.

Similarly, the Chicago post office went up in smoke when fire swept through that city on October 8 and 9, 1871, forcing postal officials to temporarily set up shop in a Methodist church. The following year fire destroyed the Boston post office, then

The Chicago post office was severely damaged during the "Great Fire" there. The heat was so intense that stamps literally fused together into charred blocks. One such block is part of the National Postal Museum's collections.

housed in the Merchant's Exchange Building. For a time following the fire, the post office was located in the Old South Church.

Despite such problems, there always seems to have been some sort of near mystical attraction to a post office. The November 1, 1882 issue of *Our Continent* described the lure of a big city post office when it observed, "There is, perhaps, no more promising field for the study of human nature in all its phases than a large post-office. Many and curious are the characters who daily resort hither to inquire for letters which never arrive, or who find in the bustling corridors a fascination which they cannot resist."

The Expanding System

HE ARRIVAL OF THE MAIL was one of life's great pleasures. Work stopped and church services occasionally ended early, just so that the mail could be collected. Typically this was an orderly process, but occasionally near riots erupted when things took longer than those waiting in line thought that they should.

The arrival of overland mail in the mid-19th century was dependent on the East/West mail corridors, a cross-country link that was served primarily by stagecoach routes and railway mail trains. Missouri was the acknowledged gateway to the West. It was the westernmost point reached by the railroads and telegraph in the late 1850s, and also the strategic starting point for the "Overland Mail" by stagecoach and the short-lived Pony Express. The Overland Mail, which started in 1858, initially followed a Southern route to California, dropping south from Missouri into Texas and then up through Arizona and New Mexico into California. The fact that the Overland Mail ran over a Southern route made Northern politicians uneasy, especially as the tensions between the North and the South mounted. Northern leaders were anxious not to allow California, with its vast gold resources, to be wooed toward the South, especially if push came to shove and open hostilities erupted. The Pony Express was a perfect alternative. It operated over a central route that totally skirted Southern territory, running from St. Joseph, Missouri, through Kansas, Nebraska, Colorado, Wyoming, Utah, Nevada, and into California. The Pony Express, begun in 1860, lasted 18 months, replaced by the transcontinental telegraph line. With the Pony Express gone, overland stagecoaches operating over roughly the

Railroads began transporting the mail in the 1830s, when mail remained in closed pouches between terminal points. Beginning in 1862 mail pouches were opened in transit to sort mail en route aboard "Railway Post Office" cars.

same route as the Pony Express continued to serve as the primary mail movers in the West.

The North/South mails were somewhat different, relying largely on a combination of steamboats, trains, and stagecoaches. By 1857, New York City was one of the nation's two largest import/export points. New Orleans was the other. Mail service between these commercial centers was crucial. The mail was conveyed over "the great Southern mail" route. The link was by railroad in relays from New York to Philadelphia, Washington, Richmond, Petersburg, Weldon (North Carolina), Wilmington, Kingsville, August, Millen (Georgia), Macon, and Columbus to Montgomery (Alabama). From Montgomery the mail went by coach to Stockton, where it was transferred onto steamboats for transport to Mobile and New Orleans. The whole relay was scheduled to take 11 days, but even Postmaster General Aaron V. Brown admitted in his *Annual Report*, "the instances in which [such] speed is actually attained constitutes rather the exception than the rule."

The cities along the principal East/West and North/South mail routes benefitted substantially in mail service frequency until the outbreak of the American Civil War. The service was twice daily between New York and Montgomery, Alabama, for example, and daily between Montgomery and New Orleans.

Postal Service in the Civil War Years

DURING THE CIVIL WAR, New York City continued to receive fine federal mail service, as did New Orleans after it was forced back into the federal fold by May of 1862, although the intermittent towns south of Washington, D.C., fell under the Confederate postal administration.

The Confederacy was organized in February 1861, and by June

included 11 states. John H. Reagan was appointed postmaster general in March 1861, and began establishing an independent Southern postal system. None of the lessons learned by the federal postal service during the first 60 years of the 19th century were lost on the South. On the contrary, the Southern postal administration was a quick study. It had to be! Mail service in the South was adequate prior to the war. This fact alone prompted several candidates for the position of Confederate postmaster general to decline the post. The common sentiment was "why saddle yourself with the possibility of failing to furnish the same caliber of service provided by the North?"

This same attitude was held by John Reagan. Not wishing to be remembered as the man who failed to provide good Southern mail service, he repeatedly declined the job of postmaster general, but Reagan ultimately relented. He proved to be an exceptional choice. One of his first acts was to consult with Union postal officials having Southern roots. He persuaded many to come South to help run the Confederate postal system. Furthermore, part of the deal was that these recruits were to bring as many examples of Union postal forms and contracts with them as they could. These documents were copied pretty much verbatim, except for the designation of the country of issuance: The Confederate States of America.

Former postal facilities remained in use in the seceded states, but communications between North and South soon became difficult. All regular exchanges of mail between Confederate and Union territories ended officially on June 1, 1861.

"Ladies Window" at the New York City post office, site of many traumatic moments during the early years of the Civil War, as sad news arrived from the battlefields. The emotional environment created by such scenes prompted the introduction of City Free Delivery Service in the North in 1863.

The Confederacy—blockaded, divided, and short of supplies—began to feel the mounting pressure of Union forces on its mail service by 1863. Union gunboats took control of the Mississippi River in 1863, dividing the Confederacy and forcing the South to devise a remarkable "trans-Mississippi" mail service that conveyed letters by rowboat under cover of darkness back and forth across the river. Other vital transportation centers were permanently lost, including Savannah, Georgia, which fell to the Union on December 21, 1864; Columbia and Charleston, South Carolina, captured on February 17, 1865; and Wilmington, North Carolina, taken five days later. After Richmond fell and General Robert E. Lee surrendered the Army of Northern Virginia, substantial Southern resistance soon came to an end. The Confederate government collapsed in May, 1865, and all fighting ceased in June.

The North experienced few war-related problems. On the contrary, the Civil War produced many new mail services in the North, services that have had a lasting impact upon American life, including Money Order Service and City Free Delivery Service.

New Delivery Service

REE HOME DELIVERY OF MAIL was a direct outgrowth of the Civil War. Its origins were humane reaction to the "Ladies Windows," provided in many major post offices more than a century ago. During the American Civil War "Ladies Windows" were often scenes of great emotional trauma. According to one wartime recollection, it was not uncommon for "packets of unclaimed letters, dictated by the loving, patriotic hearts [to be] returned to the mother, wife, or sweetheart, bearing the formal, but terrible endorsement of the adjutant of the regiment [that the soldier had been killed]." This cold notice was often the first word the family and friends behind had of the horrible fate of their beloved. For postal workers, returning such mail was said to be "almost like stabbing the recipient in the heart to hand them such a fatal gift." The looks of unutterable anguish that followed haunted mail clerks long afterward.

Joseph Briggs, a Cleveland postal worker who witnessed these heartbreaking scenes, convinced the city's postmaster that the humane thing to do was to deliver the mail to these anxious families at home, so that if they had to grieve, they could do so in privacy. To test his notion, Briggs even volunteered to serve as the city's first free letter carrier, and his idea proved to be an instant success.

The Post Office Department soon duplicated Brigg's system of home delivery elsewhere. On July 1, 1863, City Free Delivery Service was inaugurated in 49 Northern cities. Within a year, 17 additional communities were being served; and by 1880 the number had grown to 104. By the start of the next decade, 454 cities offered free delivery. This was a boon to business, a convenience for postal patrons, and a great enhancement to the local political power base and patronage-dispensing position of large urban postmasters.

City Free Delivery Service was confined to urban centers with populations of 10,000 or more or with annual postal receipts amounting to at least $10,000. By the early 1900s only about 1,500 cities were able to meet those requirements. These urban areas had combined populations of 45 million.

Rural Free Delivery, which began in 1896, served another 20 million residents, leaving approximately 30 million small town and village dwellers without adequate free delivery service until 1912, when "Village Delivery Service" was introduced.

The start of Rural Free Delivery at Lafayette, Indiana.

The primary objective of City Free Delivery Service was to prevent the congestion at general delivery sections of larger post offices. Rural Free Delivery Service and Village Delivery Service, on the other hand, was provided to patrons of smaller post offices, with slight exceptions to provide greater frequency of service and access to the mails, keeping customers from having to travel to their local post office for their mail. However, by the early 1900s rural and city letter carriers were not permitted to deliver mail to inhabitants dwelling less than a quarter mile from a post office, those living in an unincorporated village, or residing within the incorporated limits of any town or village. The elimination of these restrictions, which finally came about with the introduction of Village Delivery Service in 1912, meant that all Americans received free home delivery of their mail.

Political Patronage and Post Offices

MOST AMERICANS KNOW that Abraham Lincoln was a postmaster, but few are aware that he was appointed by Andrew Jackson. Lincoln did not think much of the political aspects of his postmastership. He thought that patronage was laughable, particularly since he had not even voted for Andrew Jackson. He had voted instead for Henry Clay, but was willing to accept a commission from the Jackson administration as a loyal Jackson supporter, his first job for the federal government, because he viewed the position as "too insignificant" to really make "politics an objection." His post office salary, a percentage of his gross receipts, probably amounted to somewhere around $55 a year, yet Lincoln enjoyed some of the other perks of the office, including the ability to send letters for free under the franking privilege and being exempt from jury duty or military service. Yet the benefit he appears to have enjoyed most was the opportunity to read other people's newspapers.

Although Andrew Jackson is generally credited with "inventing" the spoils system, in fact, it was Thomas Jefferson, who, observing that federal workers seldom die and never resign, introduced this system by replacing 10 percent of the federal workforce with individuals who supported him. For Jackson, however, 10 percent was just a beginning. By 1829, the number of post offices had grown to 8,050, a ninefold increase since 1800; and the newly elected President included William Barry as the first Postmaster General in the President's Cabinet. Under Jackson and his completely loyal Postmaster General, the mail service became an integral part of the political machine, the principal patronage-dispensing agency for the party in power. With this, politics and the spoils system became an invasive way of business for the Post Office Department and the Government as a whole. According to a House of Representatives Report for 1835, "since the 4th of March 1829, removals of postmasters have not fallen much short of 1,300 and in a great majority of the cases [the removals were made] without assignment of any cause."

Political appointments, however, worked against the postal system, dominating the attentions of postal officials, to the detriment of much needed operationally related concerns. By 1840, Postmaster General John Niles was so overwhelmed by requests for patronage that he claimed that visits by office seekers and their Congressmen took up half of each day. He believed that his only hope for getting any work done was to wait for Congress to adjourn.

Other presidents and their postmasters general enlarged the practice of patronage. Following Zachary Taylor's inauguration, 30 percent of all federal jobs were redistributed. When Abraham Lincoln took office, he

Many small-town postmasters, such as the one who operated this Illinois post office in the 1890s, were political appointees, selected for supporting the political party that won the White House.

swept out 1,457 of the 1,639 officeholders under his control. Despite the numbers of positions filled, there were always more office seekers than positions available. It seemed that nearly everybody expected a federal job in exchange for political favors. While traveling to Gettysburg to make his historic address, Lincoln contracted a mild, short-term, yet highly contagious disease. The fever did not keep the job seekers away. When he returned to Washington they descended upon him anyway. Jokingly, President Lincoln told his secretary, "Let them all come in. At last I have something I can give to everybody."

Lincoln was among the first to admit openly how intrusive the issue of political patronage had become. It was impossible to please everybody. New politicians soon discovered the meaning of the old Washington adage about dispensing patronage: Every time you got someone appointed to a federal position you created one ingrate and 20 enemies.

Shortly after his inauguration, Lincoln confided to a friend:

> I have trouble enough; when I last saw you, I was having little troubles; they filled my mind full; since then, I have big troubles and they can do no more—what do you think has annoyed me more than any one thing? Now, I tell you; the fight over two post offices—one in Bloomington [Illinois] and the other in Pennsylvania. That is the thing that is troubling me most.

Local postmasters were the leading political figure in many small communities. This particular post office was at Marta, Texas.

Lincoln's first postmaster general, Montgomery Blair, was equally beset with requests for patronage. At one point, job petitioners so besieged Blair that his brother-in-law complained: "Blair is nearly run to death with office seekers. They left him at 2 this morning and commenced at 8 this morning."

Political patronage was a curse. Each new administration was plagued by job seekers who flocked to Washington like locusts. The attention they demanded sapped much of the creativity of newly elected politicians and freshly appointed postal officials.

These postmasters, once appointed, were a potent force. As noted in a 1905 issue of *McClure's Magazine,* "In every community, the postmaster was usually a leading representative citizen." At the start of this century, the American Academy of Political and Social Science called them a powerful political army that was at the beck and call of the President and could exact great influence in securing favorable legislation for the party in power. These were the grassroots stalwarts. However, while this cadre represented the lifeblood of the prevailing party, its members were often careless, ignorant, and defiant when it came to postal affairs, and perhaps for good reason.

To keep their jobs, it was not uncommon for postmasters to contribute anywhere from a small portion of their annual postal income to many times their yearly postal salary, to their political party machine. A typical letter was sent to postmaster John B. Decker by the New Jersey Republican State Executive Committee in 1872. This particular "Dear John" letter conveys a none-too-subtle threat:

> I see that you are postmaster of Clove, Sussex County, and that your income thereof amounts to $13.00 per annum. Of course you desire the re-election of Grant—as all other good office-holders do—and we will expect that you will practice your desire thereof by forwarding your salary for the past four years. Viz. $52.00. Please remit to Joseph Soor, Jr., Treasurer, Newton, New Jersey. In case you do not get a leg over the traces [which roughly translates to "support the right candidate"] I will be obliged to have [someone else] appointed in your place.

The average compensation of the 20,000 fourth-class postmasters in 1905 amounted to less than $50. There was clearly a lack of incentive. The "lack of attention to their duties, for lack of knowledge as to laws and forms, and for an occasional display of independent spirit is a legitimate outgrowth of poorly requited service," stated *McClure's Magazine.*

General stores were common sites for small post offices.

Henry A. Castle, the auditor for the Post Office Department from 1897 to 1904, complained publicly in 1906 that [fourth-class postmasters] ignorance of postal rules and regulations was far more noticeable to the postal officials than to the public; but, their indifference was obvious to both. It was hard not to notice how some kept their own office hours. For many, it seemed that Friday was sort of a day off to go fishing.

But, despite the poor pay, these postmasters were more than willing to make do with that meager amount in exchange for keeping their post. The real boon for these fourth-class postmasters was that the post office brought folks into their shops. Most post offices were located in general stores, and patrons would, more often than not, do their shopping at the same time and place where they picked up their mail. This was particularly important because storekeeping was risky business, with a high rate of turnover. Most village shopkeepers were typically general merchants who sold homegrown or homemade goods bought in as barter, as well as manufactured items bought from eastern wholesale houses. Sales principally consisted of food, particularly coffee, tobacco, spices, molasses, and flour; household items, such as clocks, cutlery, crockery, and tin ware; clothing items, such as suspenders and shoes; fabrics; luxury items, such as ribbons and decorative combs; and notions, such as needles and thread.

Many small merchants failed because they operated on a shoestring, financed by borrowed money that had to be paid back typically within six months to a year. At the same time they often had to sell things on credit or through barter. These types of transactions often did not provide enough ready cash to pay off the store owner's debts when notes came due. Because of this, it was not uncommon for shopkeepers to occasionally disappear in the night, abandoning their businesses, often leaving what remained of their merchandise behind, or to sell out cheaply to some other optimistic entrepreneur. Clearly, because of the financial risks involved in keeping a shop, politics was only one reason for the high rate of turnover among postmaster/merchants.

There tended to be a high rate of turnover among those postmasters who operated small general stores.

Purchased jobs and patronage permeated nearly all aspects of the federal government, especially the Post Office Department, which was Uncle Sam's largest civilian employer. During 1881 the total federal work force reached 100,000. The practice of patronage was a prime concern

of political parties prior to the 1880s.

Change was sorely needed. As Ulysses S. Grant observed: "The elevation and purification of the civil service of the government will be hailed with approval by the whole people of the United States." And so it would be. The change came literally with the speed of a bullet.

On the morning of July 2, 1881, a dejected office seeker—Charles J. Guiteau—shot President James Garfield in a Washington, D.C., railway depot. Guiteau's motive was revenge for not receiving a federal job he felt he had earned through his efforts as a loyal campaign worker.

Spurred by the public outrage over the shooting, Ohio Senator George H. Pendleton introduced a reform act in the Congress designed to "Regulate and Improve the Civil Service of the United States."

The Pendleton Act—enacted January 16, 1883—was a beginning, a foundation upon which much needed and overdue reforms could be built.

It helped ensure efficient and stable government operations by gradually placing more and more federal jobs under a system of competitive selection and promotion. It forbade the payment of assessments for employment or political purposes, eliminated much of the needless personnel turnover, provided a degree of job security, and provided for the creation of a three-member bipartisan commission to administer the law.

Appropriately enough, the appointment of the first employee under the merit system was a postal worker, Ovington Weller, appointed to a Maryland post office as a clerk on August 29, 1883. However, progress was slow.

The importance of the extension of the federal Civil Service Act cannot be overemphasized. As President William McKinley observed during his second inaugural address, "Honesty, capacity, and industry are nowhere more indispensable than in public employment. These should be fundamental requisites to original appointment and the surest guarantees against removal."

Politics, however, continued to play a part in federal appointments during the early 20th century. At the end of his four-year term, from 1909 to 1913, President William Howard Taft was more than happy to be rid of the office. He confessed to his replacement, Woodrow Wilson, "I'm glad to be going. This is the lonesomest place in the world." After leaving office Taft suggested firing all postmasters in one fell swoop. All of them, he said, "are, as a class, uneconomic and superfluous." To his way of thinking, such a move would save $4 million; and besides, it would be easy "doing away with them and paying only the deputies, who do most of the work anyway."

According to Taft, "the deputy postmaster, named under the civil service, could and should be the chief executive, and we would have an end to this system of interminable politics and waste."

Thousands of letters and resumés began arriving at the offices of Democratic congressmen and senators following the election of Woodrow Wilson. One contemporary magazine observed "Every Democrat who did the slightest bit of campaigning is reminding his

Congressman of the fact, and the demands are just beginning."

A key Democrat told *R.F.D. News,* the journal of the National Rural Letter Carriers Association, "There will not be more than one out of a thousand seekers who can be rewarded. It is too bad, of course, but there won't be enough pie to go around." The real prize for many of these Democratic pie-hunters was a fourth-class postmastership.

Wilson's choice for postmaster general was Albert Burleson. A fanatic on efficiency, Burleson replaced 5,765 postmasters within the first 176 days of his administration. Of these postings, 2,203 were "Presidential Postmasters," officeholders who received in excess of $1,000 annually and whose appointments had to be confirmed by the Senate. Burleson's actions drove rank-and-file postal workers crazy.

Much to the relief of postal employees, with the election of Warren G. Harding, Will Hays replaced Albert Burleson. Hays, however, stayed only one year. During that brief period he learned firsthand how hard it was to please not only office seekers, but party functionaries. Republicans faulted him for not dumping as many Democratic postmasters as they believed he should, while the Democrats charged that he had made too many Republican replacements.

Hubert Work, who became postmaster general in 1922, oversaw the appointment of 17,774 new postmasters. He boasted that "those entering the service have been carefully selected and are taking an interest in, and making a success of, their new duties to a degree that is most gratifying to the Department."

In 1922 the nation had 834 first-class postmasters. These were high-paying positions, with salaries ranging from $3,200 to $8,000. Salaries were not constant; they were largely based upon the receipts of the individual post offices for the previous calendar year going into effect at the beginning of the regular fiscal year in July. Only five postmasters made the highest amount.

The postmaster at Fort Wayne, Indiana, received an increase from $5,000 to $6,000 in 1922 as a result of increases in receipts of over $119,000. He was one of the 66 postmasters who received the second highest level—$6,000. Ten first-class postmasters received $5,000, including those at Long Island, New York, and Augusta, Maine. Twenty-one postmasters, such as those from Camden, New Jersey; Lansing, Michigan; and Lancaster, Pennsylvania received $4,500. Twenty-five received $4,200, and 36, including the postmasters at Poughkeepsie, New York, and Asheville, North Carolina, received $3,900, while those at East St. Louis, Illinois; Champaign, Illinois; and Parkersburg, West Virginia, were among the 49 who received $3,800. Of the rest, 52 postmasters received $3,700; 69 received $3,600; 70 received $3,500; 101 received $3,400; 116 received $3,300, and the remainder received the lowest amount paid to first-class officeholders.

During the Great Depression federal jobs were a coveted prize, a trophy that Postmaster General James A. Farley dispensed with particular relish. Farley, who was a remarkable postmaster general in many respects, had the astounding ability to always remember a name.

Postmasters would meet him once, and when they went eye to eye again, even if it was years later, Farley would remember their names. Rarely did this trait fail him, although renowned journalist Sander Vanocur knows of one occasion when Farley suffered a lapse. Vanocur recounted the event in 1996, while moderating a panel discussion of former postal officials in conjunction with the 25th anniversary of postal reorganization. At a memorial for Al Smith, Vanocur recalled, "James Aloysius Farley, the man who never forgot a first name, came over the rope, puts his fingers in my chest, and hits me a couple of times and said 'It's going just like I told you two weeks ago, isn't it, Stanley.'" This slip got back to John F. Kennedy and the folks running the Kennedy campaign, who from that point on out began referring to Sander Vanocur as "Stanley."

As has already been noted, politicians were always at risk of making one person happy by making a political appointment, while at the same time making a boatload of enemies because of that same job. Hence, over the years, some in Congress became so fed up with the constant bickering over patronage-related positions that they elected to let their constituents decide. This idea was a long time in coming. In 1894, *The Arena* estimated that the average postal appointment was decided in a matter of minutes, prompting the publication of an article urging "The election of postmasters by the people." Opponents claimed that the strongest argument against this idea was the Constitution itself, which did not provide for popular elections of postmasters.

Many Congressional leaders simply did not care. They only wanted to be rid of the hassles associated with supporting postal appointments. Such elections proved popular. Residents of Fishkill Landing, New York, were given the right to vote for their postmaster in the early 1900s. A similar election was held in 1912 in Leroy, Kansas, at the urging of Congressman Fred S. Jackson. The winner, with 554 votes, was Esther Abbott, daughter of the town's recently deceased postmaster. Her opponent received 71 votes. This process proved to be so easy that Congressman Jackson pledged to fill all postal vacancies in his district by popular election.

Others in Congress favored the exact opposite approach: They cherished the ability to appoint postmasters, and rural letter carriers, and were willing to stop at nothing to keep such perks in place. Timothy May, who served as the General Counsel for the Postal Service in the late 1960s, remembers all too well the reaction he received from Senator James Oliver Eastland, one of the most influential senators and the chairman of the powerful Judiciary Committee, when he was asked to allow the postal service to sack one of the employees under his patronage. Timothy May went to Senator Eastland and dutifully laid out the problem as nicely as he could. May remembered that Eastland was gracious and attentive, but when it was time for his response, the Senator stood his ground, saying something to the effect that "You go back and tell Postmaster General Larry O'Brien and his boss, the President, that there will never be another Federal Judge confirmed for the remainder of the Johnson Administration" if that employee was fired. The troublesome employee stayed.

Politics versus Prejudice

FREQUENTLY IT WAS DIFFICULT to separate politics and prejudice. In August 1884, Postmaster Thomas G. Robinson hastily resigned his post in Bamberg, South Carolina. In his resignation letter to Postmaster General Walter Q. Gresham he explained the cause, saying that on August 10, an armed band of 10 to 12 men besieged his house. They fired shots into the home and demanded that he either resign or die. Robinson, an African-American who had become postmaster on December 27, 1883, did not have much choice. According to Robinson: "One of them said that if I would resign the office at Bamberg within 30 days and sign a petition in favor of Mrs. Varr, widow of the late postmaster, I could have that chance; if not, I would be killed at once. I was well near frightened to death and accepted the proposition. They finally concluded that I should not return to the office, and if I dare come they would kill me without a doubt."

Postmaster General Gresham was furious over the attack. He dispatched a postal inspector to investigate. To his surprise, the inspector discovered that the intimidation in Bamberg was not due to racial prejudice. It was politically motivated. "The moving cause of the whole trouble is that another party desires the office and his friends took this course to get the present incumbent out," the inspector advised postal service headquarters:

> I learned from Postmaster Robinson that trouble for some time had existed between himself and Frederick Nix, another [black] Postmaster at Blackville, South Carolina, on account of the Chairmanship of the Republican County Committee, both of them being aspirants for the position. I also found that Postmaster Nix was particularly friendly to the brother of the lately deceased Postmaster at Bamberg, and they desired his appointment to the place now occupied by Robinson, all of which, I am of the opinion, had something to do with the attack upon Robinson.

Robinson was temporarily persuaded to hold on to the postmastership, ultimately being replaced by D. F. Hooten on April 21, 1885.

While patronage was admittedly a poor way to fill the federal ranks, it did afford one opportunity; it provided many minority Americans with a chance at the American dream. Today, tens of thousands of minorities work with pride for the United States Postal Service, but such dedication was not always welcome, or possible. In the first half of the 19th century, federal law prohibited African-Americans from handling mail. The ban that barred Blacks from handling mail was first recommended in 1802 by Postmaster General Gideon Granger, a Southerner who, along with Southern members of Congress, evoked visions of potential bloody slave uprisings if such steps were not taken. Granger's thinking was captured in a letter to a Georgia Senator. He said that a Black employed in the carriage of the mails would soon "get to know too much to know his rights." This recommendation became law in 1810 and was finally repealed during the American Civil War.

Even after legal barriers fell, prejudice and injustices frequently remained. F. B. Baker, an African-American from Lake City, South Carolina, was lynched on February 22, 1898, for accepting an appointment as postmaster, and the postmaster at Humphreys, Arkansas, was forced to resign in 1904 when his post office was dynamited. Despite this and other atrocities, Black Americans continued to accept postal positions.

Most of these early Black postmasters were storekeepers who held appointments as fourth-class postmasters, conferred by the postmaster general of the United States.

John T. Jackson, Sr., received his commission as postmaster for Alanthus, Virginia, from Postmaster General John Wanamaker on March 23, 1891. As postmaster of a fourth-class office, Jackson was not paid a salary. Instead, he received a commission that was based on the value of the stamps he sold. His commission for his first partial year of service in 1891 was $12.18. The following year he received $107.95.

Jackson, who was 29 years of age at the time of his appointment, proudly served as Alanthus's postmaster for 49 years. When he retired as postmaster on January 31, 1940, he was one of the oldest Black postmasters in the United States.

Lillie G. Jackson, John Jackson's wife, served as acting postmaster for Alanthus from February 1, 1940, until July 28, 1940, when the fourth-class post office was closed. Mail service for the residents of Alanthus was then transferred to Brandy Station, Virginia.

In 1989 the National Postal Museum acquired the sorting case used by John Jackson at Alanthus, Virginia, from 1891 until 1940. The case was provided under the terms of the Will of Sara Jackson Tut, John and Lillie's daughter. She willed this family relic to the Smithsonian because she believed it symbolized her family's access to mainstream America, access ensured by the postal services' willingness to appoint her father because of his integrity and ability, not his race.

John Jackson's countertop post office cabinet, like countless others of that time, was produced by the Corbin Cabinet and Lock Company of New Haven, Connecticut. By the late 19th-century, post offices were common in the general stores of small communities. Merchant/postmasters, such as Jackson, typically purchased mass-produced countertop post office units for their postal business.

The Cost of Doing Business

THE COST OF FURNISHING their own post offices was a considerable hardship for many postmasters. Interior window units varied. Most tended to be simple arrangements, but others might have elaborate lobby units, known as "screenlines." When fourth-class postmasters lost their jobs most had to figure out what to do with their post office window units. Often these were purchased by the next postmaster, who simply moved it into his or her business establishment.

The Post Office Department did not furnish much. Fourth-class offices were supplied with eight-ounce balance scales, plain facing slips for identifying the destinations of bundles of mail, canceling ink, stamp pads, and marking devices. If the annual receipts topped $100, twine and wrapping paper were also provided. Other than that, the local postmaster furnished everything else.

John T. Jackson's sponsor, John Wanamaker, successfully managed the financing of the 1888 Republican campaign. Wanamaker was appointed Postmaster General in 1889 by President Benjamin Harrison. At the outset Wanamaker stated the policy that guided his entire term as postmaster: "The post office is not a money-making enterprise. It is not intended to be, and it is a mistake to expect it to be self-sustaining until it is perfected." He believed that reliable mail service was in the public's interest, and concentrated his efforts on improving this service. As a result, the number of post offices increased, and so did the volume of mail and the revenues of the Post Office Department.

Women in the Postal Service

WOMEN HAD A SOMEWHAT easier time gaining employment than did Blacks. The British Crown appointed several female postmasters, including Mrs. Lydia Hill, who is said to have served as postmaster at Salem, Massachusetts, prior to her death in 1768.

Appointed by her brother, William, in 1775, Mary Goddard served as the postmaster for Baltimore, Maryland. She was the only female postmaster to serve under the short-lived "Constitutional Post," which William created. This system provided service for several months prior to the creation of the American postal system under the Continental Congress. Mary Goddard's service was continued until 1789, when she was removed from office for purely political reasons by Postmaster General Samuel Osgood. Her dismissal angered many in Baltimore. A petition bearing the signatures of 230 citizens was submitted to Osgood, but he refused to consider reinstating her. Appeals were also made on her behalf to President Washington and members of the Senate, but no one bothered to intervene on her behalf.

Elizabeth Cres(s)well is probably the only other woman to serve as postmaster before 1789. Postal Service records show her serving at Charleston, Maryland, in 1786.

On September 27, 1792, Mrs. Sara DeCrow was appointed postmaster at Hertford, North Carolina. She was the first female appointed following adoption of the United States Constitution.

Several other women accepted postmasterships within the next decade, but the appropriateness of each appointment began to be questioned. Although he had no personal reservations about her capabilities, or those of any other woman, Postmaster General Gideon Granger was reluctant at first to appoint Rose Wright as postmaster at Harrisburg, Pennsylvania, in 1814. His reluctance was based upon the counsel of others. "Doubt has been suggested to me from a source that I ought to respect as to the strict legality of appointing a female and on a careful examination of the Law, I incline to ... believe that the doubt

Female postmasters served with great distinction in many communities.

may be well founded," Granger advised N. B. Boileau, secretary of the Commonwealth of Pennsylvania.

The traditional use of the masculine pronoun throughout the text of the Post Office Law of 1810 gave rise to questions about women serving as postmasters. While the law does not specifically forbid women from serving, the use of masculine pronouns as substitutes for "postmaster" appears to have been construed as eliminating females from consideration for the post. Granger hastily resolved this issue in favor of Mrs. Wright, who was appointed within a month of the initial dispute. However, Postmaster General Cave Johnson interpreted the intent of the law differently. In 1847, Johnson maintained that women could not handle the responsibilities of running larger post offices, although they could perhaps manage smaller offices just fine. He wrote in a letter:

> It has not been the practice of the Department to appoint females... at the larger offices; the duties required of them are many and important and often of a character that ladies could not be expected to perform; the personal supervision of the duties within the offices; the receipt and dispatch of the mails at all times of the day or night; the constant watch necessary to be kept over the conduct of contractors and carriers and other agents of the Department; the superintendence of mail service generally within the vicinity of the office; the pursuit and arrest of mail depredator; the prosecution for violations of the Post Office laws; are duties that could not be dispensed with at such an office as Columbus [Ohio] without serious injury to the public service and could not with propriety be exacted of a lady.

The distinction between a "larger" and "smaller" post office was open to interpretation and was perhaps further blurred by politics. At the same time Cave Johnson wrote the letter cited above, women were serving as postmasters at Lancaster, Pennsylvania, and Columbia, Missouri. Both of these offices were the fifth largest in those states. In addition, Greenville, South Carolina's postmaster was a woman who had that state's tenth highest postal income.

Female postmasters increased in number during the latter half of the 1800s. By the turn of the 20th century, roughly 10 percent of the nation's 70,000 postmasterships were held by women. These postmasters could be just as effective in dealing with difficult situations as their male counterparts, although occasionally some unruly customers thought that because they wore a dress they could be toyed with.

That mistake was made by two patrons who frequented the post office run by Mrs. Gustave A. Root. When the two became unruly in her fourth-class Colorado office in 1912, she produced a pistol and threatened to "blow the tops of their heads off." She took up a horsewhip and chased the boys out of the office, ordering them never to return. One of the banished pair complained to postal service headquarters in Washington, D.C., stating that he was afraid to get his mail after that and wanted the matter attended to at once. Instead, postal officials in Washington thought that congratulations were more likely in order, since other postmasters were having similar problems, but were not as assertive in handling them.

A particular case in point was Bernard Isaacs, who appealed to the Postmaster General for permission to close his post office at Gueydan, Louisiana, during mail distribution time because he believed that the post office was in danger of "annihilation" on account of the actions of patrons who insisted on punching each other while waiting for their mail. "I have called on the civil authorities to put down these riots in my office," he wrote, adding that "I have used every threat in my power in the hope that order might be restored. I believe that if you write an order

Rural letter carrier, 1993.

to close the office in event such disorders continue it will have the desired effect."

Whether male or female, small town postmasters sometimes went too far, treating patrons at worst as if they were criminals, or at best like constant pests. The repercussions could be quite dramatic, as in the case of one town in the Southwest, where the entire population went on strike in 1904. All 1,200 residents boycotted the post office because of the postmaster's attitude. The citizens held a town meeting and elected to neither send nor receive mail until they either received a new postmaster or were assured of better service. Postal officials in Washington hastily appointed a new postmaster.

By 1943, the number of female postmasters was up to 17,500, followed by a slight decline by 1958, when the Post Office Department observed that "lady postmasters" served in 15,751 offices.

Today, many of the nation's largest mail-processing points, known as Management Sectional Centers, are headed by women. A mail center typically is located in different sections of the country at key transportation junctions that are served by rail, truck, and plane. These facilities handle vast amounts of mail, typically worth $500,000 or more per year in postage.

Whether the candidate was a woman or a man, the appointment of postmasters based solely upon political favoritism ended forever in 1971, with the creation of the United States Postal Service.

"Uncle Jerry's" Legacy

NYONE VISITING NORWOOD, GEORGIA, today would probably wonder how anything of importance to the nation could ever have happened there. It has nothing to commend itself to anyone traveling along U.S. Route 228, unless your car is running low on fuel. It is an aged hamlet with little more than a tiny post office and a town hall, both set well back off the highway, and two gas stations that front onto opposing sides of the same two-lane thoroughfare.

Miss Emmie Jones, one of the town's oldest living residents, admits that time has been unkind to Norwood. "It has changed so much," she says. Miss Emmie knew Norwood in its greener years, when its streets were lit by acetylene lamps, and telephone service was furnished by five separate companies. When cotton was still king, Norwood was one of the brightest jewels of Warren County. It was a thriving mill town located along the Georgia Railroad tracks, part way between Augusta and Atlanta. It had two drug stores, a fine hotel, two mercantiles, a grist mill and cotton gin, a Y.M.C.A. Hall (a rarity for any rural southern town at the time), two physicians, and more than a dozen other small businesses.

In a reflective moment in 1993, Miss Emmie Jones recollected the passing of the families that were so prominent a part of her youth.

Most of the town's founding families now reside in the Norwood cemetery at the end of Massengale Street, just within the Norwood city limits. Miss Emmie's hometown is teetering on the edge of extinction. Time has defaced all of Norwood's former luster. It has laid waste to the antique plantation houses that once were served by "Uncle Jerry," the town's unofficial letter carrier. Gone, too, is his daily starting and stopping point—the Massengale general store, which also once served as the post office. Massengale's was replaced by a brick bank building early in this century, which, in its own turn, now stands derelict, half fallen down. Time has also wreaked havoc upon the boarding house where Tom Watson, an ambitious young man, humble in origin but great in destiny, lodged while clerking for old man Massengale.

In spite of its faded glories, the town of Norwood is very important to our American heritage for two reasons. First, Norwood remains the home of some 280 Americans, and second, something did happen in Norwood nearly two lifetimes ago, something that changed the face of the nation. Only Miss Emmie and a few others living in Norwood have any real memory of what Uncle Jerry, "Dosh" Massengale, and Tom Watson did for Norwood and for the nation.

Uncle Jerry is not included among those honored dead that lie in the Norwood cemetery. Blacks were not buried there! No one knows for sure where he was finally laid to rest, although the general consensus is that he lies buried somewhere on the Ray family plantation. In life, nothing gave him the appearance of greatness. He looked every inch a raggedy man: with a patch over one sightless eye and tattered clothes that others once owned. He was born a slave, the property of Mercer Elliott of Warren County, Georgia, in the days before the Civil War. He began life as Jerry Elliott, but after Emancipation, "Parsons" was the name he chose for himself, although no one is sure why. He settled with his freed wife Julie in a raw log cabin on the plantation of Shadrack and Albert Ray. To the children around Norwood, Jerry was known as "Skushman." To most of the adults, he was affectionately known as "Uncle Jerry."

The earliest known attempt to provide rural mail service was a home-brewed delivery scheme involving Uncle Jerry. Jerry was never actually a full-fledged postal worker. He carried mail as part of his keep. In 1868, he began delivering the mail to six of the leading families around Norwood. Among his patrons were former Congressman John H. Hall, the Ray brothers, Jerry Scott, George Parham, and Henry W. Smith.

Uncle Jerry's years of slavery had taken their toll. By the time he started delivering the mail, he was already becoming an old man. His gait was stooped and labored, and the heavy mail sack, slung over one shoulder, did not help his back much. Yet in spite of all this, his patrons never knew him to complain. According to George Ray, one of Shadrack's grandsons, Parson's days began with pretty much the same meager breakfast. In 1961, Ray told Gene Ownes of the *Chronicle State,* "He used to love to take coffee—he did not care how old it was or how many grounds there were in it—and crumble cold or hot biscuits in it. Then he would pour molasses in it to sweeten it and sprinkle it with black pepper. That was his breakfast."

For Uncle Jerry, the average day began at sunrise. After breakfast, Parsons would chop wood in town until about 11:15 a.m. Then, he would walk down to the Georgia Railroad tracks, which ran straight through town, to recover the pouches of mail as they were kicked from the passing railway mail trains. By 11:30, he would hand off the mail pouches to the postmaster, Theodosius Massengale, who separated the mail in short order. By noon, Uncle Jerry was back on the road. Day after day, for nearly four decades, Jerry Parsons trudged his ten-mile route, carrying letters and parcels from town, and bringing the outgoing mail back to Norwood.

Parsons was not one for taking the long way around. If he had been, his daily circuit around Norwood would have been an exhausting ordeal. In the peak of summer, Norwood's reddish clay roads were parched and dusty. In the deepest winter, those same paths were transformed into muddy rivers resembling flows of thick blood-toned gumbo. To avoid these conditions, Parsons devised his own shortcuts, which included cutting across a creek. Of course, Parsons was in no physical shape to wade the creek or jump from rock to rock each day. So, with some rudimentary engineering, he constructed his own crude bridge and maintained it throughout his letter-carrying career.

Even when Rural Free Delivery Service was officially offered to Uncle Jerry's families, shortly after the turn of the century, Uncle Jerry's patrons declined government service. They had grown attached to this weary, broken old man, and they did not want anyone else carrying their mail. In all his years of service, Uncle Jerry never delivered a letter to the wrong family. This always amazed the heads of the households since it was always assumed that Uncle Jerry was illiterate, which was one of the conditions of his "employment." Postmaster Massengale assured his customers that Uncle Jerry was completely illiterate but that he possessed a fine memory that prevented him from making mistakes.

A letter carrier who could not read? Even William Shakespeare, who lived more than 300 years earlier, saw the irony of a mailman who could not read the address on an envelope. In Act I of *Romeo and Juliet,* when Lord Capulet sends his illiterate servant to deliver invitations to a dinner party, the hapless servant chances to meet Romeo, who deciphers the invitations for him. This unfortunate encounter between Romeo Montague and this servant of the Capulets sets the whole play in motion: If Capulet's messenger had been taught to read, it probably would have saved the lives of those four fresh corpses (Tybalt, Paris, Romeo, and Juliet) that lay in the Capulet family burial vault at the end of Act V (not to mention Mercutio and Lady Montague, who died elsewhere in Acts III and V, respectively).

Fortunately, no such catastrophe ever befell the rural families of Norwood, at least not on account of Jerry Parsons. That's because Parsons probably could read, at least well enough to know the name on an envelope. The children along his route suspected this all along. You see, Uncle Jerry was the sole agent of their "underground mail." The local children had created their own clandestine system of distributing messages, especially missives of affection, and the duty of delivering these very personal letters fell to Uncle Jerry.

One of these children was Leonard R. Massengale, the son of the local postmaster in Norwood. In 1908, Massengale wrote an article, summarized in *The Postmaster's Advocate,* in which he describes the role that Uncle Jerry played in their secret communications network. According to Massengale's article:

> Along his route lived many of the prettiest and sweetest girls in all Warren County, and many letters and notes has (Parsons) carried from the boys in town to some expectant maid in the country. All of these girls are married now and many of them are grandmothers. I have heard one of these ladies relate how "Uncle Jerry" used to bring her notes from her sweetheart in town, and although her parents objected to her receiving notes (Parsons) would always faithfully deliver them, never making a mistake, and always doing so in a way the old folks would never catch on. If the old people were present when he passed by, he would never let on that he had a letter at all, but would go on by to an (outbuilding) behind the "Big House," where he would place the love epistle in a secret crevice, and, returning in the morning, would always find another in its place to deliver to the waiting lover in town.

Under such circumstances, any mistake on Uncle Jerry's part would have been disastrous for the young Romeos and Juliets of Norwood, but Massengale insists that no such accidents ever occurred. Not bad for a man who, supposedly, could not read!

Another one of the Norwood children was Tom Watson. Watson was not originally from Norwood; he came from Thomson in the neighboring county of McDuffie. With his family suffering from the hard times following the Civil War, the 14-year-old took a job with Theodosius Massengale as a clerk in the Massengale grocery store and post office. "Dosh" Massengale, as the old store owner was known, watched over red-headed, freckle-faced Watson, treating him much as he would one of his sons. The shopkeeper felt a special kinship with the boy. Massengale had been about Watson's age when his own father died, leaving him to take up clerking for his Uncle Alfred's mercantile in Thomson, Georgia. Now, the tables seemed reversed. Old man Massengale was finally able to repay Uncle Alfred's kindness by helping another young man in the same predicament.

The elder Massengale shared other traits with Watson. Like the boy, Massengale had a quick temper, especially when it came to the local children pestering his guinea fowl. He also possessed a keen sense for always doing the honorable thing. Watson shared both of these characteristics, earning him a reputation for being something of a crusader. In truth, he simply respected people for who and what they were. He especially felt protective of those who were unable to fend for themselves. Once, when a drunken bully, described by Watson as "of robust size and strength," attacked an old cripple in the Massengale store, the teenager came to the lame man's rescue, brandishing a knife used for cutting cheese, and rebuking the bully sharply: "Don't you hit him again!" While Watson's verbal authority was impressive, it was probably the knife that was the real persuader.

Tom Watson worked hard for old man Massengale, and when he was ready for college, Massengale loaned him enough money for books. Unfortunately, Watson was born with more ambition than assets; Halfway through his sophomore year, he had to withdraw from Mercer University for lack of funds. Watson, however, was not that easily defeated. He continued to pursue his education with the same passionate intensity that he had shown years earlier when he nearly got himself into a knife fight with the town drunk to save the life of an aging cripple. After Watson left the university, he began to study law under the Honorable W. R. McLaws, a judge from Augusta. After less than a month of studying, Watson was admitted to the Georgia bar.

As a youth, Thomas Watson knew all about Uncle Jerry. He saw him every day when Uncle Jerry came into Massengale's general store with the mail sacks. Watson's knowledge of this early attempt to provide rural mail service would be useful to him later in life. In the early 1890s, Congressman Thomas E. Watson introduced a bill before Congress to create an experimental Rural Free Delivery Service.

At that time, national Rural Free Delivery was a hotly debated issue; almost nobody believed it could work, much less pass through Congress. But Watson's firsthand knowledge of Uncle Jerry's years of service was a constant reminder of how important such service really was, and that it really could work.

Many members of Congress dismissed the idea of providing any type of rural mail service, arguing that the costs involved with such a system would bankrupt the nation. Watson did not agree. He believed that it was not simply a matter of money, as so many of his contemporaries believed. Watson argued, "We are collecting enough money in this country by taxation to extend this free-delivery system to every hamlet and every cottage in all the broad limits of the Republic." Sufficient funding was available; it only needed to be properly redirected. Furthermore, Watson was certain that Rural Free Delivery would generate enough additional postal revenues from rural customers to cover a significant chunk of the costs associated with the system.

In a debate, when an opponent condemns essential and inexpensive national services under proposal as being too expensive, the logical counter is to point out existing nonessential services that cost more than they're actually worth. Watson set out to do just that. His target: harbor, river, and building projects. He questioned how the nation could afford to spend so much money on outlandish "pork barrel" projects like the dredging of harbors and rivers and building opulent structures, while ignoring the need for universal nationwide free delivery.

Watson's view was that "when there are 48-percent of the custom-houses of this country which cost more to maintain than they collect, it must be apparent that those custom-houses, maintained sometimes at a distance of a thousand miles from the seacoast, are maintained for the special benefit of the importers, and not for the general benefit of the citizens at large." In 1892, these operations cost approximately $3 million. This was money, Watson said, that could be applied "to the further extension of mail facilities, the spreading of intelligence, education, and refinement among all the people." It was simply a matter of setting the correct priorities: goals that provided the greatest good for the greatest number of Americans:

> I am not asking for special favors to be granted to a few. But I would like to see a general system inaugurated that would provide an equal distribution of the mails all over the land, in cities, in town, in hamlets, and at the cottages of the people, where all the taxpayers would get some of the benefits of that magnificent system. Let us have one efficient system for the rich as well as for the poor.... I say that if we save ... a fair percentage that could be saved on river and harbor appropriation bills, for instance, we would have an aggregate sum of between five and ten millions of dollars at our disposal with which we would be enabled to distribute the mail to all parts of the country.

This was what Watson argued.

Rural delivery would truly be a democratic enfranchisement. Wealthy planters, as well as sharecroppers, Black farmers as well as White, all could equally avail themselves of this service. In this respect, it would become the nation's greatest rural empowerment, one that helped to foster farm alliances across racial and economic boundaries. This was an important goal for Tom Watson, a Populist who saw rich and poor, Blacks and Whites in the same boat on most agricultural-related issues. His view was that "You are kept apart that you may be separately fleeced of your earnings. You are made to hate each other because upon that hatred is rested the keystone of the arch of financial despotism which enslaves you both."

RFD was something that worked to the farmers' advantage for once. This was a substantial change, especially since in the past such things as credit, freight charges, and fair market prices had oftentimes been stacked against them, particularly the smaller farmers.

In an ironic twist for Watson, one of his political enemies, Lon Livingston of Georgia, a man who Watson hotly accused of betraying farmers, struck one of the first effective blows in the fight to gain nationwide rural delivery. He asked for Congress to earmark $100,000 "for experimental rural free-delivery outside of towns and villages." While many objected to the cost, Livingston defended his proviso by saying that:

> Millions of laboring people in this country are clamoring for free delivery. Suppose they think it is practicable. Have they no right to have the experiment made? Are they not the taxpayers of this country? Do not the burdens of this country chiefly fall upon their shoulders? If they believe it to be practicable, why not let the experiment be made at this trifling cost of $100,000?

Whether it was a trifling amount or not did not much matter. Livingston's amendment was ruled out of order because it could not be carried out within the framework of the existing law. Now Watson acted. In place of the Livingston amendment, Tom Watson proposed a more moderate approach that would have used a portion of an existing allocation, approved on October 10, 1890, while keeping Livingston's idea of service "outside of towns and villages" intact.

The original 1890 action called for the Postmaster General "to test at small towns and villages the practicability and expense of extending the free-delivery system to offices of the third and fourth class, and other offices not now embraced within the free delivery." John Wanamaker, the postmaster general in 1890, had done just that, instituting an experimental free delivery in 48 small towns and villages. But this was not rural enough for Watson. It excluded, he said, the:

> Absolutely rural communities, that is to say, in the country pure and simple, amongst the farmers, in those neighborhoods where they do not get their mail more than once in every two weeks, and where these deserving people have settled in communities one hundred years old and do not receive a newspaper that is not two weeks behind the times.

Watson's proposal, initially introduced during the first session of the 52nd Congress, called for an amendment to an existing expenditure to provide "for free-delivery service, including existing experimental free-delivery offices, $11,254,900, of which the sum of $10,000 shall be applied, under the direction of the Postmaster General, to experimental free-delivery in rural communities other than towns and villages."

But others argued that there was nothing to amend. The joint resolution that was approved in 1890 allowed for the use of $10,000 to test the feasibility of experimental delivery in small towns, and that amount had indeed been spent in fiscal year 1891. There was no getting around this fact, and it became the anvil upon which Watson's idea was beaten to a pulp. On this score, Congressman Blount of Georgia hammered home the fact that "those tests have been made, the money has been used, and the Postmaster-General has reported the results to Congress."

The following year, Congress passed a unanimous resolution to allocate another $10,000 to continue testing on Rural Free Delivery. These funds were in the process of being spent while Watson was making his pitch. Watson's opponents, hoping that the approval of another $10,000 would be enough to keep Watson quiet, insisted that with nothing to spend, there was nothing to discuss. Watson and many of his allies refused to accept this tactic. Among his supporters, Watson's approach was seen as a reasonable follow-up to the 1891/1892 tests. Representative Compton, for one, could not believe what was going on. "What do you make experiments for?" he exclaimed. "What is the object of an appropriation [totalling] $20,000 on the part of the Government to make an experiment? Is it simply to squander a sum of money in an unprofitable and fruitless venture and expect, as soon as it is ascertained that it is advantageous or desirable it is to be dropped and discontinued?" Common sense, he said, dictated the opposite view. Watson's amendment sought to build upon a good thing by expanding the approach slightly to include more rural communities. To Compton it was plainly a case where "the purpose of the experiment is to try it in the interest of the people, and with the money of the people, and if successful to continue it thereafter."

Despite Compton's passionate attempt at persuasion, Watson's amendment did not come to a vote. Undaunted, Watson tried again during the second session of the Fifty-second Congress, requesting an appropriation of $10,000 to be used to provide much-needed mail service. On the second go-round, he was joined by the powerful Chairman of the House Committee on Post Office and Post Roads, John Steele Henderson, and this time the effort succeeded. It was a small win. Certainly $10,000 would not go far, but Watson was a patient man. He realized that his modest RFD measure was only the beginning. It was simply a matter of getting one foot in the door.

Unfortunately, the battle over rural delivery was played out against Watson's populist beliefs. This did not sit well with the leadership of the Democratic Party, which strongly doubted his loyalty. The loyalty issue quickly degenerated, taking on the form of a steady stream of deeply personal insults leveled against Watson. Many of his Democratic colleagues picked over his past, like ravenous vultures at mealtime.

The Georgia congressman had nothing to hide. He was particularly proud of who he was. He was unashamed of the fact that, like most middle Georgia families in the wake of Sherman's march to the sea, his was particularly hard hit by the Civil War. He was proud of receiving a common-school education, a level of instruction that he jokingly boasted was "very common." He felt privileged to have attended Mercer University in Macon, Georgia, with the help of his mentor, Theodosius Massengale, even though he had had to drop out half-way through his sophomore year because of a lack of money. He was thankful for the opportunity to read law for a few weeks under Judge W. R. McLaws of Augusta and for promptly being admitted to the Georgia bar. In later years the relative ease with which he was admitted to the bar prompted a fellow member of the Congress from Kentucky, who also was a lawyer, to tease him about the admissions process. Characteristically, Watson unsheathed his wit and went on the attack. "It is not very hard to get admitted to the Georgia bar—not much harder than it is to get admitted to the Kentucky bar [and] I believe you are a member of that," he curtly retorted. His law practice began in Thomson, Georgia, the place he considered home, in November 1876.

The red-headed Watson was also proud to have served as a member of the Georgia legislature in 1882/1883. And he was equally honored to have been a Democratic elector for the State at large in 1888. Some years later he admitted that he had not been all that devoted to politics and great reforms. "Like a thousand other young men in Georgia, I had my hands too closely to the work of making a living to know much on these questions, which I had never understood before," he confessed in 1892. At that time his greatest accomplishment was having been elected to the 52nd Congress as a Democrat pledged to farm reforms, receiving 5,456 votes to 507 for his opponent.

Watson was not the least bit ashamed of his populist views. They were never a secret from his party, and they certainly were not unknown to the people who elected him—they were at the heart of why he was elected! "I was nominated and received the standard of those people," he proudly told fellow Democrats. "The nominating convention told me to stand by the subtreasury plan, to stand by the Ocala platform, subtreasury and all, no matter where it carried me, whether with the Democratic party or out of it," he told those that questioned him. The Ocala platform emerged from the 1890 meeting of the National Farmers' Alliance and Industrial Union, held in Ocala, Florida. The Ocala convention was attended by voting delegates from 25 states. It passed planks calling for, among other things, the popular election of U.S. senators, the application of a graduated income tax, and the establishment of federal subtreasuries that could furnish low-cost loans that could be secured by farm commodities, not land. Watson believed that the reform movement was the key to strengthening the party. His view was that "the time is coming when the Democratic party of the South, if it wants to save its life ... will wrap the Ocala banner around it and 'come in out of the wet.'"

Watson's youthful pluck with the cheese knife in Massengale's store some years earlier was nothing compared to his mature form whenever he was confronted over the question of party loyalty. Said to be able to "talk like the thrust of a bowie knife," to those Democrats who sniped at him on the floor of the House or in committee chambers, Watson would go for their political jugular veins—drawing into question their honor and integrity—by asking if they, as men who were expected to possess those qualities of leadership, would do any less than he in standing behind the wishes of those they served. "If you had been elected by a constituency of farmers upon the Ocala platform ... and you had seen that platform denounced by the very Democrats who had organized this House, would you have stood by your principles or would you have stood by your party?" Watson stood by his principles! He also stood by the countless small farmers in Georgia, and elsewhere who rooted him on. Despite the fact that he had become a large land owner, with about 3,000 acres, he spoke with great passion and fervor particularly for little planters, farmers who had been voiceless before.

More and more he grew dissatisfied with the Democratic Party, so much so that he jumped ship, promptly joining the newly formed Populist Party, which was more to his liking. The Populist movement owed a great deal of its strength to militant farm groups, such as the Farmers' Alliance. He was that party's nominee for Vice President in 1896 and was its candidate for President in 1904. When the Populist Party fell apart a few years later, Watson returned to the Democratic fold and subsequently served in the United States Senate.

For his efforts, Watson is often hailed as the creator of RFD service, but Watson was not the first to support rural mail service. The man who is perhaps most commonly known as the "Father of Rural Free Delivery" was Postmaster General John Wanamaker. It was Wanamaker who set out in 1891 to test the feasibility of a "country mail service." This was the experimental delivery system that was being tested in selected small towns when the Watson amendment was initially proposed. Wanamaker saw his limited tests as only the beginning. In this respect, Wanamaker's views coincided with Watson's.

As postmaster general, Wanamaker believed that "The extension and improvement of no branch of the public service has proved so universally successful and satisfactory in modern times as free delivery of mail to addressors at their door."

Like Watson, Wanamaker believed that rural Americans were being ill served as far as the postal service was concerned. Rural families were paying the same postage as city dwellers, but were they receiving the same level of service? Clearly not.

Wanamaker's charitable view was not appreciated by everyone. Some critics carried Wanamaker's benevolence to the extreme, claiming that, in addition to providing rural mail service, Wanamaker would give out a free telephone and telegraph to every bumpkin and rube in the country, if he were given half a chance.

The major difference between Wanamaker and Watson was more than a question of outlook or strategy, it was a question of motive. Even though Wanamaker was instrumental in getting RFD up and running, his motives were suspect from the start. Not only was Wanamaker the Postmaster General, but he also presided over *Wanamaker's,* a Philadelphia-based department store with a formidable mail-order division. Many critics charged that Rural Free Delivery was merely a self-serving scheme by Wanamaker to expand his business. Others accused him of attempting to bankrupt the countless, small country stores that relied upon farm families for their trade.

These were grave allegations, but they were hard to disprove—except, of course, the sneers about incorporating telephone and telegraph services into the postal system: Wanamaker did not even have those services to give away. The other accusations, however, were not so easy for Wanamaker to shrug off. It was true, Wanamaker stood to gain immensely from Rural Free Delivery initiatives. Even without rural mail service, the mail-order operations at *Wanamaker's* were averaging about 1,000 orders a day by the mid-1880s. Wanamaker boasted that his department store could provide "Everything from Everywhere for Everybody" and the proprietor wanted to ensure that this boast included rural Americans and towns folk alike.

In fact, Wanamaker had long cultivated the support of Pennsylvania's farmers through his sponsorship of *The Farm Journal* and, apparently, his patronage of that publication extended far beyond advertising support. According to a letter found by Herbert A. Gibbons while researching a book, Wanamaker himself created *The Farm Journal* in an attempt to reach farming audiences. In a 1920 letter that Wanamaker wrote to Wilmer Atkinson, the *Journal's* publisher, Wanamaker writes:

> You will remember that I began the publication of *The Farm Journal* in 1877. You were my first editor until the little Journal had so grown that I felt the object I had in starting it was accomplished and turned the publication over to you without any price... .

First published in 1877, Wanamaker's *Journal* was mailed to 25,000 farmers and other rural residents within a day's ride of Philadelphia, an ideal marketing audience for *Wanamaker's* department store.

Even though the benefits of RFD to Wanamaker were enormous, many historians still believe that Wanamaker's support for RFD was not fueled by his desire to create business for himself, but rather, it was the product of his earnest desire to promote the greater public good. According to William Allen Zulker, author of *John Wanamaker: King of*

Merchants, "Though [Wanamaker] firmly believed in private enterprise, he felt the government should control and operate some public services lest private investors take advantage of the public and extract exorbitant fees for their services."

To his political allies, Wanamaker's designs for rural service seemed ideal. Throughout 1890 and 1891, he consulted with the leadership of his principal allies, the National Grange, the National Farmers' Congress, and the State Farmers' Alliances, for ways to push his plan for country mail service. Armed with the October 1, 1890 Congressional authorization, and backed by his farmers' coalition, Wanamaker began experimental service between February 1 and September 3, 1891.

Others tried to build upon this momentum. The following year Michigan congressman James O'Donnell introduced "A Bill to Extend the Free Delivery System of Mails to Rural Communities." This measure sanctioned $6 million for the extension. This was an astronomical amount, far more than his colleagues wished to support. O'Donnell's bill was subsequently amended to $100,000; but this too was rejected.

In February of 1893, however, Congress approved Thomas Watson's bill to create rural mail service, and in March it passed a $10,000 rider appropriation bill to cover the costs of testing the service. However, by then John Wanamaker was no longer postmaster general. His successor, Wilson S. Bissell, rejected the idea, believing that such a system would bankrupt the nation and that the spending of the money was at his discretion; this however was not the case. Watson's resolution was mandatory. Choosing to ignore that fact, Bissell reasoned that "the department would not be warranted in burdening the people with such a great expense." Bissell's boss, President Cleveland, believed the same way. Cleveland's view was that "The estimated cost of rural free delivery generally is so very large that it ought not to be considered in the present condition of affairs."

In some respects, the timing for such an important initiative could not have been worse. The economy was a mess. In 1893, the failure of the Philadelphia and Reading Railway and of the Erie Railroad prompted a collapse of the stock market. This led to rampant bank failures, particularly in the South and West. In domino fashion, there was widespread unemployment, farm prices hit the bottom of the barrel, and businesses were failing in record numbers.

Then, too, Uncle Sam's three-year effort to keep faith with the holders of paper currency, by redeeming greenbacks with silver or gold, further retarded the economic recovery, especially since the nation's gold reserves were alarmingly low.

Politics also played a part in all of this. Republicans saw RFD as largely a Democratic initiative, one that they were not overly keen to see become too popular. The power of rural voters was only now beginning to be properly mobilized. If the Grange had demanded rural mail service in the mid-1870s, when its membership was at its peak, rather than in the mid-1890s, when it had declined dramatically, the start of RFD might well have come two decades earlier. However, during that 20-year period Grange membership had fallen from 858,050 in 1875 to less than half that by 1895. Moreover, the base of membership shifted during that period, going from a truly nationwide organization to a fraternity dominated by members in only nine states. By 1900, the northeastern quarter of the country held 83 percent of the organization's strength. These two factors drastically weakened the Grange's clout during the crucial period when RFD had its greatest chances of starting.

On March 1, 1895, William L. Wilson succeeded Wilson S. Bissell as postmaster general. Again, Congress approved an appropriation, this time for $20,000, but Wilson was skeptical and declined to implement the plan. He believed that free delivery was "wholly impracticable" with the low level of funding that Congress was providing. He thought that he had assumed control of the postal service too late in the fiscal year to take full advantage of this appropriation. But he was willing to try the service experimentally if Congress would make a more reasonable amount of money available in the near future. Congress responded by approving $40,000 the following year. With that increase, Wilson thought that the idea could be pulled off successfully, if only on a limited basis. Wilson chose to test Rural Free Delivery in his own hometown of Charles Town, West Virginia, as well as in two other West Virginia villages: Halltown and Uvilla.

Although these routes were officially introduced on October 1, 1896, this was not the first time that Rural Free Delivery had come to Charles Town. Earlier in the year, the postal service had conducted a preliminary trial of RFD in Charles Town to see if there would really be any interest in such a service. Harry C. Gibson served as a rural carrier for free during that brief RFD trial. Earlier in 1896, Gibson and his parents, John and Mary, visited Washington, D.C. The young man was fascinated by city letter carriers. At first he thought that the carriers were door-to-door salesmen, distributing free samples. When he learned what they were really doing, he began to think of ways to do the same thing in rural Jefferson County, West Virginia.

To make his ideas a reality, Gibson arranged a meeting with Postmaster General Wilson. He offered to try furnishing mail service to rural families in Jefferson County at no cost to the postal system. Wilson smiled, nodded his head, listened politely, but made no commitment. Later, during a visit to his home state, Wilson called in on young Harry. Wilson had not forgotten their previous meeting. He wanted to know how many families Gibson thought that he could serve each day and whether Gibson's neighbors were really all that interested in the idea. Gibson promised to find out the answers to both questions during August and September. During the waning summer months Gibson visited each local family. According to Gwendolyn Aaberg, secretary of the National Association of Rural Letter Carriers, writing in the 1940s, "His manner was so pleasant and the idea of rural delivery as he presented it seemed so feasible, that the would-be patrons were greatly pleased. Before long they were asking him to bring their mail if he came along that way again, or sending their letters with him for posting."

Postmaster General Wilson kept up with Gibson's little experiment. He liked what he was hearing, and, when it appeared possible to start

RFD, he focused upon Jefferson County for the first five routes. Each of the first carriers was personally selected by the Charles Town's local postmaster, Captain George H. Flagg, after conferring with several of the county's leading citizens, (and, in the case of Gibson, listening to the preference of the Postmaster General). The nominating committee gathered at Rouss Memorial Hall in Charles Town on September 17, 1896. Among those in attendance were Colonel H. B. Davenport, Samuel J. Boyd, S. Howell Brown, Gustav Brown, George W. Haines, Colonel John Gibson, George W. Washington, and Colonel R. P. Chew and his brother Robert. The Post Office Department's representative at this meeting was Colonel Thomas G. Marche, who was the chief clerk for free delivery service. Colonel Marche informed the committee of the postmaster general's decision to create rural mail routes in West Virginia, and he asked the panel who they thought the carriers should be. Selected to serve with Harry Gibson from Charles Town were Frank Young and John W. Lucas. I. Keyes Strider was chosen to serve as the sole carrier from Halltown, and his younger brother, Melvin T. Strider, carried from Uvilla. Melvin was underage when he started serving on October 1, 1896, so he was forced to work for his first week-and-a-half without pay. As soon as he turned 16, he started receiving a paycheck. The West Virginia routes proved extremely popular. During the first month of service, the three Charles Town carriers delivered 2,226 pieces of mail to the 87 families they served. For their service they received $200 annually. The two other carriers did about the same amount of business. Each carrier's route was about 20 miles long, twice the length of Uncle Jerry's daily walks, but they were furnished with carts and wagons.

At about the same time, Wilson asked various members of Congress to nominate counties or portions of counties in their states where the new service could also be started. Before the end of the year, Postmaster General Wilson had chosen 41 additional routes, located in 28 states, as sites on which to continue the testing of rural delivery. One of those

Rural letter carrier in Michigan, 1914.

41 routes was in Climax, Michigan. Service started there on December 3, 1896.

To show their gratitude for being one of the nation's first routes, the residents of Climax erected the nation's first monument in honor of RFD service in 1917.

The Michigan State Grange, Michigan Rural Letter Carriers' Association, Kalamazoo and Calhoun County chapters of the Daughters of the American Revolution, and Climax Mens' Fellowship Club each furnished a bronze tablet for use on the stone monument. The four bronze plaques were imbedded on each side of the memorial. The structure, dedicated on July 26, 1917, is composed of small stones collected from each of the 238 farms served along the initial route. (In 1947 the monument was moved to the Village Park, where it stands today.)

In order to apply for a rural delivery route at the turn of the century, at least 100 families along the proposed route had to sign a petition. Petitions were then forwarded to that district's Congressional representative, or to one of the senators from the state, for their recommendation. Congressmen and Senators, eager to hold on to their seats, rarely refused to endorse a route.

The number of RFD routes grew quickly. On June 30, 1900 there were 1,214 routes, serving an estimated 879,127 people. Six months later the number had increased to 2,551. These provided mail service to more than 1.8 million Americans, and applications for 2,158 additional routes were still pending.

By 1915, there were over 27,000 rural routes in operation, and the service was being extended at a rate of about 800 routes a month. Rural Free Delivery was no longer on trial. It was well past the experimental phase of its existence. It had fast become an accepted and vital part of the American way of life, one which owed its existence in large measure to Uncle Jerry and the farm people of Norwood, Georgia.

The interior of a nicely run post office in small-town America.

Why Some Post Offices Perished

ONE OF THE GREATEST BENEFITS of Rural Free Delivery was the creation of better roads, but such service came with a price: the demise of countless small-town post offices. This outcome should have been expected, but was not given much thought until it was too late.

With RFD the nation simply did not need as many fixed post offices. This is why the reaction of the nation's rural postmasters in the late 1890s and early 1900s to the start of RFD was far different than that of urban postmasters roughly 30 years earlier when city delivery service was introduced. While urban postmasters applauded city service when it was inaugurated in 1863, small-town postmasters strongly opposed RFD and their resentment grew as the number of routes increased.

According to one 1908 commentary:

> When rural routes come in, one of the most picturesque incidents of rural life goes out. "Going to the post office" is a function highly regarded, unless the distance is too great to make it possible every day, and in that case it assumes more the proportions of an event as it becomes rarer.

Closing small town post offices hit the affected postmasters very hard. One ousted postmaster complained that "to take the office away takes part of my living away from me." This particular postmaster had a wife and two children to support so he could hardly afford being sacked. "I beg you for some kind of an appointment. I am not choicy [sic]—any place in the mail service will do," he pleaded to postal officials.

Other rural postmasters in similar circumstances asked if there was some other way to handle things. "Can not this matter be remedied, in justice to this office," observed one fired postmaster, who complained that his removal "seriously interferes with the patronage of this office."

Postal officials were not willing to mediate such complaints. "It is difficult at times to convince those whose personal interests seem to be temporarily antagonized that there is not an effort on the part of the Department to force [RFD] service upon the unwilling patrons to the disadvantage of the country store and its postmaster proprietor," was the Post Office Department's typical reply to such pleadings.

Congressmen took an equally hard stand. Wisconsin Congressman John J. Esch's attitude was that holding onto postmasters, instead of creating rural routes, "would create a revolt among the farming class."

Early on, influential newspapers were drawn into this debate. The opinion of the *New York Tribune* in 1899 was typical of the sentiments for keeping Rural Free Delivery:

> Fourth-class postmasters are in the main a worthy and useful set of men. But they ought to realize that as office holders their standing depends on the service they render. The fourth-class post offices are maintained not because of the postmasters or any of them have claims to the profits of office holding,

> but because those offices have served a useful purpose.... The idea that an antiquated system of handling mail is to be perpetuated to give some country postmasters an easy existence, untroubled by the march of improvement, is too preposterous to be entertained.

Not all farmers favored Rural Free Delivery either. As one local opponent put it in 1908, the "worst thing about one of these rural routes is that the carriers do not have much time to do much talking. I heard that from those that have 'em." This was a common complaint. Besides being the villages' grocery or dry-goods emporiums, local post offices functioned much like community social clubs, places to gather and find out what was happening elsewhere in the district or to swap gossip.

Rural mail carriers did not have much time to fill that void, in fact, they tended to add to it. "It ain't so much news from somewhere else that most 'em want. It's the news from right around town here. And how are you going to get that I'd like to know, if you stay up on the farm all the time and never come down to the post office to see somebody and talk things over," observed one turn-of-the-century farmer.

To accomplish the closing of so many small fourth-class post offices, rural America first needed to get rid of its muddy gumbolike roads. This was a prerequisite for rural delivery when it began in 1896.

Between 1897 and 1900 local governments spent approximately $72 million on bridges, culverts, and other road improvements. In one Indiana county farmers pooled $2,600 to grade and gravel a road in order to qualify for RFD.

As roads improved and more and more rural mail routes were added during the next half century, no longer was the nearest crossroad community—with its small post office, weekly newspaper, and tiny one-room school house—a farm family's main window to the world. The world quickly became far more accessible. With better roads, created in part by RFD, rural residents had the choice to either travel to larger communities with a greater variety of shopping or to take advantage of RFD service and purchase items through catalog sales. Schools increased in size and quality and became capable of serving an entire county worth of kids. Big city newspapers and national magazines could be delivered right to the mailbox.

This seemingly exciting expansion from isolated rural life to the bustling city only made matters worse for many of the nation's smallest rural hamlets by further accelerating their demise, a trend that continues to this day. It follows a pattern that was described by former postmaster Walt Borla in an issue of the *Postmaster's Gazette* a few years back:

> The local newspaper is the first thing to go in the small communities of America. The weekly issue, valued by the citizens eager for news of their town and people, is swallowed by a larger chain. Local publication is suspended and the news then emanates from a larger center of population. Next to go is a local elementary and/or junior high school. The students are transported to a distant school and local school loyalty and pride are lost. Finally, the post office is targeted for closure, the real death knell of the community.

Post Office Names

HERE ARE OTHER REASONS WHY post offices have perished, one of the most significant being the confusion associated with the place name assigned to the particular office.

Accurately addressing mail to assure delivery is one of those essential skills that we cannot live without. It is a fact as old as the country itself, as can be seen by this November 1773 notice, printed in the *New-York Journal:*

> Whereas the inhabitants of a certain village situated at Passaick-River, on the main road that leads from Elizabeth-Town to Morris-Town, found themselves under a considerable disadvantage from the place's not having a particular name, as the river runs through the country 40 or 50 miles, and letters directed to persons at Passaick River only, would be sometimes carried above and sometimes below them; upon which the principal freeholders and inhabitants assembled together on Friday, the 19th inst. and unanimously agreed to call it CHATHAM; and all persons that should hereafter direct letters, or any thing else to any person living at or near the above place, are desired to direct at Chatham, on Passaick River.

During the past two centuries, post offices came and went; the location and place names often changing every few years. During the formative years of many new communities, it was not uncommon for the name of the town to change several times. The locations of most early makeshift offices were equally transient. Such revisions were so frequent that each month the Post Office Department devoted page after page of its *United States Official Postal Guide* to listing new and closed post offices, as well as name changes and spelling corrections. The tally from 1881 to 1882 included nearly 1,000 name and site changes, 1,500 closings, and the creation of 3,000 new offices.

Denver, for example, was originally known as Auraria, Kansas Territory, when its first post office was established in the sprawling cluster of tents and shacks that was created following the 1858 discovery of gold on Cherry Creek. Later known as Denver City, the word "City" was dropped in 1864. By that time, the post office was on the ground floor of postmaster David Moffat's book store.

Oftentimes, towns were named by, or after, the local postmaster. That was certainly the case with "Adaton," Nebraska, named by cowboys in the area in honor of their postmaster Ada Foster. The "Luella," Nebraska, post office was named after postmaster Luella Keller. Another Nebraska community, "Burrough," was likewise named for postmaster John H. Burroughs, only in this case the last letter was dropped. A few of the other Nebraska towns named after local postal officials are Russell, Peters, Mosser, and Hamilton. Nebraska was not unique in this respect, nor were post office names limited to local postmasters.

Some post office names have come about in even weirder ways. When asked if he could think of a proper name for the post office, the founder of one small settlement in Montana replied "You bet!" That name stuck, although in a slightly abbreviated form: "Ubet." Such shorthand names were somewhat common. Uoll Heights, Montana, is another typical example of this type of improvisation; it was easier to spell than "You All." As for Eek, Alaska, it appears to have been named after the scream, "Eek!" made by a patron when a barrel of flour was opened and out jumped a mouse. Another Alaska town, Chicken, was originally to have been named "Ptarmigan" in honor of what became the state's bird, but the miners that first populated the town were not sure how ptarmigan was spelled. "Chicken" was a word that everyone could spell, so a quick substitution was made.

The same sort of odd naming opportunities arose in other states as well, and you did not necessarily have to be a prominent person to be honored. According to old-timers, a certain South Dakota community was originally named for a wandering cat. The owner of the mouser, Adel Labreche, could never keep up with the critter. It ran wild over much of the countryside, much to the child's upset. Every time she would spot a passing cavalryman she would ask if he had seen her cat. In time, the soldiers came to know the place as "Adel's cat." Adelscat, South Dakota, is presently known as Jefferson, South Dakota.

Usually, Uncle Sam holds all of the cards when it comes to naming post offices. Early on, the government established a simple set of rules that had to be complied with in order to name a town. Uncle Sam has been very stingy when it comes to approving place-names. A preference for plain, sincere, single-word names has taken shape over a number of years. In 1882 the nation's mail service dictated that new post offices had to have the same name as the town or village where they were located. A few years later it ordered that prefixes, such as "Old," "East," or "New" be dropped.

Many post office names were shortened to conform with a January 5, 1892 report by the U.S. Board of Geographic Names, which recommended that the names of post offices be simplified by combining multiword designations into one word. In the mid-1890s many post office names were simplified in this manner. A number of towns were upset by the postal service's idea of condensing the names of towns and villages like this, but the residents of La Mesa, California, seemed especially enraged. Here is one of the tamer letters that was sent to several California newspapers complaining of this bureaucratic act:

> The Post-Office Department at Washington is robbing California of untold thousands [in lost tourism] through their fool order that the names of post offices shall be run together into one word, as "Lamesa" for La Mesa, and scores of other beautiful names mutilated in this way. The action of the Post-Office Department is pure vandalism—nothing more nor less. Some fool clerk, with a pin-head brain, has figured that some time, and a few gallons of ink, may be saved in writing Agua Alta [as] "Aguaalta" and Big Trees [as] "Bigtrees." Why not "Sanfrancisco?" Sacra! To Alcatraz with him!

Another requirement is that no two towns in any state can have the same name. This commonsense rule of thumb was designed to keep mail from going to the wrong place.

It was not the postal system's responsibility to come up with the post office names. That was left to the town's leaders. Instead, the Post Office Department ruled on the use of names to avoid confusing duplication. Occasionally, however, the Department had to mediate disputes. In 1923 a Missouri community wanted to take the name of another town in the state. The Post Office Department said no. Alternative names were proposed, but each time the proposed name was previously owned by another hamlet in Missouri. At this point, one postal official advised the town fathers that their inability to come up with an acceptable name was "mighty peculiar." In short order, this response appeared at postal service headquarters: "Acting on your suggestion, we wish to name our town 'Peculiar.'" The name stuck.

Despite the "one name per state" limit, common names were a constant problem. In the 1920s, the nation boasted 31 "Franklins," 20 "Clintons," 22 "Buffalos," 14 "Denvers," 11 "Bostons," 7 "Detroits," and 6 "Philadelphias."

Such similar post office names have caused a great deal of confusion. Postal service headquarters was constantly reminding employees to watch out for potential mix-ups. Typical of this concern, employees were advised to be especially careful with "Painted Post," an office in New York state. A great deal of mail marked "Parcel Post" was winding up in Painted Post by mistake.

Likewise, hasty handling sent West Virginia mail for "Cameron" to "Dameron," which was also in that state. No state was immune. "Logan," in the states of Alabama, Illinois, Indiana, Iowa, Kansas, Missouri, Montana, Nebraska, New Mexico, North Dakota, Ohio, Oklahoma, Utah, Virginia, West Virginia, and Wisconsin, was a constant headache. "Barry," "Berry," and "Perry" were other frequent offenders.

On rare occasions the Post Office Department has used its muscle to veto a new town's name. An example of this occurred in the early 1900s when the residents of a new community in Kentucky proposed the name "Lower Greasy." This did not sit well with Postmaster General Albert Burleson, who flatly rejected the idea. Burleson refused to consider a name he believed to be undignified and unpleasantly suggestive. Besides, he told the residents, Kentucky already had far too many such unflattering names, including Gum, Pig, Shoestring, and Shucks. As far as he was concerned, "Offut" was by far a better choice.

Bull City, Kansas, also had to be renamed, but not because of Burleson. In this case, the town was originally named in 1870 in honor of its founder, General Hiram C. Bull, but a female patron from Illinois complained that the name was simply too vulgar to be used by ladies. She succeeded in circulating a petition to have the town renamed. Fifteen years after its founding, Bull City officially became Alton.

The rationale behind many small-town post office names was largely a local matter, and, as such, the reasoning was sometimes lost on the outside world. "Sunbeam," Colorado, is one of those hard-to-comprehend names. It was named by a prominent farmer in the Yampa Valley because he believed that the sun shone just a bit brighter there than in any other place in the valley. Although now extinct, the town of "Preparation," Iowa, was said to have been named that by a religious group on its way West because it was only a brief stopping off spot, a place where they could prepare to move on. Not everyone agreed with this interpretation. Others believed that it was named in recognition of the need to prepare spiritually for the hereafter.

Common Architecture and the Supervising Architects

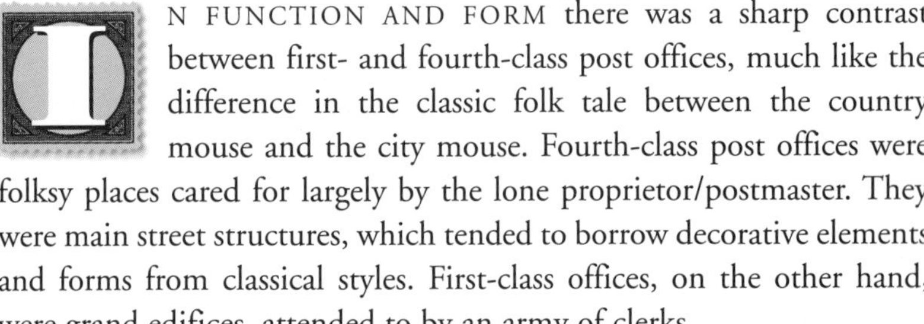

IN FUNCTION AND FORM there was a sharp contrast between first- and fourth-class post offices, much like the difference in the classic folk tale between the country mouse and the city mouse. Fourth-class post offices were folksy places cared for largely by the lone proprietor/postmaster. They were main street structures, which tended to borrow decorative elements and forms from classical styles. First-class offices, on the other hand, were grand edifices, attended to by an army of clerks.

In either case, the postmaster ruled the roost, at least on paper. As often as not, larger-town postmasters were simply absentee landlords. The pervasiveness of this situation was pointed out in Congressional hearings. First Assistant Postmaster Charles P. Grandfield advised a House Committee that the average big city postmaster would "simply show up at his desk for an hour or two each day." Most of the work of running the place fell to the assistant postmaster.

Unlike rural post offices, which tended to be small vernacular buildings built by local contractors, large urban post offices were designed by the Treasury Department's Office of the Supervising Architect for much of the nation's history. They tended to be larger, more elegant structures, such as the post office at Princeton, New Jersey.

Fourth-class postmasters were not as fortunate. They had to run the whole show largely by themselves.

Wanted: Good Accounting Skills

METHODS OF ACCOUNTING VARIED, and many small-town postmasters were not the best bookkeepers. Accurate records were important because village postmasters were paid according to the volume of stamps they sold and canceled. While accurate bookkeeping was generally a problem for every postmaster, it was a particular problem for Charles J. Liebtag, a blind man who served as postmaster of Osnaburg, Ohio, for many years. All the same, Liebtag's books always balanced, somehow, and he never shortchanged his customers. Liebtag's ability in this regard astonished postal inspectors who routinely reviewed his accounts, as well as his local customers; but his rule of thumb was simple: Whenever a patron gave him a bill he counted out change for $1. Paper currency was scarce and he realized that a one dollar bill was about the most anyone had. If the transaction was in change, he easily recognized the denominations by the feel of the coins. Besides, no one in town would want to stiff him, he was too well loved. In addition he was able to recognize all his customers by the way they walked or the sound of their voices, so he would quickly know who any troublemakers were.

As with the case of Postmaster Liebtag, the arrival of a postal inspector in New Salem, Illinois, over a century and a half ago was cause for alarm among the local population. They knew the inspector was there to audit Postmaster Abraham Lincoln's accounts. Lincoln was an easy-going fellow, and his friends were worried that his revenues might not agree with government figures. Several good friends went to Lincoln shortly before the audit to ask if everything was okay. Lincoln reckoned so, but was not the least bit concerned about the outcome. A few friends even offered money that could be used to make good any difference, but their generosity was graciously declined. At the appointed hour the audit began. It resembled a morbid deathwatch. By all accounts, Lincoln was the most composed of the lot. The inspector announced what Lincoln owed. The lanky postmaster produced a tattered sock from a locked box under the counter and began counting out coins. When the counting was finished, Lincoln's receipts were right on the money.

Other postmasters have not been so lucky. In 1912 the postmaster of Selma, a small logging community in Washington State, relied on peas and two cigar boxes to keep his business records. Small holes were cut in the tops of the boxes. One box was used to record the stamps sold, the other the stamps canceled. He deposited a pea in the sales box for every one-cent stamp sold. A pea was dropped into the other box every time he canceled a letter. The idea seemed perfect—until mice ate all of his peas.

Rats were Henry A. Pease's problem. His last! When faced with the problem of rodents many postmasters brought in cats. The Post Office Department even gave a small allowance, amounting to "milk money," as an incentive to have cats around. Pease, the postmaster at Jonesville,

Vermont, would have been well advised to handle his rat problem the same way, but he did not. Instead he kept a shotgun handy. On April 18, 1926, the shotgun accidently discharged during a rat hunt, killing him.

Rodents are not the only animals that have caused postal problems. Chief Postal Inspector Grant B. Miller was not the least bit pleased to be notified in the mid-1920s of a case involving sheep eating postal money orders. It seems that the postmaster at Tamo, Arkansas, William L. Clemmons, could not take the summer heat inside the post office, where he lived. One night he moved his bed outdoors to the nearby sheep pen, where he believed the temperature was cooler. For security he took along 16 blank postal money orders. The next morning eleven of the order forms were missing. He immediately notified postal headquarters of the loss. He told postal officials. "[The sheep] were all the time pulling at the bed when I (was) in there, and at other times, I think they ate the missing orders." Postmaster Clemmons should have known better than to have taken the money orders with him to bed. After all, he had held the job as postmaster since July 12, 1916. Luckily for Clemmons none of the money orders in question were ever cashed. Despite the fact that there was no loss to the government, William Clemmons was replaced as postmaster. His successor was Andrew J. Clemmons, who took over in an acting capacity on October 8, 1926. Andrew officially became postmaster on February 14, 1927. He was the town's sixth postmaster. In all, five members of the Clemmons family served as postmasters at Tamo between March 2, 1900, when the post office was established, and December 31, 1967, when it was closed.

There have been other types of problems, too. When postal inspectors audited the books of the Lake Bluff, Illinois, post office they found a mess. The postmaster, Miss Isabella Ross, was short $400. She knew she'd be in error, but thought that everyone would understand. "I realized all along I was making mistakes, but I was sure the inspectors would be glad to help when they came to look at the books," she said in 1915. But she was dead wrong! In her defense, she did try to compensate, but even that worked against her. She tried to make good the losses by putting the Post Office Department's money in her own bank account, but she was short there, too. The inspectors immediately went after her bond and her job. "I suppose they thought I was a regular shark at figures when they made me postmaster," she said. "If they did it was a mistake."

Postal officials tended to be an unforgiving lot, even when the excuse seemed outside the control of the postmaster. A good example of this occurred when Jasper Workman, the postmaster at Bald Knob, a part of Virginia that later became West Virginia, was taken prisoner by a Southern raiding party shortly after the outbreak of the Civil War. He remained tied up for nearly 36 hours while the raiders confiscated $16 worth of stamps and embossed stamped envelopes. Because of the war, the post office remained closed until the late 1860s, when it was again allowed to reopen with Jasper Workman again in charge. Unwilling to forgive the lost postage, the federal government deducted the missing $16 from his first paycheck.

Mother Nature also has created problems for postmasters from time to time. While weather has been a constant foe of letter carriers, now and then it affected postmasters too, such as one in Georgia, who in 1928 had just finished preparing four postal money orders when a freak whirlwind struck. The high winds broke a window and scattered the money orders. Like a primed gymnast, the postmaster was able to catch three of the airborne money orders, but the fourth, worth $1.09, eluded him. In the blinking of an eye it was sucked out the broken window pane and took flight. It whirled out over the treetops. One employee ran after the flying money order on foot, while the postmaster gave chase in his automobile. Both pursued the object for miles, before finally losing sight of the flying cash, which was never recovered.

"Yeggmen" Strike

OTHER PROBLEMS AROSE, not because of postmaster's poor bookkeeping practices, acts of war, or chance encounters with the elements, but because many small-town postmasters didn't trust their cheap safes. Instead, they took their stamps and other valuable post office property home with them over the weekends. This was not always the smartest thing to do, as Thomas H. Wallace, postmaster at Mill Village, New York, discovered in 1914. His house was broken into one Sunday afternoon and the bandits made off with about $1,000 in stamps and postal stationery charged to him. He personally had to make good the loss.

Wallace's concern about the post office safe was not unfounded, however. The word "yeggmen" is lost on our generation, but in an earlier era, it was used to describe safe blowers who struck post offices. Postal news reports were full of the accounts of such banditry, including this report:

> One of the biggest, boldest postal robberies in the annals of the Post Office Department occurred a few weeks ago at Richmond, Virginia, when yeggmen, under the glare of a street lamp, backed a wagon up to the door of the post office at that place, pierced the vault with steel drills and made off with more than $86,000 in stamps, money and certified checks.

Within a matter of weeks, the Richmond Post Office was robbed again. This time the safe was not blown, it was cracked without damage, netting a total of only $107.67 in cash and money orders.

By and large, it did not take much to gain entry into small-town post offices. The doors were easily pried open or windows were quickly smashed. As might be expected, the thieves were almost always out-of-towners.

Architectural Trendsetters

ANOTHER TYPE OF CREATIVE GANG at work during the Victorian era was comprised of 13 men who largely dictated federal architecture during that period; they were the nation's principal architects for public buildings. Their official title initially was "Federal Architect," later

"Architectural Advisor," and finally "Supervising Architect." The latter designation, which was used informally by 1852, was legislatively established in 1864. The Supervising Architects were a part of the Treasury Department's Office of Construction. The Treasury Department was responsible for overseeing the design, construction, and operation of all principal government-owned buildings, including major custom houses, court houses, and post offices.

Early on, the fledgling Office of Construction eliminated the haphazard use of local commissions to award design contracts with private architects, opting instead to employ a staff architect—presumably one of exceptional caliber—who would work directly under the supervision of the Office Chief. This approach streamlined the planning and construction processes and provided greater central control of architectural projects. But, there were drawbacks. A government worker in Washington, D.C.—even one of renown—was seldom capable of anticipating local whims, swaying public opinion, or appreciating the best available indigenous building materials. Furthermore, the nature of the work automatically thrust the incumbent into the political circus that surrounds life in the nation's capital.

During the Victorian era, the Supervising Architects were initially headed by Alexander H. Bowman, a captain with the Army Corps of Engineers, who was detailed from that job to provide "more efficient management" to the government's building program. Bowman was responsible for overseeing the design, construction, and operation of all principal government-owned buildings, including major custom houses, court houses, and post offices. Working with Bowman was his chief architect, Ammi Burnham Young. Young was a complex figure who was described by later peers as "a gentleman who had that kindly, hard-boiled, wistful, shrewd, childlike, happy, faintly melancholy expression one usually associates with architects." Another quality was that he apparently worked well with Bowman.

The Bowman/Young team streamlined planning and construction processes and provided greater central control of architectural projects. Aided by six draftsmen and a bookkeeper, who also doubled as a draftsman in a pinch, Bowman and Young embarked upon a totally unprecedented building program.

There was much work to do. The enormous volume of mail generated during the Civil War emphasized inadequacies of small or poorly planned buildings. In 1863 at Chicago, some 400 employees handled 125 million pieces of mail. At New York City mail clerks complained about working 10 to 12 hours daily, including Sundays and holidays, without extra pay under terrible conditions, citing ventilation and lighting as the worst.

Over the years, the government's architects were men of mixed talents and tastes. Overall, their works mirrored the rich diversity of major architectural trends in vogue throughout the age. They translated the nation's evolving tastes into large-scale projects for hundreds of communities.

During the Victorian era, the architectural "trendsetters" included: Robert Mills (1836–1842), Ammi B. Young (1842–1862), Isaiah Rogers

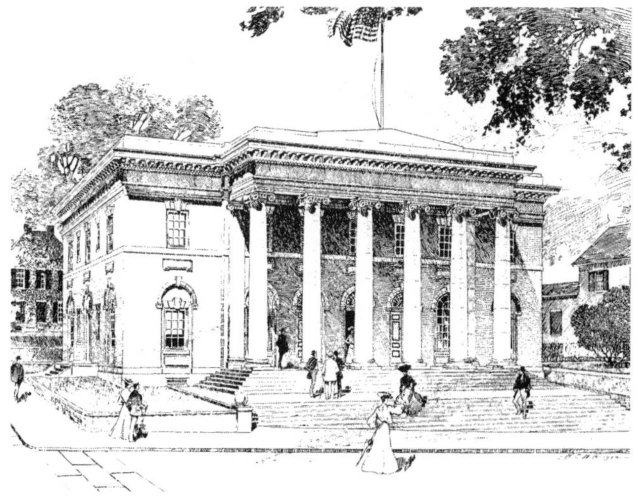

TOP ROW, LEFT: *Renaissance Revival was the style preferred by Ammi B. Young, which he used in designing the federal building at Wheeling, West Virginia.* TOP ROW, RIGHT: *The Second Empire post office at Philadelphia was designed by Alfred B. Mullett, who served as Supervising Architect from 1865 to 1874.* MIDDLE ROW, LEFT: *Supervising Architect Will A. Freret's design for the Wilmington, North Carolina, federal building.* MIDDLE ROW, RIGHT: *The federal building at Eastport, Maine, as designed by James H. Windrim, 1890.* BOTTOM ROW, LEFT: *Mifflin Bell's design for the La Crosse, Wisconsin, federal building, completed in 1890.* BOTTOM ROW, RIGHT: *James Knox Taylor preferred Beaux-Arts and Georgian styles. This was his design for the federal building at Charlottesville, Virginia.*

(1862–1865), Alfred B. Mullett (1865–1874), William A. Potter (January 1875–July 1876), James B. Hill (August 1876–September 1883), Mifflin E. Bell (November 1883–July 1887), Will A. Freret (1887–1888), James H. Windrim (1889–1890), Willoughby J. Edbrooke (1891–1892), Jeremiah O'Rourke (1893–1894), William Martin Aiken (1895–1896), and James Knox Taylor (1897–1912).

The architectural preferences of these men were apparent in many of the post office buildings they helped to create. For example, Mills concentrated on Greek Revival forms; Ammi B. Young favored Renaissance Revival styles; Alfred B. Mullett preferred Second Empire structures; William A. Potter liked High Victorian Gothic designs; and Willoughby J. Edbrooke leaned toward large-scale Romanesque buildings. This diversity of tastes represented a dramatic and democratic flow in "old world" forms. These architects absorbed the spirit of these resurrected European styles, but their works were more than simple imitations. Instead, they endowed their adaptations with a rugged appearance of permanence, creating forms that were in keeping with our democratic values.

James Knox Taylor preferred Beaux-Arts and Georgian forms. The Beaux-Arts style, which became popular as a result of the 1893 Chicago Fair, coincided with the end of Victorian-era architecture.

Unfortunately, many of the government architect's buildings amounted to little more than architectural fast food. All too often, they were lackluster structures, buildings with little if any variation. They represented the same bland diet of columns, eaves, clocktowers, and embellishments repeatedly served up in town after town. This may appear to be a damning criticism. It is not. Designwise, there were no villains. Not all of the architects possessed the same abilities, sensitivities, or grasp for harmonious proportions. In addition, there was an abundance of less-than-desirable circumstances under which they were

A design by Alfred Mullett for the federal building at Boston, Massachusetts.

forced to work, including understaffing, rushed deadlines, bleak quarters, and burdensome red tape which forced these men to cut corners whenever possible.

The workload of the Office of Supervising Architect rose and fell with the economic climate of the country. In 1853, the office was responsible for only 23 buildings. In certain other years, both before and after that, there was even less work. In 1897, the number of designs totaled 297, with another 95 buildings under construction.

The workforce also grew, and the staff also had its ups and downs. In 1857, the entire staff of the Office of Construction, including the architectural component, could be counted on the fingers of both hands. Roughly three decades later, a small—but still inadequate—army of 148 employees was assigned to the Supervising Architect's office.

Administratively, by 1896, the principal office functions had been divided up between six division chiefs. These section heads were responsible for engineering and drafting, inspection and materials, accounting, photography, law and records, computing, repairs, and tracings. The division chiefs answered to a chief executive officer, who in turn reported to the Supervising Architect.

Assembling a competent staff was not always easy. In his *Annual Report* for 1884, Mifflin E. Bell bitterly explained how "The office labors under great difficulty being unable to offer rates of pay sufficient to secure and retain in the service of the Government architects and draftsmen competent to perform the work satisfactorily." A decade later, Jeremiah O'Rourke faced the same problem. He advised the Chairman of the Senate's Committee on Public Buildings and Grounds, "The only reason for the slow progress of these works is the want of a technical force adequate to the demands of the office."

Things did not change. In 1896, William Martin Aiken complained about the disparity between the number of buildings authorized by acts of Congress and the technical and clerical assistance provided to do the work. At that time, he could not afford to assign more than two draftsmen to any particular project and, deep down, he even questioned if that number was actually available. His tiny staff had to prepare an array of required drawings for each building showing foundations, masonry, steel and iron construction, interior finishes, heating and ventilating systems, plumbing, and vaults. This was tantamount to shoestring designing. In effect, between April 1895 and January 1896, his office was occupied

Different types of contractors were often hired to do each phase of the construction of early post office projects, such as the construction of the Springfield, Missouri, post office shown here, adding to the delays and mountains of bureaucratic paperwork. Work on this federal building began in 1891. Completed five years later, the postal staff consisted of the postmaster, assistant postmaster, six clerks, and seven letter carriers. This post office was vacated in 1937.

almost exclusively with completing unstudied and unfinished designs.

Understaffing was not the only problem. Working conditions tended to be deplorable too. In his 1889 *Annual Report,* James H. Windrim complained: "Attention is respectfully asked to the fact that the present drafting room of the office is inadequate in size and poorly lighted; frequent absence of the draftsmen is occasioned by ophthalmia."

Additionally, from the very beginning the office tended to generate massive amounts of paperwork; however, more often than not, the clerical function was never properly handled. Up until about the end of the American Civil War, files were frequently never completed, deeds were often misplaced, and routine reports were late or simply never prepared.

Contracting procedures also contributed to the paperwork problems. Individual contracts typically were awarded for each step in the building process, including trench excavation, foundation casting, cut-stone work, brick work, completion up to the point when the interior finishes were applied, interior finishes, plumbing, flooring, heating and ventilating. By 1896, in an effort to simplify matters, much of the work was lumped together into single contracts, and this made a significant difference.

A lack of adequate technicians and clerical help, poor creative environment, and an excessive workload forced many Supervising Architects to economize. While William Martin Aiken claimed that his approach was to keep building designs and construction details simple, a flurry of ornately detailed styles betray such claims. Among his more exceptional approaches are the post offices for Clarksville, Tennessee; Saginaw, Michigan; and Paterson, New Jersey—all of which resemble fairy tale

Contrary to William Martin Aiken's claim that he preferred simple designs, many of his federal buildings were extremely elaborate, as was this post office, in Paterson, New Jersey.

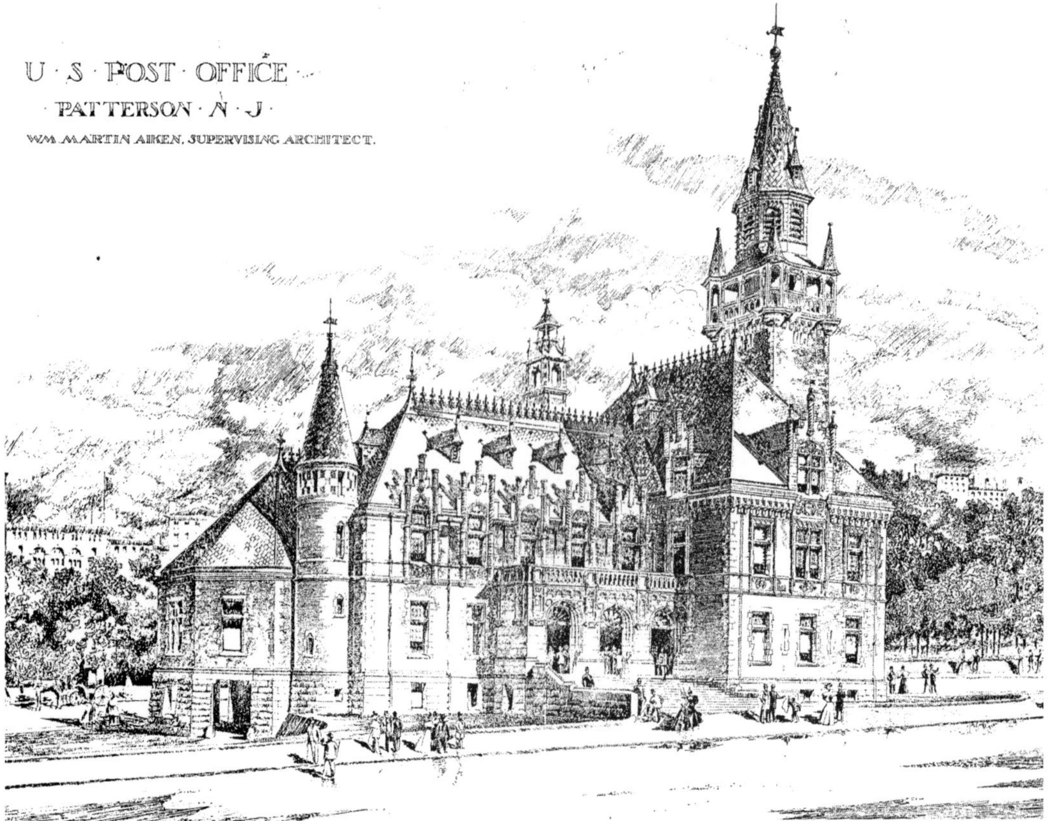

castles—and the Mission style used for the San Francisco post office and court house.

Several of the architects were artistically frugal, reusing the same basic designs over and over again. Minor cosmetic changes were sometimes made, principally to the exteriors, so as not to offend the local community, which would have been grossly insulted to think themselves worthy of only a carbon copy of another town's post office. That had to be avoided if at all possible, for unlike ecclesiastic structures, which gave pride to one segment of the local population, specifically a particular denomination or faith, federal buildings belonged to the entire community.

Understanding this was crucial to the success or failure of each architect. In this respect, no matter how talented they were individually, they shared a singular architectural purpose: To make the presence of the federal government prominent within the local community.

This had a harnessing effect upon the group. Certainly these were powerful and influential men, but they had to accept the fact that they did not always have absolute authority over the appearance of government buildings. Their opinions were frequently tempered by political considerations or local desires. Design work was commonly interrupted at the request of the members of Congress from the districts involved. When the residents of Frankfort, Kentucky, objected to the use of bricks for their new Queen Anne style post office in 1884, it was constructed of stone instead, in an effort to placate the population.

On the surface, these men's individual creativity may be hard to detect. It does not always come across when looking at existing exterior illustrations of their buildings. For this reason, they cannot be judged to have been "outstanding" or "mediocre" simply by perusing a gallery of their renderings. That would be unfair. A great deal more must be taken into consideration, including the various influencing factors mentioned previously, as well as others.

The work of the first "mass-production" architect employed by the government during the Victorian period, Ammi B. Young, for example, was carried out at a hectic pace, in many ways more hectic than was possible for those who would follow. Young was indeed a superb designer. Many of his Italian buildings, with Grecian details, were the same basic design. The post office at Galena, Illinois, is a classic example of Young's "style." Originally erected in the late 1850s as a post office and custom house for river traffic between St. Louis and Fort Snelling in Minnesota, the building is said to have been constructed from stone quarried for the Morman Temple at Nauvoo, Illinois, which was destroyed during the 1840s. Perhaps the novelty of Young's style was that, although he closely followed classical architecture, he did so with two twists: He insisted that his designs be economical—which was highly unusual and significant in and of itself—and, rather than merely copying antiquity, his approaches featured originality in interpretation.

The last Supervising Architect of the Victorian age, James Knox Taylor, boasted that his style also was marked by a return to the classic tradition. Actually, his tenure was highlighted by a boring redundance in design, a monotonous sameness, almost as if post office buildings

The Galena, Illinois, post office designed by Ammi B. Young.

were stamped out by one great cookie cutter. Taylor was prolific. He had no other choice. The sizable length of his tenure as Supervising Architect combined with the steady stream of hefty "pork barrel" government appropriations for new building started during his term of office, forced him to be architecturally frugal.

In all fairness, if the sheer number of buildings created by a Supervising Architect served as a yardstick for greatness, Taylor would rank high on the list as an outstanding success.

One thing is for certain: The impact of certain architects was greater than that of others, not because of the abundance of "their style" of buildings, but because of the individuality, uniqueness, or complexity of their designs. Assessing any of these architect's greatness is complicated by the fact that many of them served in office for just a few years. In fact, between 1866 and 1897, the position of Supervising Architect changed hands nine times. During that same period, nearly 300 projects were undertaken. In addition, there was a constant stream of renovations or enlargements to buildings designed by earlier job holders.

Because of these circumstances, many hybrid structures emerged. These buildings cannot be claimed by any one particular architect, rather, they combine the favorite styles of two or more supervising architects. Such composites are common. For example, Alfred Mullett had no qualms about redesigning the rooflines of several buildings planned by one of his predecessors, Ammi B. Young. In turn, William Potter redesigned some of Mullett's mansard rooflines and balloon and pyramidal pavilions in keeping with his Gothic taste.

The extension to the post office building at Des Moines, Iowa, is an excellent example of a hybrid structure. The overall Second Empire building, as originally designed by Alfred B. Mullett, was subsequently punctuated by the addition of a massive clocktower, a favored structural element used by James B. Hill, some years later.

Hybrid government buildings seldom escaped public scrutiny or controversy for very long. In fact the exact opposite is true: They attracted broad-based interest. As a result, most projects were hampered by outside interference, miserly appropriations, drastic cost overruns, constant contractor problems, congressional meddling, persistent investigations, shortages in essential materials, inefficiency, fickle weather, and professional jealousy from private architects desiring a piece of the action.

Such outside influences delayed construction projects for long periods and added to costs. Overly expensive government construction projects tended to take as much as three times as long to complete as private ventures. Dismissed amid outcries of overspending, Ammi B.

Willoughby J. Edbrooke preferred massive towers. Nicknamed "The Old Tooth" because of its tower, the Washington, D.C., post office also housed U.S. Post Office Department's national headquarters.

Young found this out the hard way, thereby ending a prolific public career. In just two years—1855 and 1856—Young developed the plans and specifications for 35 projects. That represents nearly twice as many buildings as were in the works when he assumed the office in 1853.

Comparison of identical sets of lithographed prints of building styles of the time indicate that, in fact, many of these projects were clones. Only the site plans varied. The use of prints in the design and construction process was one of Young's most important contributions to the architect's office, eliminating the tedious and time-consuming task of tracing designs. Young, who was not opposed to reusing his designs, supported the idea of standardization. It was not only the expedient thing to do; but, to his way of thinking, there was no reason why buildings with the same purpose should not have the same basic appearance. Consequently, in 1855, matching post offices were created for seven locations: Buffalo and Oswego, New York; Newark, New Jersey; New Haven, Connecticut; Chicago, Illinois; Milwaukee, Wisconsin; and Wheeling, West Virginia. The following year, Young repeated the same type of duplicating architecture in other cities utilizing a different set of lithographic plates.

Much like Young, both in terms of talent and productivity, Alfred Mullett was willing to reuse elements of old designs on smaller federal projects. Although a large number of designs created by Mullett were for smaller structures, several of his projects, such as the custom houses and post offices in New York, Philadelphia, Chicago, Boston, and St. Louis, were immense. The fact that Mullett was fortunate enough to design many of America's largest post offices, buildings that boldly present the Second Empire style, made the use of this style for commercial buildings and residences more common.

Mullett adorned his many smaller projects with a simple elegance, but it was his massive undertakings that allowed his tastes to run rampant. Mullett repeatedly ornamented his rooflines with allegorical

The Charleston, South Carolina, court house and post office was a hybrid project of a somewhat unusual type. The design was begun in the 1850s under the supervision of Ammi B. Young, but not completed until the 1870s, interrupted by the Civil War. This is Alfred B. Mullett's rendering of the project.

Smaller federal buildings, such as the combination court house, customs house, and post office at Omaha, Nebraska, designed during Alfred Mullett's tenure as Supervising Architect, reflected his preference for the Second Empire style.

Alfred B. Mullett utilized Second Empire styling throughout his career as Supervising Architect, including designs for some of the nation's largest post offices, including Boston, Chicago, Philadelphia, St. Louis, and New York City, shown here. Of his larger post offices, only the St. Louis building survives.

designs and eagles. Such applications today appear grossly out of place. The eagles appear to be little more than a misplaced symbol of state, declaring that the building once belonged to the federal government.

Like Young, Mullett found himself at the heart of no less than five separate investigations, largely the result of his suspected acceptance of kickbacks from suppliers of building materials. The alleged graft reportedly involved the "Granite Ring," a group of influential and politically well-connected New England stone merchants.

In the case of the Boston post office, Mullett probably had no other choice but to use New England granite. The stone for that post office came highly recommended, having reportedly been "discovered" by Massachusetts Congressman Benjamin Franklin Butler in an abandoned quarry on the property of his summer residence in Gloucester.

Hounded by the press over the allegations, Mullett fought back as best he could. He weathered these witch hunts, trying to hold on to his salary of roughly $4,500 a year. All this exacted a heavy personal toll. Ultimately he resigned because of sharp disagreements with Treasury Secretary Benjamin H. Bristow.

When John Sherman became treasury secretary in 1877, serious thought was given to rehiring Mullett, but his reappointment was delayed. Impatient, Mullett criticized the Hayes administration in a newspaper interview for what he believed was unjust treatment. His comments destroyed any chance of his being reappointed.

In failing health, due largely to severe rheumatoid arthritis, Mullett filed suit against the federal government for $300,000 for services in connection with his design of the State, War, and Navy Department Building (known today as the Old Executive Office Building). In the end, he spent much of his family's savings, lost the case against the federal government, and ruined his health. Mullett became despondent; within a year of losing the federal lawsuit, he committed suicide. He died as a result of a self-inflicted small-caliber gunshot wound to the head. The cause of death was officially attributed to "melancholia."

What would prompt talented men, such as Mullett and the others, to accept such a job? A portion of Alfred Mullett's letters of resignation, submitted on November 21, 1874, provides a clue. In it he confessed, "My health as you know is broken down. I am consequently nervous and perhaps more irritable than I am aware of. You are also aware that I consider the salary so inadequate that the office is of no value except so far as it affords an opportunity for making a reputation."

Many Supervising Architects believed that they had made a mistake in accepting the job. Among them was Mullett's successor, William Potter, who told those attending the American Institute of Architects convention meeting November 17–19, 1875, that "Experience has shown that it is difficult, if not impossible, to separate the Office of Supervising Architect from political control to a greater or lesser degree...." Within a matter of months, Potter expanded his view of "political control" to include the possibility that even an incompetent could get the job, if he was politically connected. Potter wrote that if that were to happen, as he feared was likely, then:

> The country is liable thereby to be burdened by structures utterly lacking in those architectural qualities which should be found in the works of a great nation. The stamp of inefficiency so imprinted in the national architecture is not of a nature soon to pass away, for not only will it remain itself a monument to a vacuous system, but its teachings for evil can never be fully estimated. But should this evil be escaped, there remain yet others.

The additional evils to which Potter was referring included the voluminous administrative tasks routine to the position, the variety of projects to be evaluated, the constant stream of interruptions, which gave him no opportunity to really study the designs he was required to produce, and the always present potential for corruption.

The Mullett scandals permanently tainted Potter's opinion of his predecessor, and Potter wound up disliking Mullett personally and professionally, and publicly shared his opinion without hesitation. The August 12, 1876 edition of *American Architect* reported that "if half [Potter] tells of Mr. Mullett, his predecessor in office, be true, that individual has shown a most remarkable pertinacity in underhanded dealing." Likewise, an acquaintance of Potter's, Montgomery Schuyler, recalled him saying that Mullett "knew a little something of everything, excepting architecture." The ill feelings were mutual; there was no love lost on Mullett's part for Potter either.

The mutual dislike appears to have been well earned. In 1878, long after Potter had resigned from the architect's office, he and several others were indicted on charges that they conspired to defraud the government of $850,000 on the stone supplied for the Chicago custom house and post office. Like the building itself, the case was flimsy. The alleged conspiracy occurred on September 1, 1876, several weeks after Potter had left the architect's office, at which time Potter was not in any position to influence a contractual agreement aimed at defrauding the government. Because of the overall lack of evidence everyone involved in the case was acquitted. Actually, the construction flaws in the Chicago post office building, which was begun in 1872, were basically Mullett's responsibility. By the

Alfred Mullett's original design for the Chicago post office, 1870s. Reaching a peak in popularity during the Grant Administration, this building style is also referred to as the "General Grant style."

time Potter was appointed, the inferior stonework was already in place. His principal involvement was in trying to correct the serious cracks and defects, which he initially observed early in 1875. Despite Potter's efforts to reinforce the crumbling structure, it had to be demolished within only 16 years.

For Potter, the inability to really study his designs was perhaps the worst drawback to the job, leading him to explain:

> Architecture is an art, and, like all arts, he who practices it successfully must give himself unreservedly into the contemplation of the problem. And, furthermore, the objects for which the buildings erected in this Office are constructed, with slight exception, so nearly alike, that the difficulty, the impossibility, of endowing them with variety and individuality must be apparent.

Furthermore, Potter hated the sweatshop mentality that dominated the position. He thought that the duties of the government's architect were larger than one man could adequately handle. He wanted to make changes. He thought that the responsibilities should be significantly redefined and much of the design work delegated to qualified architects around the country. In his typically blunt and honest fashion, Potter hammered home his view in his *Annual Report* for 1875, stating:

> I owe it, first, to myself, for I am before the people to be judged, as other men of my profession are who do not labor under the same difficulties as myself, and if my works fail of that artistic merit which the public have a right to expect, the blame is laid upon me, and not the false system under which I work, and where it belongs. I owe it, further, to the profession of architecture, whose members have right to their share in the honor of increasing the dignity and beauty of the art of this country, and whose work must do infinitely more to this end than the endeavors of any one man, be he ever so gifted. And, lastly, I owe it to the public, whose money I am placed here to watch, that it be faithfully and wisely expended, and that the best results attainable from it are achieved. I fail to do my whole duty in this if I remain inactive in this direction; for by some other system than that now obtaining, much better, more artistic and worthy work can be done.

Potter's position was wholeheartedly endorsed by his boss, Treasury Secretary Benjamin H. Bristow, but little came of the architect's call for action.

Potter's openness and honesty shocked no one, least of all Bristow. It was one of the principal reasons he had been given the job in the first place. Roughly a year before the comments just quoted, Potter's selection was heralded in the December 30, 1874 edition of the *New York Times,* which said:

> Mr. Potter brings to his new position ... qualities more valuable than any merely technical excellencies in his possession. Of honorable lineage and blameless record, it may reasonably be expected that he will not convert his position into a convenience for securing "fat" jobs or large commissions. He is, fortunately for himself, without political associations, and will have no friends to reward nor party pledges to redeem. Whether he will find this new position sufficiently attractive to induce him to retain it long, we are not quite sure. But whether he leaves it sooner or later, we venture to predict that he will do so without having filled his pockets or stained his hands.

In all honesty, William Potter was not the first candidate for the job, nor was he even the second choice. His older half-brother, Edward T. Potter, apparently had refused the position, as had John MacArthur, Jr., but William Potter proved to be a wise selection, despite his short stay. His tenure was like a long overdue, yet peaceful, revolution. In addition to revitalizing the outward appearance of the nation's buildings, a move which was proclaimed as long overdue, he tried to refine the inner workings of the office. At the same time, he labored to restore the office's severely tarnished reputation, which had suffered under Mullett.

All of this proved to be an excessive undertaking, for William Potter's term of office lasted only a year and a half. Upon leaving, he observed that "the office is no sinecure by any means; and I doubt whether you could get a capable architect, in good practice, to give up his office for the post. It needs to be made more distinctively artistic, and many of the mere routine duties lopped from it."

An even more telling comment about the post of Supervising Architect is to be found in a letter from J. M. Carrere to the Secretary of the Treasury. Carrere never held the position. He turned down the job in 1895, noting:

> The work itself is scattered over the entire United States and is absolutely beyond the reach of any one man excepting by proxy, and practically beyond his control... . The present condition of the work is in such a disorganized state, that it would take the best part of any man's time to organize the work itself, irrespective of the department. The accumulate waste of money is beyond belief. The department, in the main, seems well organized though cumbersome.... The tenure of the office is controlled either by civil service rules or political influence, and with this state of affairs the Office of Supervising Architect, legally, is mainly that of a clerk of the department, appointed by the Secretary of the Treasury, and though his responsibility is supposed to cover all of the above work, his authority is absolutely dependent on the Secretary of the Treasury, and much of it is divided with heads of departments.
>
> My examination of the office and its possibilities convinces me that the underlying principle upon which it is based is radically wrong, and that it is beyond the power of any one man to make a success of it. The system, not the man, should be changed.

Types of Post Offices

AT THE TURN OF THE LAST CENTURY post offices were divided into four groups: first-class, which were the largest; second-class; third-class; and fourth-class. The class designation was determined basically by the office's receipts and mail volume, with postmasters in certain classes keeping a portion of the proceeds in lieu of a salary. There was another difference. While fourth-class postmasters were appointed by the postmaster general, first-, second-, and third-class postmasters were appointed by the president and were usually confirmed by the Senate. These latter three classes were known as "Presidential class offices."

Many of the nation's fourth-class post offices were located in tiny general stores or other such small quarters, cramped little confines that made serving the public somewhat unpleasant, often requiring the postmasters to be downright improper. A case in point was the first post office in the tiny hamlet of Creede, Colorado. It was housed in tight quarters in a surveyor's hut. The general-delivery unit consisted of empty canned-fruit boxes stacked one on top of the other. No more than one customer could fit inside the post office at any given time. Postmaster C. C. Meister realized that this sort of arrangement simply would not do, so on his own he moved the post office to his cabin, which could accommodate as many as ten people, although then there was not any room left for him. The arrival of each new mail shipment was a nightmare. For weeks the postmaster worked to distribute the mail, cramming as many customers as possible into the post office to collect what was coming to them, but the massive backlog of unclaimed mail, given the amount of space available at ten customers at a time, soon made things impossible. In an effort to resolve matters a notice was posted outside the post office which read: "All mail uncalled for after thirty days will be burned." As might be expected, this only made matters worse.

For all of their rough edges, small town post offices did tend to set the trend when it came to office automation. Until about the turn of the century, office equipment was almost unheard of in most large government-owned post offices. This was due in large measure to the traditional use of handwritten forms and ledgers. In contrast, typewriters were rapidly being introduced into the private sector in the 1880s. The growing use of typewriters in commercial offices was emphasized in an 1887 report in *Penman's Art Journal,* which observed "five years ago the typewriter was simply a mechanical curiosity. Today its monotonous click can be heard in almost every well regulated business establishment." No such clatter

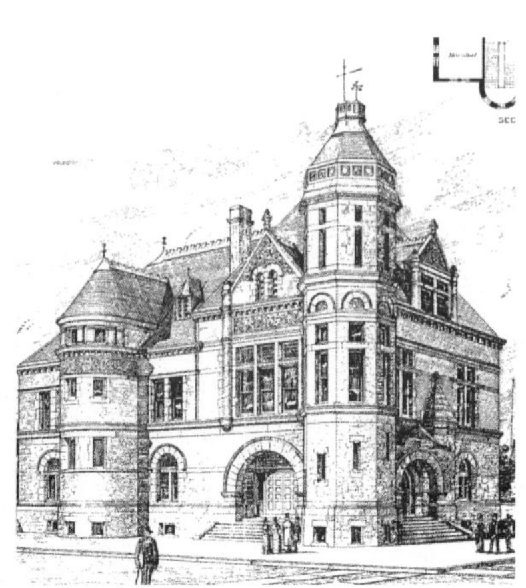

Supervising Architect renderings for three larger federal buildings: William Martin Aiken's design for the Richmond, Kentucky, post office; Will Freret's rendering of the federal building at Los Angeles, California; and Mifflin Bell's design for the federal building at Auburn, New York. These designs reflect the grandeur expected of larger postal facilities. These designs, however, do not always resemble the final appearance of these buildings.

typically resounded in government offices. Instead, the federal government remained content to rely upon a "scribe-system" to maintain ongoing operations. The reliance upon clerks tended to stifle the introduction of federal office automation in large cities. Small town postmasters had no scribes. Here they led the way. Many turn of the century rural postmasters purchased their own typewriters for official use.

First-class offices are the largest class of post offices. They typically had more than enough room for patrons, and their physical size and shape reflected their importance. Architecturally, they are grand, and unlike fourth-class offices, which largely were located on private property, first-class post offices have traditionally been government-owned. First-class post offices symbolized in the biggest way possible the prominence and the presence of the federal government on the local level, regardless of whether the post office stood alone or shared space with a court house or customs house.

The post office at Port Townsend, Washington, a massive Romanesque-style building, is a structural beacon, a prominent visual focal point, situated on a bluff overlooking the Straits of Juan De Fuca. Its placement proclaims the federal presence. The massive sandstone exterior and copper-covered hipped roofline of this 30,883 square foot structure originally dwarfed its immediate surroundings. It was far grander structurally than was necessary; at best, it was intended to serve a population of 6,500, which was the count in 1889. By the time of its completion the population had dwindled to under 2,000, thanks to local economic failures and the Depression of 1893.

The commanding site of the Romanesque-style federal building at Port Townsend, Washington, dominated the community.

Supervising Architect Mifflin Bell's design for the federal building at Aberdeen, Mississippi, gives the impression of being a prominent town house.

Secure in their ability to carry out their work, these clerks were photographed in 1891 sorting letters inside the "fortified" post office at St. Louis, Missouri.

The Trappings of Power

AS THE REPRESENTATIVE of the federal government, the post office building had to be impressive, yet in keeping with the style of the times, and they usually were. During the 1880s and 1890s, one trend was for post offices to resemble opulent town houses. These structures would not be too out of place along any grand boulevard, except perhaps for the telltale loading dock, which frequently was tastefully concealed.

In other cases, post office buildings were nothing less than glorified "secular cathedrals." In at least one case, however, it might be more appropriate to use the word "fortress," rather than describe the building as a "federal cathedral." Because of the fear of fire, and the large amount of money collected from the traffic along the Mississippi River, averaging $2 million per year, and in an attempt to protect gold deposits, the St. Louis post office and customs house was virtually designed as a fireproof and attack-resistant fort.

Towers dominate the designs of many 19th century post offices, such as Bridgeport, Connecticut, and Rochester, New York.

As well as being grand structures, many large urban post office buildings were grand sights. Tall towers were quite the fashion, even though the towers and embellishments served little functional purpose; they did not move the mail any faster or farther, but they did make the building stand out. Many of these towers were massive things, frequently overpowering the rest of the building in terms of their height or breadth. These grand buildings in small cities were a tangible symbol of the federal government's presence.

American eagles were often incorporated into the designs of federal buidlings during the 1890s and 1900s, as were one or more tall flagpoles for the display of the Stars and Stripes. This use of the American flag was another telltale sign of the federal presence. This was, and is, true of both urban offices and those in tiny hamlets. However, even after World War I, there was no uniform way of presenting the flag. This troubled some postal officials, especially Postmaster General Harry New, who was irked by what he viewed as irreverence. In New's opinion, the flag was not always as prominent as it should have been. In 1924 he advised all postmasters:

> At a number of offices the flag is not raised in the morning and lowered in the evening and at others the flags are not in a satisfactory condition. The failure of the postmaster to display a flag in the prescribed manner reflects adversely upon the service and I shall appreciate it if you will give this matter special attention.

In addition, New provided each postmaster with excerpts of the War Department's circular on the proper methods for displaying the flag and told them to follow the Army's instructions.

There was a cost for all this. The post office at Windsor, Vermont, for example, constructed in the 1850s, cost $71,347. That was a high price tag for a town with a population of only about 2,000 inhabitants.

Instead of producing useful structures, the nation was building extravagant edifices. A report published in a popular magazine shortly before World War I took exception to such expenditures, highlighting the example of a post office building that was constructed for $60,000, when a $5,000 structure would have been entirely adequate.

Between 1900 and 1916, according to Treasury Secretary William McAdoo, the nation spent roughly $180 million for public buildings. In his 1916 *Annual Report*, McAdoo stated "the major part of this great sum has been expended on costly structures in small localities where neither the Government business nor the convenience of the people justified their construction." McAdoo's sentiments were that, instead of being exceedingly expensive and wasteful of space, government buildings needed to be practical, cost effective, and built for the right price for the specific site. His views found a more and more receptive audience, particularly among congressional leaders, prominent citizens, and postal officials who were beginning to realize that architecturally opulent government "temples," of the types that had been built for decades at great government expense, were simply not always the best types of buildings for housing such an important function of the government as the postal service. Taking McAdoo's cue, an important government commission rationalized that "The kind of building best adapted to the needs of the government is the modern office-type structure, designed with due regard to the safety, health, and comfort of the people who are to use it."

Opposing McAdoo's notion of proportional spending was the general tendency of party politics, and the desire of each incoming administration to outshine the previous one. Republicans and Democrats alike were quick to point with pride to the dedication of new post office

In the 1890s and 1900s, American eagles and tall flagpoles were often used to enhance the sense of a federal presence. The Waterloo, Iowa, post office features a prominent display of both icons. It was designed by James Knox Taylor.

buildings as representations of their tenure in the White House. Consequently, the construction of post offices became a contest of sorts to see which party could outshine the other, but by 1915 even this was beginning to change. Reason was beginning to take root.

Trends Along the Way

BUILDING STARTS often coincided with upward trends in the economy, as well as nationalistic fervor. The rise of Americanism at the turn of the century resulted in a frenzy of construction. Many of these 1900s post offices looked alike. Indeed, in many cases, if you peeled away the outer facade and compared the interiors you would find floor plans that were often very much the same.

This tendency toward look-alike government buildings did not sit well with private architects, who thought that greater creativity and individuality could be attained by using practitioners, like themselves, instead of the government stable of designers employed by the Supervising Architect's office. The Tarsney Act, a piece of 1890s legislation, was designed to encourage outside commissions among private architects. This legislation, backed by the American Institute of Architects, was expected to make the government more architecturally competitive, while at the same time achieving a greater array of appealing building designs. The AIA hoped that this would be good for its members, which included about one-fifth of America's architects at that time, but the Treasury Department was less than enthusiastic about this legislation. It awarded outside commissions only reluctantly, claiming that the language of the legislation was vague, that private architects were slower and more expensive than their counterparts at the Office of the Supervising Architect, and that the resulting buildings were certain to be more expensive to produce. There were also claims that AIA members would almost certainly be favored over other private architects in receiving such commissions, but too few projects were actually undertaken for that to be determined statistically. Only about three-dozen commissions were actually awarded to private architects, with assignments going to such prominent names as Daniel Burnham, Cass Gilbert, and Albert Kahn, before the act was repealed in 1912. Much to the regret of the Supervising Architects, some of the nation's biggest post offices, almost all of which are still standing, were designed by these outstanding outsiders.

After decades of overtly or covertly sabotaging the Tarsney Act, the Treasury Department could afford to be magnanimous in its demise, even to the point of saying that it would be missed. In his 1912 *Annual Report* Treasury Secretary Frank MacVeagh expressed the opinion that "the repeal of the Tarsney Act was received with great regret by the Treasury Department, and by great numbers of people who are especially interested in the art and fitness of government buildings." MacVeagh's opinion was that it was absurd to think that any one government office should, or could, design the number of buildings that the Office of the

Supervising Architect was being asked to prepare.

MacVeagh genuinely believed that there was value in collegial exchanges between the Supervising Architect's office and private practitioners. His view was that "no architect's office, such as [the Supervising Architect's office] should be thrown in upon itself or should be taken out of constant association and competition with all the other successful architects and architectural offices."

Excessive workloads and outside competition were not the only problems confronting the Supervising Architect's office. Between 1890 and 1910, government officials from the different agencies that occupied these grand federal buildings began to doubt the wisdom of having such multipurpose structures. The practicality of combining a customs house, court house, and post office together into one big building became an issue for a number of reasons. For the postal service, space was a constant concern, especially as mail volumes grew. Then too, the location of the federal building, typically in the heart of the commercial district, where traffic congestion was fast becoming unbearable, constantly made moving the mail much more difficult. The location and space issues were compounded by the fact that a variety of rival railroads usually had terminals in different parts of the city. Like an urban spiderweb, the mail transported by each of these competing rail carriers had to be collected by wagon and brought to the central post office for distribution. The alternative was to create a separate post office adjacent to, or right on top of, the tracks of a union station, a station that could unite rival tracks at one point, as was uniformly done after 1910 in most large cities.

Postal officials applauded this type of location as a major convenience, and they came to regard those cities that failed to create a union terminal as great frustrations. Chicago, with its numerous depots, was perhaps the postal service's greatest headache in the years before World

One of San Francisco's post office stations, about 1894.

War I. By the mid-1890s, Chicago's postal workers were handling about one-sixth of the nation's total mail volume, which at that time amounted to 5.5 billion pieces of mail.

Another trend occurring at about the same time, the growth of urban populations and the corresponding urbanization of the areas surrounding the city, led to the creation of smaller city postal stations and substations to serve the geographically spreading populations. Chicago, in 1893, was served by the main post office, 13 postal stations, and 22 substations; by 1917, it had 52 large postal stations and 306 smaller stations, plus the main office. Because of the convenience of these branch post offices, city dwellers profited greatly from this growth.

The growth also included the use of larger and larger numbers of letter carriers. In 1893, 610 cities provided free door-to-door delivery by 11,625 carriers. Seventeen years later, this same service was being provided in over 2,000 cities by over 36,000 carriers. Post office facilities had to accommodate this growing workforce. Larger break and locker rooms began to become a serious consideration.

Air quality within postal facilities was another concern. The mere act of dragging heavy mail sacks from the loading docks, where they arrived by horse-drawn wagons, into the buildings gave the entire office an foul odor that many old-time clerks likened to a stable. These same mail pouches were covered with copious amounts of horse manure, dust, and debris, which came loose from the sacks and fell onto the clerks in a constant shower as the mail bags were transported about the facilities on overhead conveyors. By the turn of the last century the Post Office Department found that costly ventilating systems were needed to simply keep the air in many urban offices breathable. Newer facilities opened in the 1910s in St. Louis, New York, Washington, D.C., and elsewhere, providing state-of-the-art air handling systems, as well as artificial lighting.

All of these changes, occurring nearly simultaneously, greatly affected the architectural face of the postal service. In less than one generation, urban mail services more than tripled, and with that increase came a corresponding need for new architectural standards and structures.

Major Building Sprees

NOT ALL POST OFFICE changes involved the Supervisory Architect's office; some minor alterations were decreed or improvised locally. As more and more Americans took to the roads for pleasure, Postmaster General George von L. Meyer was struck with a brilliantly simple, yet overdue, idea in 1908: "As an aid to travelers, local postmasters should include the names of their towns on all post office signs." Always quick to save a dollar, Meyer insisted that such signs were the postmasters' or property owners' responsibility.

Construction of the Georgetown, South Carolina, post office, 1905.

Congress was not as thrifty. During James Knox Taylor's tenure as Supervising Architect, Congress went on a "pork barrel" binge, spending extravagantly on post offices and other public buildings. The phrase "pork barrel," coined by Democrats in the early 1900s, was rooted in the Southern custom of giving out slabs of salted pork, cured in large barrels, to slave families on plantations.

Congressman Morris Sheppard of Texas was one of the "Kings of Pork." During one session he sponsored bills to buy sites and/or build post offices for constituents at Pittsburg, Jefferson, Cooper, Mount Pleasant, Dangerfield, Paris, Atlanta, Texarkana, Mount Vernon, and Clarksville. These lard-laden bills amounted to an appropriation of $910,000. Not to be outdone, Congressman Louis B. Hanna of North Dakota offered appropriation bills for offices at Mandan, Jamestown, Dickinson, Williston, and Valley City. These five projects had a combined price tag of $500,000.

The majority of the members of Congress, such as Leonidas Felix Livingston of Georgia, were no more kind on Uncle Sam's wallet. Restrained by comparison with most others, Livingston "limited" himself to the introduction of bills worth $150,000 each for post office projects at Fairburn, Conyers, Jonesboro, Decatur, Douglasville, Covington, and Monroe.

Excessive building bills became so common, that in 1909 Senator Nathan Scott of West Virginia introduced a measure to enable the Secretary of the Treasury to borrow $100 million to pay for "pork barrel" projects built in towns with populations of 5,000 or more.

The spending spree continued; a major raid on the public treasury came in a midnight session in 1910. This was like a feeding frenzy at the public trough. During that session over 900 separate building bills were introduced, amounting to $225 million, which was far too much for serious consideration. Conferees whittled down the projects by a third, and then lumped them together. The omnibus building bill, covering everything from the purchase of building sites to the erection of new buildings or the expansion of existing structures, and containing nearly 50 pages of projects, passed easily in the House, with only five opposing votes. Twenty hours later, with $5 million more added by the Senate, the measure passed without major debate or dissenting vote. President William Howard Taft balked at signing the legislation, but only briefly.

One member of Congress boasted that the omnibus legislation was not really "pork barrel" politics, but was rather "a masterpiece of geographical distribution." And, in a way, it was. Two hundred and ninety-six Congressional districts out of 391 were represented in one fashion or another. But this reflected only the excessiveness of the plunder, not the appropriateness of the appropriations.

Such Congressional camouflage did not fool the public or the press, which advised:

> Call it "pork barrel" legislation if you want to. There is nothing that entices votes in a given community more than an appropriation for a federal building or the improvement of a river or harbor. So Congressmen must get all the "pork" possible to help their own cause along when election time comes around.

And, in 1910, greasing the way for elections was crucial for many politicians. Republicans realized that they would be facing a hard fight for control of the House of Representatives. The passage of two major "pork bills" in one session—one for river and harbor projects, the other for public buildings—was considered a sure vote-getter.

There was even a sort of gentlemen's agreement concerning such bills; those members of Congress who did not have rivers or harbors to improve in their districts voted for such spending measures anyway, with the understanding that they would get their fair share of "pork" in the form of building legislation. One commentary observed, "It looks now as though the promise for their support is going to be kept, and that practically every good Republican will get a good slice in one bill or the other to help out in the campaign."

Although the postal service constantly needed more space to keep up with growing mail volume, many of the post offices created during the late 1890s and early 1900s were "pork barrel" projects, such as the federal building at Los Angeles, California, designed by James Knox Taylor in 1906.

Other comments were less kind. One stated that "some members of Congress clamor to loot the Treasury in this nefarious political game for personal gain. Many would no doubt have a federal building at every crossroad town in their district if they could possibly put the projects through Congress, and thereby win favor in the community affected."

That's nearly what one Congressman from Missouri tried to do. Rather than watch individual members of Congress tack on a steadily growing number of building bills to one major appropriation, he proposed a gigantic, one-time raid on the U.S. Treasury. His idea was for Congress to authorize a new post office for every county seat in the country. That would have amounted to an estimated 4,000 post offices.

With only slight variation, many of James Knox Taylor's designs were reused, as can be seen from the post offices at Macon, Georgia, and Deadwood, South Dakota.

Unfortunately, the country could hardly afford the extravagance. The fact of the matter was that for many of these proposed government-owned buildings in small cities and towns, the costs of janitorial service and building maintenance alone would—and often did—exceed the annual rent previously paid for being in a nongovernment-owned building.

There were other things to consider on the minus side. Because of such "pork barrel" bills, by 1910, the Supervising Architect's office had a backlog of about two years' worth of work, making it impossible to take on any additional projects, even if additional appropriations were made.

But that did not stop Congress. During subsequent sessions, hundreds of public building bills continued to be introduced. The snowballing effect grew to such proportions that by 1912 the House Committee on Public Buildings and Grounds voted to limit members to one "pet" project each.

At the time James Knox Taylor's staff had a number of pet building styles and sizes. These comprised a common cast of architectural characters that were repeatedly called upon to suit different sites, subject only to a slight change of exterior costuming. There was nothing architecturally wrong with rolling out the same old troop of designs time after time. This certainly was the expeditious thing for Taylor to do. Besides, it created a range of standard designs, which could be used to create post offices in similarly sized cities with relative ease. This sat especially well with Senators and Congressmen, because it treated their constituents as equals, irrespective of where they lived or how much they mailed. This approach, however, did not always make sense to postal officials.

Many of Taylor's designs bear an unmistakable resemblance. Despite variations in window treatment and ornamentation, many overall patterns are replicated. Lincoln, Nebraska, and Butte, Montana, represent one case in point; as do Yankton, South Dakota, and Waterloo, Iowa. In the latter case, oversized eagles, with outstretched wings, perch prominently on the roof lines. Such eagles were more than an architectural gesture. They helped give the buildings a "federal" persona which set them apart from similarly styled commercial buildings, such as banks. Ogden, Utah; Deadwood, South Dakota; and Macon, Georgia; represent still another example of look-alike designs that were popular among Taylor's team.

It was clear to Treasury Secretary William McAdoo that spending limits and standardization were sorely needed. On June 29, 1915, he advised the Office of the Supervising Architect that it was to observe a strict policy when it came to "giving effect to authorizations for the construction, enlargement, extension and special repairs of public buildings under control of the Treasury Department." The key to McAdoo's position was that the designs for public buildings were to be in keeping with the types of structures already in the communities. The amount authorized for such projects by Congress was not to be the driving force behind the type of structure that was constructed. "Effort should always be made to conserve rather than unnecessarily to expend appropriations," he told the nation's chief architect; adding "This does not mean that savings are to be effected at the expense of space and facilities, or that the designs employed are to be stripped of ornamentation." Instead, McAdoo insisted that the buildings provided should be of adequate size, properly planned for the convenient transaction of public business, feature modern facilities, and be in keeping with the architectural designs and materials used within the communities in which they were to be placed.

To achieve this, McAdoo devised a general classification system that was to be observed for the foreseeable future. Four categories of construction were covered under this scheme, which would determine the size, style, materials, and embellishments to be used for a particular building. Each of the four categories was based upon the total annual receipts for the particular post office in question.

These four classifications included:

CLASS A

Definition

Buildings that include a Post Office of the first class with annual receipts of $800,000 or over; the site forming part of a city development plan or situated on an important thoroughfare of a great city; improvements on adjoining property reaching the higher valuation of metropolitan real estate.

Character of Building

Marble or granite facing; fireproof throughout; metal frames, sashes and doors; interior finish to include the finer grades of marble, ornamental bronze work, mahogany, etc.

Public spaces to have monumental treatment, mural decorations; special interior lighting fixtures.

CLASS B

Definition

Buildings that include a Post Office of the first class with receipts from $60,000 to $800,000; valuation of adjoining property somewhat below the higher valuation of metropolitan real estate.

Character of Building

Limestone or sandstone facing; fireproof throughout; exterior frames and sash metal; interior frames, sash, and doors wood; interior finish to exclude the more expensive woods and marbles; ornamental metal to be used only where iron is suitable. Restricted ornament in public spaces.

CLASS C

Definition

Buildings that include a Post Office of the second class with receipts of $15,000 or over, and of the first class up to $60,000 receipts; valuation of surrounding property that of a second-class city.

Character of Building

Brick facing with stone or terra cotta trimmings; fireproof floors; non-fireproof roof; frames, sashes and doors wood; interior finish to exclude the more expensive woods and marbles; the latter used only where sanitary conditions demand; public spaces restricted to very simple forms of ornament.

CLASS D

Definition

Buildings that include a Post Office having annual receipts of less than $15,000; real estate values justifying only a limited investment for improvements.

Character of Building

Brick facing, little stone or terra cotta used; only first floor fireproof; stock sash, frames, doors, etc., where advisable; ordinary class of building such as any businessman would consider a reasonable investment in a small town.

McAdoo stressed that speed should be observed in the creation of standardized plans and specifications, advising the Supervising Architect that "work on the standardization of full sized details should be carried forward as rapidly as possible; and similar attention should be given to the completion of the work that has been undertaken in preparing standard specifications." Realizing that time was money, McAdoo stressed that "in the preparation of specifications special consideration should be given to such changes as may be practicable to shorten the contract time."

Besides being a logical response to the unreasonable demands that were being placed upon his department, McAdoo's classification system was a perfect way to shield the Treasury Department from charges of favoritism and extravagance.

In issuing this policy Treasury Secretary William G. McAdoo restated his firm belief that competitive pricing, not local or Congressional pressure, should determine the sources of the materials and manpower that were used on public projects. McAdoo's opinion on this in 1913 was that the Treasury Department "is always gratified whenever local materials and labor are found to answer its requirements, but it cannot undertake to restrict competition by limiting bidders to local materials and labor." His opinion two years later was the same, characterized by this requirement that "while I recognize the fact that frequently strong sentiment is expressed in favor of the use of local materials in the construction of public buildings, I do not feel justified in limiting competition to such materials, or in awarding contracts for materials so produced at prices which amount to subsidizing local industries."

McAdoo's evenhanded position on local versus out-of-state materials angered many a local politician who did not care much for his concept that bids on materials should encourage the widest possible competition for the class of materials that were called for.

Eight leaders of the marble and granite industry also were quick to express their displeasure with McAdoo's classification system, one that restricted marble and granite to only the finest structures. "This ruling on classification is, in our opinion, unfair, in that it limits competition regardless of local conditions governing availability and price, which if considered might result in all these materials being competitive in many localities," said a committee representing the marble and granite industry. What prompted this reaction was not only the fact that the industry wanted a bigger piece of the public-works pie, but also the realization that "this ruling is also adversely affecting the use of other materials in private buildings, because architects are following the precedents established by the Government in this movement, which results in the discouragement of the development of the natural resources and manufacturers of the country."

The granite and marble lobby wanted concessions, claiming that McAdoo's classification system discriminated against two fine building materials. Supervising Architect Wetmore met with leaders of the granite and marble industry and reached an agreement, which in effect, conceded very little. It was agreed that "bids on granite and marble will be taken only in case the Department thinks the material suitable" and that "it is not contemplated to approve granite or marble unless it is offered at the same or lower cost than limestone or sandstone." Wetmore passed on the results of his meeting with the granite and marble men in a memorandum to his boss, William G. McAdoo, in which he closed by observing that "it is extremely improbable that bids will be received for any of these buildings with dressed granite or marble facing and trimming as at low a cost as on limestone or sandstone,but as the Association evidently believes otherwise and considers the amendment a concession, the office sees no objection to its adoption." McAdoo accepted this compromise, authorizing bids for granite and marble to be accepted for B,

C, and D class buildings, along with sandstone, limestone, and brick. The result was almost precisely what James A. Wetmore predicted.

In May 1917, the Treasury Department broadened its building categories to include the use of stone facings for buildings in communities where the post office had gross annual receipts of at least $45,000. A further condition, that the post office's receipts for the past 10 years had to show an increase of not less than 75 percent, also applied to this new category. America's entrance into World War I in April 1917 reduced the likelihood that this amendment would be broadly implemented.

Two months after the United States entered World War I, the Treasury Secretary advised his supervising architect to take whatever steps were necessary to ensure that those responsible for building and supplying government facilities "exercise patriotic judgement and caution in their demands" until prices returned to their prewar levels.

By 1923 Postmaster General Hubert Work wanted to get away from the practice of building common-sized offices. The notion that "a few sizes fit all" ignored the basic fact that different-sized communities sent and received different amounts of mail. Roughly 35 percent of the post offices built between 1912 and 1922 were in the South, an area of the country that was responsible for only about 15 percent of the nation's mail. This placed a greater burden on equal-sized facilities in the North.

Postmaster General Work realized that many of the buildings designed by the Treasury Department for major business centers were totally inadequate almost as soon as they were completed, which convinced him that business mail was about to enter an unprecedented period of growth. With this in mind, Work began to anticipate the growing pulse of mail marketing; he wanted to be ready, rather than merely playing catch-up. He protested plans to rent the buildings required to keep pace with that growth. His view was that "being compelled to pay in rental the first cost of such a building during the life of a 20-year lease, is subversive of good business methods."

To a degree, postal automation was also beginning to play a part in Postmaster General Work's plan to move more mail. Although the technology of the time was primitive, mechanical canceling machines,

The main city post office for Washington, D.C. for many years, and the adjacent Union Station railroad terminal, were designed by Daniel Burnham, in the early 1900s.

crude sorting devices, postage-meter machines, and conveyor systems were beginning to have an impact upon postal facilities. And, the 19th century notion of housing post offices with federal courts and custom houses in common structures was gradually being abandoned in favor of building government-owned postal facilities adjacent to "Union" railway stations.

The next serious building binge after the pre-World War I activity did not occur until the late 1920s with the passage in 1926 of another piece of omnibus building legislation, a Congressional authorization of $165 million over an 11-year period. This spending limit was raised to $290 million in 1928 and, with the onset of the Great Depression, was further increased to $620 million by the early 1930s. Added to this figure was the income from the sales of obsolete government properties, which amounted to nearly $70 million. In all approximately $700 million during the Depression era was used in creating new federal buildings. Once again Congressional leaders and government officials gladly assumed the role of latter day Johnny Appleseeds, sprinkling post offices all over the countryside.

How Services Affected Design

THE CREATION OF EACH NEW postal service has brought about some sort of physical change in America's post offices. Because of the unprecedented number of innovations introduced since 1900, this has been especially true of this century. These evolving services reflected the federal government's willingness to become more and more involved in the daily lives of the average citizen, particularly in the areas of banking and shopping.

As the mail-order business grew, provision had to be made in many facilities for increased storage space, including refrigeration units for perishables. No longer did one clerk, a single window, and some pigeonholes constitute a post office.

A plank in the Republican Party platform of 1909 called for the creation of a system for public savings to stem the flow of cash from immigrants out of this country and into accounts abroad, a drain of an estimated $75 million

A minor adjustment to the post office interior was all that was needed to accommodate Postal Savings—placing a new sign over an existing service window. Theodore Roosevelt is represented by the "Teddy Bear" in this 1900s editorial cartoon depicting the inauguration of Postal Savings.

annually. The proposal was also intended to lure countless hoards of cash out from teapots and cookie jars and into a Postal Savings System. Local post offices would become banking centers in communities that had no banking institutions. Socks would be emptied of their stash and money would be deposited into postal savings plans through the newly constructed banking windows. The presumption was that those Americans who, by their nature, distrusted banks, would have confidence in banking with the Post Office Department. That assumption proved correct.

Although this portion of the platform was largely ignored by many Republicans following the presidential election, it was championed by President Taft. Taft's insistence on adhering to this plank of the party platform resulted in the passage of an Act of Congress, which was approved on June 25, 1910.

Theodore L. Weed, who helped organize and manage this country's Postal Savings System when it was established in 1911, described its purpose this way:

> "Uncle Sam" will be extending kindly hands to the widows and orphans, to the old and young in the most inaccessible regions of the country. The dimes of the school children, as well as the dollars of the thrifty, will be securely guarded by a benevolent Government against panics and disasters of all kinds.

Cartoonists were quick to lampoon Weed's remarks and ridicule the system. One drawing showed Uncle Sam as the Pied Piper leading a parade of cash-filled socks, tin cans, and fruit jars on their way to the post office for deposit. But in this case the satirical art was not extremely harmful because the system worked.

Intended to serve predominantly small-scale depositors in places not adequately served by other savings institutions, the system was initially introduced at 48 second-class post offices, one in each state and territory. The sites included:

Bessemer, Alabama
Globe, Arizona
Stuttgart, Arkansas
Oroville, California
Leadville, Colorado
Ansonia, Connecticut
Dover, Delaware
Key West, Florida
Brunswick, Georgia
Coeur d'Alene, Idaho
Pekin, Illinois
Princeton, Indiana
Decorah, Iowa
Pittsburg, Kansas
Middlesboro, Kentucky
New Iberia, Louisiana
Rumford, Maine
Nebraska City, Nebraska
Carson City, Nevada
Berlin, New Hampshire
Rutherford, New Jersey
Raton, New Mexico
Cohoes, New York
Salisbury, North Carolina
Wahpeton, North Dakota
Ashtabula, Ohio
Guymon, Oklahoma
Klamath Falls, Oregon
Dubois, Pennsylvania
Bristol, Rhode Island
Newberry, South Carolina
Deadwood, South Dakota
Johnson City, Tennessee
Port Arthur, Texas

Frostburg, Maryland	Provo, Utah
Norwood, Massachusetts	Montpelier, Vermont
Houghton, Michigan	Clifton Forge, Virginia
Bemidji, Minnesota	Olympia, Washington
Gulfport, Mississippi	Grafton, West Virginia
Carthage, Missouri	Manitowac, Wisconsin
Anaconda, Montana	Laramie, Wyoming

Most of the sites hosting the Postal Savings System were small industrial centers where wage earners were thought likely to benefit from this kind of banking. It was logical to assume that the deposits from mining and isolated communities would be greater than those in the more densely settled communities in the eastern and central states. As a result, Colorado, Montana, and Arizona had the largest receipts during the first few months of operation.

The Postal Savings System proved popular. Receipts collected during the first four months of operation exceeded $250,000. By July 1911, Postmaster General Frank Hitchcock was authorizing nearly 150 additional offices a month to provide the banking service. By January 1912, the Postal Savings System was extended to 5,185 post offices, including those of major urban centers, and preparations were being made to establish the system in all fourth-class post offices that handled money-order business. Such preparations included remodeling the interiors of many offices, adding additional window units to accommodate banking business.

The Postal Saving System had certain restrictions, only accepting individual accounts; corporations, societies, and civic groups had to bank with state chartered or national banking institutions. The minimum amount required to open a Postal Savings account was $1. Not more than $200 could be deposited in any one month. Depositors had to deal with only one post office, which was not bad if there was only one office, but where there were several branches in the same community, it was troublesome for postal officials, who insisted that if depositors wished to set up accounts elsewhere in the same town, they first had to close the original account. Interest was 2 percent per annum, computed from the first business day of the month. This meant that deposits made after the first of the month could not begin to earn interest until the first of the next month. The fact that the government was paying 2 percent interest had a beneficial impact upon the banking industry in general by prompting many state and national banks to raise their interest rate from 2 to 3 percent in order to attract and retain customers.

Money deposited into Postal Savings accounts was reinvested into state and national banks at a 2 1/4 percent rate of return, with Uncle Sam keeping the difference over the 2 percent that was paid to account holders. The deposits were backed by a guarantee of security furnished by the national government.

By January 1915, the system had over $59 million in deposits, savings that belonged to nearly a half-million patrons. "Substantially all deposits in the Postal Savings System," said Postmaster General Albert Burleson in 1915, "represent the savings of wage-earners who will not patronize private institutions, but who have confidence in the government."

During the first few years the savings system grew to a point where service was provided at 9,631 post offices. New York City maintained the biggest bank, with nearly $9.5 million on deposit. In addition to New York, roughly one-third of the system's $59 million was attributed to five other offices—Chicago, Brooklyn, Boston, San Francisco, and Portland.

The outbreak of World War I had a profound effect on the Postal Savings System. It greatly curtailed the flow of funds overseas and resulted in an increase of more than 100,000 depositors in the first six months of the European war. During that period, deposits amounted to $3 million a month. According to a boastful Post Office Department statement, "When Europe's paralyzing conflict broke out, withdrawals fell off and thousands of strange faces appeared at post offices to entrust their soiled and tarnished savings to Uncle Sam." At the Indianapolis post office, for example, by the middle of 1915, American citizens owned $103,658, while foreign nationals held $63,664.

In the years between the end of World War I and the start of the Great Depression, deposits varied from about $131 million to $167 million. With all of the bank failures that accompanied the Depression, small savers turned increasingly to the Postal Savings System. The number of accounts rose dramatically from 674,728, the high during the previous decade, to 770,859. During the first six months of 1930, over 104 times as much money was deposited as during the same period in 1911, when the system started. Public confidence was that great! And it was growing. By the middle of November 1931, about $575 million was in Postal Savings accounts, up by over $66 million in just one month. One New York Congressman called this "sleeping money," savings that had formerly been hoarded in tin boxes, tobacco cans, trunks, privies, barns, stoves, and socks. The number of depositors grew to over 2.5 million by 1935. The Postal Savings System was ideal for cautious savers. Postal officials said it was the perfect financial "refuge for the timid."

Little changed until after World War II. By the late 1940s Americans had greater trust in federally insured commercial banks. Local banks also were paying much higher rates of interest on deposits, prompting the Postal Savings accounts to drop. The Postal Savings System was formally discontinued on March 28, 1966.

Parcel Post

PARCEL POST, WHICH WAS BEGUN in 1913, was another story. On the eve of its inauguration it was easy to visualize the array of barnyard animals that might find their way into the mailstream once Parcel Post started. Stalls for cows and pigs were expected to become just as much a permanent part of post office architecture as lockboxes and loading docks. Jokesters also envisioned the addition of hitching posts alongside street-corner letterboxes for the convenience of those mailing or receiving sheep or horses, and a new category of postal employee was jokingly predicted: the flock herder.

Despite such predictions, Parcel Post was a phenomenal success. During roughly the first five days of service, over 4 million packages were mailed. Over 300 million packages were handled during the first six months of service, and the inauguration of Collect-on-Delivery and Insurance services, later in 1913, only added to the popularity of Parcel Post.

All of this had an immense impact upon postal facilities. To handle the influx of package mail, the Post Office Department needed to do some hasty remodeling.

The inauguration of Parcel Post on January 1, 1913, caught the government's Supervising Architect, the person responsible for major post office construction projects, by surprise. By February of that year, it was obvious that the plans for countless buildings would have to be revised to accommodate the popularity of the parcel business. At that time 174 public buildings were under contract and 233 others had been funded. None of the buildings on order or under way, amounting to about $50 million worth of work, provided adequate space for processing the number of parcels the Post Office Department began handling.

According to the postal system, "the plans for these buildings having been prepared without regard for the establishment of a Parcel Post, it is necessary now to have changes made in their architectural construction in order that the necessary volume of mail may be handled to the best advantage."

Many existing post offices were also hard up for space. In 1913, post offices were located in 759 government-owned buildings, none of which

Editorial cartoonists had a field day with the way they envisioned the Post Office Department's reaction to Parcel Post and the effect that it was expected to have on the interiors of post offices.

were capable of handling the amount of parcels they were receiving. Postmaster General Frank Hitchcock was anxious to confer with Supervising Architect Oscar Wenderoth, who headed that office between 1913 and 1914, concerning the addition of floor space in all of these offices.

Space and growing volumes remained a problem. Denver, for example, was swamped with packages. In April 1914, the *Rocky Mountain News* reported that "packages were piled ceiling high in [the post office], aisles were blocked and still there was not enough room for the parcels." In response to the crush, postmaster Joseph Harrison asked for permission to rent a store building to accommodate the overflow, until a new post office could be built. Harrison was lucky in that Denver was already in the process of getting a new post office.

Other urban centers, like Brooklyn, had to cope as best they could. By the late 1920s parcel mail was so heavy there that it was necessary to take over a Brooklyn armory to accommodate the Christmas rush.

The nation's big mail-order houses, on the other hand, were not caught napping. They were geared up to deal with the onslaught of Parcel Post business by 1913 and they kept well up with demand.

The Original Shop-at-Home Club

FROM THE INSTANT PARCEL POST was inaugurated, nature's most fragile package, the egg, was a mainstay of the service. Half a dozen eggs were the first objects sent by Parcel Post from St. Louis, Missouri, at 12:05 a.m. on January 1, 1913. They were mailed to Edwardsville, Illinois, where they were baked into a cake and promptly returned to St. Louis the same day.

Like countless other communities, Emmitsburg, Maryland, also received eggs as its first Parcel Post shipment. These eggs were just for eating though, not for ceremony. They were sent from Motters, Maryland, around midnight on January 1, 1913, and arrived in Emmitsburg at 9 a.m.

The popularity of sending eggs by Parcel Post was evidenced by the following poem, published in the March 1913 issue of *The Postmaster's Advocate:*

She stands besides the open gate
To wait the postman's coming
Her eyes with expectation bright
A little measure humming.
The flush upon her dainty cheek
Tells how the heart is beating,
And likewise of the thought it keeps
Repeating and repeating.
The postman comes! He stops! He waits!

He searches through his burden;
He finds something she receives
And gains her thanks for guerdon.
She clasps it to her bosom close
As if to still its aching
And cries with joy; "Thank Heaven, the eggs
Have come in time for baking!"

It was literally only a matter of minutes before eggs were joined by other good things from the farm. All kinds of farm-fresh produce were being shipped by mail from the farm to the city by way of Parcel Post. Of course, mailing eggs and cheese and chickens and carrots was a little more complicated than sending furniture, clothes, and department-store goods. Expedience was the key. But when Parcel Post was first inaugurated, the postal service had not given too much thought to the issue of safely conveying such produce. It was more than a year and a half before the postal service came up with a comprehensive plan to handle this deluge of farm goods.

The "Farm-to-Table" program, inaugurated in August 1914, was designed to allow city dwellers to buy directly from farmers, with the postal system acting as an impartial broker. The Farm-to-Table program was launched as a test program in ten cities: Washington, D.C.; St. Louis; Boston; Baltimore; Atlanta; Birmingham; San Francisco; Rock Island, Illinois; Lynn, Massachusetts; and La Crosse, Wisconsin.

The underlying goal of the Farm-to-Table program was to expand the Parcel Post customer base so that it catered not only to the big mail-order houses, but also served thousands of previously untapped grassroots entrepreneurs as well. In this respect, the system was an instant success, creating an anxious swarm of what Postmaster General Albert Burleson called "mail-order farmers."

From the start, farmers were urged to rely upon friends and relatives to help them find customers, and this strategy did pay off for a while.

Shoppers at a post office looking for "Farm-to-Table" deals.

More than 75 percent of all the products marketed by mail were sold to customers located through the help of relatives and acquaintances. This made sense from the the standpoint of both the buyer and the seller. Neither party relished the idea of doing business with a stranger. City dwellers wanted some assurances about the quality of the farmers' products, and farmers wanted guarantees about the integrity of the buyer.

Seeing the popularity of this new program, the postal service wasted no time in extending the service to other cities, including Chicago, Philadelphia, Brooklyn, Denver, and Seattle. Postmasters in the targeted areas bent over backwards to ensure the success of this new venture. Each postmaster was responsible for circulating lists of farmers with produce to sell, as well as current prices and descriptions of the goods offered. But most postmasters went even further. In Brooklyn, school children were given "take home" lists of farmers who were willing to sell goods by mail. In Philadelphia, 60,000 "consumer application blanks" were distributed to potential buyers in an attempt to create a data bank of possible clients. In Boston, urban mail-order cooperatives were established so that groups living in the same apartment building or working for the same company could buy produce in 50-pound lots at bulk rates.

Realizing that the Farm-to-Table program could greatly increase advertising revenues, newspaper publishers were eager to ally themselves with it. Publishers hastily set up "matchmaking" agencies to bring potential buyers and sellers together. Like many other papers, *The New York Tribune* created a "Parcel Post Information Bureau."

Special "Buy by Parcel Post" sections were published in the classified pages, offering an array of farm-fresh commodities: candies, eggs, butter, and poultry, to name a few. Eggs, though, were by far the most salable. In the same few column inches, J. M. Bronson offered eggs at 45 cents per dozen, and so did Rock Ridge Poultry Farm. Shady Lawn Poultry Yards outpriced them both, charging 60 cents per dozen, but in all fairness, the Shady Lawn folks did promise to pack the eggs within four hours of receiving the order, so maybe that was the reason for the higher price.

Other times, sellers played hard to get. The Allicedall Farm of Salisbury Mills, New York, announced that it was only soliciting "a few additional orders," although at 60 cents a dozen it's doubtful that it received many responses.

Despite the best marketing efforts of postal officials, the Farm-to-Table program was not universally warmly received. The arch nemesis of Parcel Post, country and city shopkeepers, opposed the Farm-to-Table program. Merchants argued that it was another case of the government creating unfair competition, which would be ruinous to their business. But the hostility toward mail-order farming died down by the end of 1915. Small-time merchants were beginning to see the flaws in the system, flaws they believed would bring about the end of Farm-to-Table. Unfortunately, they were right.

The Farm-to-Table program did not last beyond 1917. Oddly enough, the one thing that was expected to contribute to its downfall—spoilage—was not nearly as much of a problem as was initially expected. It is estimated that less than one-half of one percent of the products shipped were lost to spoilage, and what spoilage there was could be attributed to poor packing, rather than delays in delivery. Many large city post offices were equipped with refrigerators, keeping waste to a minimum. Instead, the Farm-to-Table program failed for a number of other reasons.

First of all, packages could not contain correspondence. Descriptions of the contents and invoices were okay, but a letter or greeting card would bump the package up to first-class mail. This was a costly mistake. In one instance, 200 turkeys and 500 chickens were sent by Parcel Post from a Kansas City farm as Thanksgiving Day treats. Roughly one-third of the birds were accompanied by sealed holiday greetings. This increased the postage from about 12 cents to $2.50. The unexpected increase was passed along to the gift givers.

Price gouging was another common concern. The sellers priced their goods as high as market vendors, thereby eliminating one of the key incentives to shopping at home. Despite being urged to keep costs competitive and reasonable, one farm wife charged 50 cents for a pound of butter through Parcel Post, when the same thing sold at the corner market for only 20 cents. The difference was not due to mailing costs. Postage, insurance, and Collect-on-Delivery charges all had to be paid in advance by the buyer.

Most mail-order farmers also did not appreciate the importance of consumer buying habits, treating consumer preferences as though they were whims or fancies that did not have to be recognized. They failed to recognize that in areas like Boston, for example, brown eggs brought a premium, while in New York, white eggs sold best. Most farmers were indifferent to such preferences, and as a result, they lost customers.

Probably the greatest problem facing the Farm-to-Table program, however, was poor customer relations. According to the *Farmers' Bulletin,* published by the Department of Agriculture, "The bringing together of these persons into business contact is one of the most difficult problems in marketing by parcel post." There should have been no limit to the number of potential customers living within a day's train journey from farmlands. But again, the trust issue came into play. Most city dwellers did not like the idea of buying from an anonymous vendor they did not know and never saw. Faulty business practices all but destroyed the credibility of those participating in the Farm-to-Table program, turning many buyers off entirely to the idea of buying produce by mail.

In many cases, mail-order farmers were too successful for the program's own good. Some sellers found themselves sold out in just a few short weeks. To maintain good customer relations, postal officials asked farmers to inform expectant buyers when the cupboard was bare. But such notifications cost time and money, eating into what meager profits there were. As a result, such etiquette was soon ignored, creating a marketing nightmare for the Post Office Department. This led to enormous ill-will among hopeful buyers, another reason for them to give up on mail order.

Other customer relations nightmares included careless bookkeeping, which sometimes led to double and even triple billings; failures to observe state and federal pure-food laws; and poor labeling and packaging, which often resulted in rotting vegetables and mashed eggs.

Both sides had horror stories. For sellers, remittances were sometimes made late, if at all. Buyers sometimes got "taken," too. Postal Inspection Service records include a report of mail fraud in San Francisco involving eggs that were supposed to come by mail. Because the price was so cheap, the vendor requested payment in advance. Those that paid up front got scammed; the eggs never arrived because they were never sent.

Best of Times, Worst of Times

WITH THE NATION REELING under the devastating impact of the Great Depression, President Franklin Delano Roosevelt realized that the Post Office Department was the visible form of the federal government in every community. The postal service's activities were the only ones that touched the individual and collective lives of the local residents, the social interests of the overall community, and the business concerns of every neighborhood; and, he recognized the role that post office construction could play in revitalizing America during the Great Depression. This was a decisive way to put countless Americans back to work. When FDR took office nearly one-third of the nation's work force was on relief, and he was committed to finding meaningful jobs for these 13 million willing workers. Beginning in the early 1930s, the nation embarked on a massive government-financed building binge, much of which was part of the national work relief program sponsored by the Public Works Administration to alleviate the effects of the Depression. During the economic crisis, 40,000 new public buildings were constructed and more than 85,000 existing buildings were improved in an effort to get the country working again.

The newly constructed post office at Wakefield, Rhode Island, December 1936.

The post office at Ellenville, New York, constructed in 1940.

The vast majority of these New Deal buildings were "Starved-Classical" style post offices, an architectural form that matched the Roosevelt Administration's propensity for simplicity and thrift.

Such thrifty times required frugal fashions and the "Starved-Classical" form was the ideal thin diet, one that featured symmetrical designs with classical proportions, but without the popular classical elements, such as bold porticos, columns, and pediments. With this style, utility and economy outweighed exterior opulence. The term "Starved-Classicism" was used by Louis Craig, Director of the Federal Architecture Project for the National Endowment of the Arts, in describing the "modern" architecture style that was derived from the Classical, but stripped and simplified to provide "a gaunt, underfed, 'starved' classicism, denoted as much by white masonry and the rhythm of wall and window as by vestigial columns."

Several other important characteristics of this architectural style, which has also been referred to as "Public Works Administration Moderne," were described by Postal Service's Federal Preservation officer John Sorenson, when he observed:

> "Starved Classicism was the dominant mode of government construction during the 1930s and it is a direct descendant of the Treasury Department's Supervising Architect's earlier Beaux-Arts-inspired buildings. The facades and plans of these buildings remained symmetrical; the primary shift is in the ornament. Starved Classicism, in an effort to reduce costs and speed construction, eliminated or reduced architectural ornamentation to a minimum. The ornamentation that was used often owed a stylistic debt to the Art Deco of the 1920s.

Responsibility for these "starved" post offices principally goes to Louis A. Simon. Simon, an 1891 Massachusetts Institute of Technology graduate who headed up the architectural section of the Supervising Architect's office throughout the tenure of James Wetmore from 1915 to 1933, replaced Wetmore in 1933, serving as Supervising Architect until 1939. Known as a conservative designer, Simon oversaw the design and construction of the majority of the post offices projects carried out during the "Starved-Classical" period.

Many of the "Starved-Classical" post offices built between 1930 and 1942 look much the same outwardly; their greatest differences are often concealed inside. Typically, the interiors of many such post offices were uniquely decorated with colorful lobby murals, giant works of art that were sponsored by the federal government. Unlike the art created under the largest of the New Deal era art programs, the Works Progress Administration Federal Art Project created under the Emergency Relief Appropriations Act of 1935, the artworks created for post offices were not commissioned in order to provide financial relief to artists or to preserve their skills during the critical years of the Depression. Instead, the works in post offices were virtually all commissioned under the Treasury Department's Section of Painting and Sculpture, later designated as the Section of Fine Arts, which operated from 1934 to 1943. The Section's goal was to provide murals and sculptures for newly constructed federal projects using appropriated funds that usually constituted about one percent of each project's budget. Artworks were usually awarded on the basis of national or regional competitions conducted in all 48 states, with the bigger prizes going to the highest ranking competitors, while runners-up generally received commissions for smaller post office pro-

Depression era murals are a common part of many "Starved-Classical" post offices, such as this one at Princeton, New Jersey.

jects. During the nine years the Treasury Department program was in existence, approximately 1,200 murals and 300 sculptures were commissioned for post offices around the country.

These post office murals represent "feel good" art, paintings that did not dwell on the hard times and devastation brought on by the Depression, but instead harkened back to brighter days and nostalgic images. In the December 4, 1939 issue of *Life* magazine, the murals judged during the 1939 competition sponsored by the Fine Arts Section of the Federal Works Agency, which attracted 1,475 anonymous submissions, were described as "interesting not only in themselves but also as barometers by which the everyday art taste of rural America may be judged. Designed mostly for village post offices, they represent in most cases the collective taste of the citizens of the community, together with the individual taste of the artist." The magazine characterized the opinion of small-town Americans concerning such art by observing that "apparently rural Americans are artistic 'stay-at-homes' with a preference for paintings that reproduced experiences and scenes and parts of history with which they are familiar. In spirit, many of these sketches are local American epics." This was precisely the mission of the murals, to relate to the history and prideful moments of the locality, giving such significant periods or events artistic expression, while at the same time evoking positive emotions of accomplishment and purpose.

Today, these murals and sculptures constitute a great national treasure, comprising a comprehensive public collection of artworks that portray the diverse culture and character of the American people during this period; and the buildings that house these works represent a valuable and important American asset. Only now are many of these Depression era post offices beginning to show their age and, thankfully, today such older buildings are typically accorded the status they rightfully deserve. They are generally considered as vintage assets, ideal sites for historic preservation and tasteful redevelopment.

Few new post offices were constructed during World War II. Instead, all available manpower and materials were devoted to the war effort. Following the war, however, the Post Office Department embarked on another massive modernization program, but this time something was different. During the post-World War II period, the government did not want to pay directly for the construction. Instead, the postal system utilized commercially leased spaces. As part of its accelerated commercial leasing program, between January 1953 and August 1956, 1,200 new postal buildings were constructed by private industry and leased to the postal system. By mid-1956 "new style" offices were being completed at a rate of two a day. By 1960 more than 5,000 new post offices had been built under commercial leases without the requirement of huge sums of capital investment by the government.

Many of these projects were long overdue. More than half of the nation's post offices had been built during the 1930s or before. The larger of these were described as "mostly monumental in character and totally unsuited for [coping with the current] mail-handling problems." In the case of the old mail-handling facility at Seattle, Washington, the mail volume had grown to a point where much of the mail was being sorted outside the building irrespective of the weather. A new mail-handling facility, constructed in the 1950s, was said to be only one of many needed in other major cities. The following decade witnessed the completion of dozens of major mechanized post offices in many of America's largest communities.

At that time the Post Office Department was estimating that roughly $2 billion was needed to rehabilitate the existing federally owned properties. Of this sum, the government figured that approximately three-quarters could be invested by private industry for buildings to be constructed to postal specifications and leased to the Post Office Department. According to the Post Office Department, such structures—constructed predominantly of brick, structural metals, concrete, and glass—"are designed to harmonize with the architectural pattern of the communities in which they are built—and which they serve."

Actually, this assessment represented the postal service's official opinion. While it was fine for self-serving press releases or Congressional briefings, such statements were not totally accurate. In far too many instances the heavy-handed, modern styles imposed upon local communities either overpowered or understated the prevailing architectural flavor of the host communities. In such instances, all too often it became easy to pick out the post office simply because it visually did not fit in with the rest of the buildings in town.

By 1958, the Eisenhower administration was beginning to rethink its stand on post office designs. Far too many of the early 1950s post offices were beginning to look exactly alike, especially in smaller communities. The Post Office Department, however, viewed standardization as a desirable characteristic. The intent, then, was to provide greater standardization of the interiors, with eight different sizes, ranging from 1,000 to 12,000 square feet, while greatly enhancing the exterior styling. In 1958, the Post Office Department proposed 50 "typical examples" of exteriors that should be considered as a guide to investors planning to erect building for lease to the government.

This was done for two reasons: First, to enable future buildings to fit compatibly within the architectural character of the sites, neighborhoods, and cities that had varying customs, climates and characteristics; second, to meet improved postal methods, equipment, and standards.

General mail facilities at Houston, Texas.

Designwise, this was a much-needed step, and there was much to do. In 1958 the postal service was projecting the need for 12,000 new post offices over the next three years. That year alone, construction was started on 605 projects. To date, this represented the largest number of new leased building starts in any one year in the history of the postal service. These buildings provided over 2 million square feet of floor space and, because they were constructed under a commercial leasing program, this eliminated in excess of $20 million in government-related construction costs.

Many of the large urban post office buildings constructed during this period tend to be little more than mail-processing factories. Architecturally, they have little fanciful appeal. Instead, they are practical buildings of glass, concrete, and steel, which were located away from the centers of towns.

The same "outcast characteristic" applied to attempts to rehabilitate older structures. The early Eisenhower-era renovations, for example, were often grossly out of character. Frequently, the renovations stuck out like a matron in a miniskirt. These buildings should have been allowed to gracefully look their age, freshened up perhaps, but still retaining their mature allure. Instead their interiors were absurdly made over with plastic, Formica, and buffed metals.

The interiors of many of the new Eisenhower-era buildings, as well as those large older building that were renovated during this period, were dramatically different from anything before. They featured many of the first major breakthroughs in postal mechanization. A massive machine for sorting parcels was installed in the Baltimore, Maryland, post office as an experiment and, at about the same time, another giant device for sorting letters was installed in the post office at Silver Spring, Maryland. An innovative automatic conveyor system for moving mail throughout the Detroit, Michigan, post office also was installed as part of the postal system's 1950s mechanization program.

Postal officials realized that the agency had to mechanize if it was going to keep up with growing mail volumes. For that reason, in the late 1950s the government launched a drive to automate as much of its work as possible. Several prototypes of mail culling, facing, and canceling machines were tested in 1958. That same year the first attempts to develop equipment that could optically scan addresses on envelopes were begun. This was expected to be a long-term effort. In 1958 Postmaster General Arthur Summerfield acknowledged that "a great deal of research, time, money, and manpower are required before mail-handling functions in larger postal installations will be on a fully automatic basis." In reality, the Postal Service is still striving for this four decades later. This evolutionary process in postal automation continues to influence the shape and style of postal facilities developed since the 1950s.

The post-World War II building binge continued during the 1960s, utilizing much the same styles of architecture; yet while the postal system was replacing or modernizing its buildings at a frantic pace in the 1950s and 1960s, ironically it was outdated architecture that ultimately served as the catalyst for the most radical metamorphosis in the postal system's history.

Reinventing Government: Transforming America's Postal System

ON JULY 1, 1971, the postal system underwent the most radical change in its history when the United States Post Office Department became the United States Postal Service. The transformation changed the lives of hundreds of thousands of postal workers and brought the management of the postal system from the 19th century into the 20th.

This change was long overdue. Between 1840 and 1940, roughly half of all civilian employees of the federal government worked for the Post Office Department. The department grew for good reason over those 100 years: to deliver mail to America's ever-increasing population, and to support the introduction of new services, such as City Free Delivery in 1863, Railway Mail Service in 1864, and Rural Free Delivery in 1896.

The volume of mail also grew, especially after World War II. More than 40 billion pieces of mail were processed by 1948 and 63.6 billion pieces by 1960. Increases in Congressional funding for the postal system, however, lagged behind this steady growth in the volume of mail. While the Post Office Department was targeting only 3 percent of its annual budget to finding new ways to move the mail, major corporations were typically devoting up to 30 percent of their budgets for research and development.

At a time when private industry was embracing new management ideas, postal employees were typically left with outdated equipment, obsolete business practices, deteriorating buildings, stagnant salaries, and plummeting morale.

The seriousness of the problem confronting the Post Office Department became all too obvious in October 1966, when 19th-century management practices collided with 20th century reality. Work at the Chicago post office—the world's largest postal facility—ground to a halt for three weeks, stranding 10 million pieces of mail. In Congressional hearings over the shutdown, President Lyndon Johnson's Postmaster General, Lawrence O'Brien, admitted that "no human being can efficiently manage the nation's postal service as it is now constituted." O'Brien had no control over workloads, postal rates, and pay scales; and only marginal control over working conditions, a state of affairs that was unthinkable for the head of any private corporation. O'Brien warned Congress that unless things changed, the Post Office Department "was in a race with catastrophe."

In response to Congressional and public outcries over the Chicago shutdown, Postmaster General Lawrence O'Brien established a task force of postal officials to consider alternative organizational forms that might strengthen postal management. The group identified four alternatives: Making gradual changes to the existing organizational structure;

asking Congress for rate-making authority and bargaining power; creating a private company with stock shares; or establishing a public corporation. The task force selected the final option, and also recommended that the Post Office Department should be removed from Cabinet and Congressional oversight.

In addition, in 1967, President Lyndon Johnson created a commission "to determine whether the high-quality postal service which Americans have come to expect can better be performed by a Cabinet department, a government corporation, or some other form of organization." After 15 months of study, the commission called for the chartering of a "Government-owned Corporation to operate the postal service" and the removal of the Post Office Department from the Cabinet. Led by retired AT&T Chairman Frederick Kappel, the commission was composed of leaders of organizations as varied as General Electric, Campbell Soup, the Bank of America, and the AFL-CIO. The commission members came to believe that the Post Office Department had failed as a business primarily because it was run as a political institution. The Kappel Commission also concluded that "only a basic change in direction can prevent further deterioration of this essential public service and bring to an end its huge and wholly unnecessary drain on the national budget." In summarizing the situation to President Johnson in June 1968, Frederick Kappel emphasized that "you asked us to determine whether the postal system, as presently organized, is capable of meeting the demands of our growing economy and our expanding population. We have concluded that it is not."

Postal wages, which were always low, were a major contributing factor that led to the creation of the United States Postal Service in 1971.

The Chicago Post Office, site of the major shutdown that helped bring about postal reorganization and the creation of the United States Postal Service.

Business Week magazine described the challenge facing President Johnson, and later President Richard M. Nixon, in transforming the old Post Office Department as "the most comprehensive overhaul of a U.S. public institution ever considered."

When President Nixon took office in January 1969, he and his postmaster general, Alabama businessman Winton M. Blount, embraced the Kappel Commission's report, but no sweeping change in an organization as large as the Post Office Department is ever free of conflict, and postal workers did not instantly embrace the recommendations of the Kappel Commission. The Department had over 700,000 employees, making it the largest nonmilitary employer in the United States government, and many of the postal workers believed they had good reason to be skeptical about the Kappel Commission's findings.

The starting pay for a letter carrier in 1969 was $6,176, and after 21 years of service the salary rose only to $8,442. Eighty percent of postal employees ended their careers in the same grade they began in, and 85 percent had jobs in the five lowest-paid classifications. There was little opportunity for advancement, few salary increases, and high employee turnover.

In early 1970, postal workers learned of a proposed 3 percent pay raise in one piece of legislation, found the raise inadequate, and reacted dramatically. Postal employees in New York City went on a wildcat strike on March 17, 1970. The strike reached its height on March 21, when 152,000 workers walked out of 671 of the nation's largest post offices. Businesses lost billions of dollars each day.

As federal employees, postal employees were forbidden to strike and could have been fired for taking such action. But President Nixon chose not to fire the strikers; instead he mobilized the National Guard. Guardsmen were not trained for this type of duty, and little mail was distributed. After one week, the striking workers went back to work at the urging of their leaders. In response to this show of good faith, the administration and the unions agreed to an immediate and retroactive pay hike, with another increase to accompany postal reorganization.

Many of the Kappel Commission's suggestions for improving the postal system were incorporated into the Postal Reorganization Act, which became effective July 1, 1971. Provisions of the Act included:

- Establishing a postal corporation with an 11-member Board of Governors, which would appoint the postmaster general.
- Empowering the government-owned corporation to mechanize the mail, improve working conditions, and make the postal system responsive to the needs of its customers.
- Establishing collective bargaining, with binding arbitration.
- Setting postage rates after hearings by an independent Postal Rate Commission. The ultimate implementation of postal reforms also ended many practices a century old or more.

Among the changes were these:

- The postmaster general, a powerful political position since Andrew Jackson's administration, was removed from the president's cabinet and was no longer appointed by the president to reward political service.
- Political patronage was eliminated from the postal service. Elected officials in Washington no longer had the opportunity to fill thousands of positions in the postal system with their own appointees.
- The Post Office Department was given the opportunity to break away from federal tax subsidies.

Dramatic changes swept through the United States Postal Service 25 years ago, but they are no more dramatic than the changes in the 25 years since. Today, the Postal Service finds itself in competition with toll-free phone lines, messenger companies, private overnight delivery services, fax machines, and even the Internet. Shaping the future of the Postal Service is now a task for the dedicated men and women of today's postal system—and for the American people—to accomplish.

SECTION II

Regional Guide to American Post Offices

THE POST OFFICES HIGHLIGHTED in this section are literally the tip of a giant architectural iceberg. Nearly every town in America has, at some point in time, had its own post office building, and, more often than not, the post office has had more than one location. The trick is trying to track down as many of these sites as possible. In my own community of Takoma Park, Maryland, for example, there have been nearly a dozen post office buildings, and many of the structures still stand. This book, then, is only a starting point for some pleasurable gumshoeing. Finding these post offices is like one grand game of "seek and ye shall find," an enjoyable exploration that involves using old street maps, photographs, newspaper articles, and recollections from long-time residents.

The author encourages readers to do a little hometown sleuthing on their own, to try and locate as many post office buildings as possible in their own backyard, as a preliminary to using this book. After finding as many hometown post offices as possible, readers can use this book to begin to explore other communities as well.

It is often difficult at first glance to separate a post office from a city hall, railroad depot, or county courthouse; they often possess the same architectural characteristics. In larger towns, cornerstones can be helpful in uncovering a former post office, but it is important to remember that many of these bigger buildings have undergone renovations over time, so they many not look like what you would expect a "post office" to look like, particularly in their current configuration. The contemporary disguises that hide many post offices are varied: They may be masked now under the boarded-up grime of dilapidated, abandoned buildings; they may be simply aging structures consigned largely to use as storage areas, or they may be totally made-over gems that continue to serve the needs of the community in some other meaningful way. Those searching for old post offices often have to look deep beneath the current surface.

One important thing to keep in mind is that many one-time post offices are now private property. Proper respect must be given. Searchers must not improperly trespass upon the current owner's time, patience, and property.

This volume is divided by region and then alphabetically by state and town. (In a few cases, post offices have been moved from one location to another. These have been listed in their original state, with the new locations indicated as well.) The listing here contains an array of different architectural styles and building sizes.

In describing these buildings, simple language has been used. Architectural nomenclature has been avoided to the greatest extent possible.

Whenever possible, the National Register listing dates are furnished, as are the names of the builders or architects. Hopefully, those credited with creating the design or construction of these post offices have been correctly identified. (The author expects that he will no doubt hear about any errors in attribution, and that is as it should be.) The dates listed for each post office typically reflect the year the building was first occupied by the postal system.

PRECEDING PAGE:

The post office at Memphis, Tennessee, as it appears today.

New England

CONNECTICUT

East Windsor Hill

1865 Main Street

UNKNOWN – ABOUT 1750

STILL HOUSED IN THE SAME L-shaped wooden building where it has been since 1810 when the post office was established, the East Windsor Hill post office is a Dutch Colonial structure that is locally known as "Bissell's Store," in honor of David Bissell who built the original two-story structure as a residence and tavern, and later attached the one-story storehouse and shop. Besides housing the post office, over the years the building has served as a dry-goods store, goldsmith shop, barber shop, saddle shop, and print shop. George Washington was one of the customers to be served from this building, purchasing a two-blade pen knife in 1779. Over the years the Postal Service has attempted to discontinue this office, but such efforts have been strongly opposed by the local community. Commercial use of the building ended in 1963, leaving the post office as the sole tenant of the building.

Hartford

135-149 High Street

MALMFELDT, ADAMS, AND PRENTICE – 1933

ALTHOUGH THIS SYMMETRICAL BUILDING has many outstanding characteristics, one of the significant features of the federal building at Hartford is that it was designed by an outside architectural firm, Malmfeldt, Adams, and Prentice. Although the government had the capability of using outside architects, a power granted under the Public Works Acts of 1926 and 1930, the government's general preference was to keep the work for itself, assigning both large and small projects alike to the Office of the Supervising Architect instead of farming the work out. In this case, however, intense public and political pressure prompted the government to award the project to Malmfeldt, Adams, and Prentice, a local firm. This was a good decision, one that significantly expanded the architectural "gene pool" of creative ideas, a benefit that is evident in the firm's resulting design.

PRECEDING PAGE:

Now known as the "John W. McCormack Post Office and Court House," this Art Deco style federal building in Boston, Massachusetts, was constructed between 1931 and 1933. It is a massive structure, designed by Cram and Ferguson, that is dominated by three towers that loom above a five-story base.

Details of the frieze carving on the Hartford Post Office.

In effect, this building affords something for just about every mid-20th century taste in that the resulting design represents an eclectic architectural palate that includes classical elements, such as the massive columns that accentuate its two principal entrance pavilions, and Art Deco features such as the cast aluminium American eagles with uplifted wings that perch at either end of the main facade's cornice.

Constructed between 1931 and 1933, the building is sheatherd in light-colored marble. The High Street facade includes the following frieze inscription:

Across unbounded reaches of the sky
Over long trails upon the land
By lakes by rivers and the trackless sea
In tempest and in calm by day and night
We speed at your command and bear
The tidings and treasures of mankind.

The main frieze also contains a low-relief carving of two mounted post riders exchanging the mail; this carving divides the inscription in half.

‖ *National Register listing 10/19/81* ‖

Hebron

4 Main Street

AUGUSTUS POST – ABOUT 1820

KNOWN LOCALLY as either the "Augustus Post House" or the "Hewitt House," this two-and-one-half-story brick and frame house reflects the Federal style of architecture. The brick portion of the house was constructed by Augustus Post about 1820. Its appears as though Post was forced to sell the property in 1824. It then passed through a succession of owners, including Dr. John S. Peters, who served as Governor from 1831 to 1833. The house was acquired in the late 19th century by W. S. Hewitt, who operated a general store and post office here for a number of years. The building remained in the possession of the Hewitt family until the 1970s, when it was converted into professional offices. [*National Register listing 06/28/82*]

Norfolk

Greenwood Road West and Station Place

ALFREDO S. G. TAYLOR – 1905

THIS BUILDING WAS ONE of the first multipurpose structures in the center of the village, built by James T. Levi for the Royal Arcanum, a fraternal health insurance organization with offices on the third floor. Besides the post office, in the early 1900s this structure also housed the volunteer fire company, telephone exchange, a plumbing and heating contractor, Masonic Lodge rooms, and a drug store.

One of the postal workers employed in this building in the 1900s, Assistant Postmaster Myra Silvernale, created a stir when she insisted that she lost part of her tongue from licking postage stamps. She believed that her case of blood poisoning was due to the adhesive used on stamps. Postal officials promptly rejected her claim as utter nonsense, saying that the glue then used on stamps was derived from harmless corn dextrin.

When the post office moved from the Arcanum Building in 1961, the space formerly devoted to the mails was taken over by a hardware store. Today, that space is a dining area of a restaurant.

MAINE

Old Town

Center Street

OSCAR WENDEROTH – 1914

THE POST OFFICE AT OLD TOWN was designed in 1912 and constructed between 1913 and 1914. It is one of 40 buildings constructed that year under the supervision of Oscar Wenderoth. The head of the American Institute of Architects did not much care for Wenderoth's leadership of the Office of the Supervising Architect. Wenderoth was accused of "not [being] an architect in any sense of the word" and was further characterized for his lack of vision, which was described "unsympathetic to an unfortunate degree." Wenderoth was seen by the AIA as being at the heart of the environment that led to the repeal of the Tarsney Act. Despite such negative comments, the general public tended to like his creations, including this two-story stone post office, built under the provisions of the Tarsney Act and the first Omnibus Building Act of 1902. [*National Register listing 09/25/86*]

Portland

125 Forest Avenue

JOHN CALVIN STEVENS – 1934

UNTIL THE 1930s when Portland's current post office was built, the town had a steady stream of bad luck with its post offices. On January 8, 1853, fire destroyed the town's business exchange building which had housed the post office since 1849. The same site was used for a new custom house and post office. Congress authorized funds for this project on April 4, 1854, with a price tag of $200,000. The new building was occupied on April 1, 1859. Nine years later another fire did extensive damage to the stonework, so much so that the building was torn down. Once again Congress came up with the money to replace the facility, this time spending $392,214.64. The post office moved into the first floor of the new structure during the middle part of 1871. Work on the project continued for nearly two more years, however, and the upper two floors of the Vermont-marble-faced building were not completed until 1873. This building also subsequently burned.

The current post office is a striking red-brick, Georgian-style structure built during the Great Depression. Of particular interest to visitors are the two murals by Henry Elias Mattson that adorn each side of the building's main entrance. [*National Register listing 05/09/86*]

Wells

Bragdon's Crossing

UNKNOWN – ABOUT 1763

DESPITE THE FACT that it is difficult to verify precisely when this one-and-one-half-story 18th century Cape Cod building housed the post office, post office pigeonholes were found in the right front room of the structure during a major renovation. [*National Register listing 12/27/79*]

MASSACHUSETTS

Attleboro

75 Park Street

JAMES A. WETMORE – 1916

BUILT AT A COST OF $85,000 by the King Lumber Company, this is an exceptional "Class B" first-class post office, constructed in accordance with Treasury Secretary William MacAdoo's 1915 instructions to the Office of the Supervising Architect. This classification applied to first-class post offices with annual receipts between $60,000 and $800,000. Attleboro just barely qualified, reporting slightly over $60,000 in income. In keeping with this classification, the character of the building was to reflect "Limestone or sandstone facing; fireproof throughout; exterior frames and sash metal; interior frames, sash and doors wood; interior finishes to exclude the more expensive woods and marbles; ornamental metal to be used only where iron is suitable. Restricted ornament in public spaces." This description fits the former Attleboro post office almost exactly.

[*National Register listing 10/19/87*]

Becket

Main Street

UNKNOWN

SERVICE TO A LARGE PORTION of the Northeast, including Becket, was severely disrupted by a flood on November 4, 1927. Overnight numerous bridges and roadways disappeared or became inoperable, post offices were submerged or swept away, and railway mail service connections severed. Despite the havoc, for the most part, the mail reached its intended destinations. Becket was never without mail service. Although the post office was literally washed from its foundation during the deluge, the local postmaster had the forethought to transfer the mail to a town outside the immediate danger area as the rain waters began to rise. Under makeshift conditions, he prepared whatever incoming mail he received for next day delivery.

Great Barrington

222 Main Street

LOUIS A. SIMON – 1936

THIS BUILDING REPRESENTS a "Class C" style post office, built in accordance with Treasury Secretary William McAdoo's classification system for federal construction for a second-class post office. This meant that the building would have a brick veneer with stone trim, wooden doors, frames, and sashes, and simple interior ornamentation. This type of standardization reduced the number of drawings that were required for different projects, helped to standardize material lists, and significantly speeded completion of projects. Some latitude was occasionally afforded to local architects employed to oversee the actual work.

Using a standard plan for this class of building devised by the Office of the Supervising Architect, local architect Lorimer Rich adapted the government's basic 1935 design somewhat, giving the Great Barrington post office a unique "temple-like" appearance through the use of Tuscan columns that support the central portico. Construction of the post office was carried out by D. A. Sullivan and Sons of Northampton, Massachusetts.

[*National Register listing 01/10/86*]

Lynn

360 Washington Street

L. L. LEACH AND SONS – 1898

BUILT LARGELY OF light-colored buff brick by L. L. Leach and Sons of Chicago, Illinois, between March 1897 and February 1898, on a square plot bounded by Washington, Willow, and Liberty Streets and costing $34,000, the federal post office at Lynn is a stunning two-story, oblong building with a round tower over each entrance. Each rotunda is 15 feet in circumference and opens onto a 15-foot wide vestibule that runs the entire length of the building. Postmaster General Frank Hitchcock, who served from 1909 to 1913, consolidated the Lynn post office into the Boston post office. Hitchcock's replacement, Postmaster General Albert Burleson, quickly reversed that action, restoring the independent status of the office in the summer of 1913. The post office remained at this location until 1933. The building currently houses the multiservices center for Lynn economic opportunity. [*National Register listing 09/14/81*]

Provincetown

217 Commercial Street

JAMES A. WETMORE – 1932

DESIGNED IN 1931 under the supervision of James A. Wetmore, and constructed of brick in 1932, the two-story central core, with one-story wings on either side, reflects a Georgian style of architecture that is in keeping with the community. A windowed cupola surmounts the high pitched roof, giving the building added prominence, a feature that has been described as providing a "visual beacon" on Commercial Street.

[*National Register listing 10/19/87*]

Weymouth

103 Washington Street

LOUIS A. SIMON – 1941

THE POST OFFICE AT WEYMOUTH is an outstanding example of one of Louis Simon's more popular cookie-cutter designs, one that was especially used in locations where there was an abundance of field stone or quarried rock. Although the overall design is far from unique, the individuality comes from the particular stone that was used for the exterior. The use of local stone was a welcome concession, one that tended to outweigh concerns over the individuality of the design in that it added significantly to the local economy through bolstering employment and the purchase of the stone. Besides saving money on the transportation costs associated with the use of more expensive stone, in this particular case, the use of local material added to the workload of the local granite pit, an operation that at its peak in the 1920s employed over 200 workers and shipped approximately 500,000 square feet of stone. The use of local "seam-face granite" also meant that the post office, built at a cost of $78,000, would blend in with other structures in the community, such as the central fire station and two area library buildings.

[*National Register listing 05/27/86*]

NEW HAMPSHIRE

Concord

North State Street at Park and Capitol

JAMES R. HILL – 1889

CONSTRUCTED BETWEEN 1884 and 1889 by a local contractor, Giles Wheeler, principally of Concord granite, the old post office and court house is an eclectic combination of Romanesque Revival and other Victorian styles that together give the structure a strong castle-like appearance, a look that was well suited to Concord's postmaster in the 1890s, ex-state senator and U.S. Congressman Henry Robinson, who believed that "at no point does the machinery of government come so closely in contact with the people as at the post office." Robinson believed that Supervising Architect James Hill's design for the Concord post office was symbolic of that relationship. The federal government relinquished control of the building in 1967, allowing the state to acquire the structure for legislative offices. [*National Register listing 08/13/73*]

Old postcard illustration of the federal building in Concord, New Hampshire.

Photograph of the Littleton post office taken during construction, 1934.

Littleton

165 Main Street

JAMES A. WETMORE – 1934

A SIGNIFICANT EXAMPLE of the Classical Revival style of architecture, the 23,200 square foot Littleton post office and courthouse was constructed by the V and M Construction Company mainly of brick with marble details and trim. The main facade features a central bay with a temple pediment and marble Ionic columns, while the corners are trimmed with marble quoins. The roof is gray slate, topped by a stunning ornate cupola. While the greatest distraction is the metal fire escape, the building also suffers from the lack of any significant landscaping, a limitation that is due to the fact that the building and its adjacent parking lot take up nearly the entire plot. The public lobby, which runs the entire length of the front of the building, retains its original charm and appearance, as do the upstairs court house areas, which take up the second and third floors and include courtrooms, detention areas, jury rooms, and judicial offices. [*National Register listing 07/17/86*]

Manchester

Hanover and Chestnut Streets

MIFFLIN E. BELL – 1891

CONGRESS INITIALLY APPROVED the expenditure of $100,000 for the Manchester post office/courthouse in 1885, but added money over time. The property was purchased in 1886 for $38,602.40, with the excavation contract for the building awarded in 1887. The granite building was completed in February 1891 at a cost of $212,934.99. The entire first floor of the building was devoted to the postal service, while the upper floor housed the federal court. The postal service continued to use this as the

Mifflin Bell's rendering of the Manchester, New Hampshire, post office.

city's main postal facility until September 24, 1932, later designating it as a station. Today, the building serves as the offices of a law firm.

[*National Register listing 12/01/86*]

Orford

North of Bridge Street on Route 10

ALBERT W. FRIEDLAND – 1962

ORFORD'S POST OFFICE was established nearly two centuries ago by one of the town's earliest settlers, John Mason. Since that time the post office has operated from five different locations. Prior to moving into its current location in 1962, business was transacted from the converted garage of then postmaster Gould Richmond. In Richmond's opinion, the garage worked fine until 1962, when it became evident that it was incapable of accommodating the mail generated by one of the town's biggest mailers, the Equity Publishing Company. The garage site was replaced that year with a one-story brick structure that was designed to blend in with the community's colonial flavor.

Portsmouth

40 Pleasant Street

AMMI B. YOUNG – 1858

NEW HAMPSHIRE ENACTED its first postal legislation in 1693. That action called for the creation of a post office "in some convenient place within the Towne of Portsmouth." A tavern was the obvious site, especially since the enabling legislation "ordained that the officer of the post house [have a] Licence [sic] granted to retaile [sic] Beer, Sider [sic], and Ale within Doors according to Law... ." In 1858 Portsmouth's post office was in a more suitable building, a Greek Revival structure constructed from Concord granite.

RHODE ISLAND

Bristol

420-448 Hope Street

AMMI B. YOUNG – 1858

BRISTOL'S RENAISSANCE-REVIVAL style federal building, which originally housed the post office and customs house, is an excellent example of Ammi B. Young's architectural talents. The building is principally constructed of deep red brick, with grayish sandstone moldings that outline the triple arches defining its entrances and windows. A course of sandstone also separates its different levels. The building's low-hipped roof, with a single large attic dormer in the center of each section, should be viewed at a distance to be appreciated. The local Young Men's Christian Association now owns the building. [*National Register listing 05/31/72*]

Pawtucket

56 High Street

WILLIAM MARTIN AIKEN AND JAMES KNOX TAYLOR – 1897

DESPITE THE FACT that the city conveyed a deed for the property for the Pawtucket post office in 1892, construction of the building, which was the town's first federal facility, was delayed until 1896, pending competition to select an acceptable design. That task fell on Supervising Architect William Martin Aiken, whose final wedge-shaped design incorporated a domed circular entrance pavilion as the chief architectural focus of the building, a feature that superbly exploited an otherwise difficult triangular shaped property purchased in 1892.

Aiken's design placed the entrance at the juncture of a major Y-shaped intersection, and incorporated red brick on a granite pedestal with limestone trim, giving the building an impressive arrow-shaped appearance, which acts as a focal point terminating the vista up High Street from Main Street. Besides the entrance pavilion, other details include window arcades set within an engaged colonnade with full entablature, above which a balustraded parapet partially conceals the building's mansard roof. The design reflects Aiken's interest in European influences. A ribbed copper dome capped by a small louvered cupola and supported by a copper-clad drum is one of the structure's most notable features. The domed entrance motif was borrowed from contemporary combinations of Beaux-Arts and

Postcard illustration of the Pawtucket, Rhode Island, post office, 1906.

French-Second-Empire designs, while the remainder of the exterior treatment reflects an Italian Renaissance flavor.

Construction of the building required 14 months and $50,644 to complete. The post office opened to the public on November 1, 1897, continuing in use until 1940. In 1941 the City of Pawtucket purchased the building, transforming it in 1945 into its municipal welfare building, housing the city's public welfare administration. The building now is a library.

[*National Register listing 04/30/76*]

Providence

24 Corliss Street

CHARLES A. MAGUIRE – 1960

The nation's first fully automated post office, Providence, Rhode Island.

THE PROVIDENCE POST OFFICE was developed under the code name "Project Turnkey," because figuratively speaking it was to be turned over to the postal service fully ready for operation at the turning of a key. It was also

the site of the first fully automated post office in the United States. The facility, located on a 14.5 acre site in the 30 acre "West River" section of Providence, was constructed under a contract to International Telephone and Telegraph. Groundbreaking ceremonies were held on April 2, 1959, and the building was dedicated on October 20, 1960. Initially, the postal service held a basic 20-year lease, with three renewal options, each for 10 years.

The post office is basically a single-story structure with 126,000 square feet of space and a loading dock platform area of approximately 45,000 square feet that could accommodate 130 mail trucks. The facility was designed to handle at least 2 million pieces of mail each day. Architectural features of the building include: a 25-foot-high control tower that serves as the nerve center for the fully automated facility; over 15,000 feet of conveyors so that much of the mail processed in the facility is untouched by human hands; a mezzanine observation walkway around the workroom floor; and an unusual "clam shell" or parabolic roof.

In dedicating the building, Postmaster General Arthur Summerfield expressed the belief that "it will be a major proving ground for post offices of tomorrow, helping us break the age-old mail service bottlenecks which have slowed service in the past in our outmoded post offices using old fashioned, laborious manual methods of handling the mail."

While this project was a beginning with respect to innovations in automation and mechanization, in 1960 the postal system was a long way from finding adequate solutions to its problem of moving massive amounts of mail. However, the opening of the Providence post office was a moment of great accomplishment for Summerfield, who recalled "the very earliest days of my tenure in this office in January of 1953, and the panorama of shabbiness that greeted me on my first tour of inspection of many of the largest post offices." Not only did the new building include the finest facilities for employees, including modern locker rooms, showers, and a snack-bar cafeteria, when it opened in 1960, this facility also incorporated the latest techniques in automation and mechanization. Among the labor saving devices incorporated in the building were six giant "culling machines" that separated mail according to size and shape, six "facing machines" that put mail in the proper position for cancellation, and 11 letter sorting machines, each capable of sorting 18,000 letters an hour to 300 destinations. Two package sorting machines also were installed, each with a capability of sorting of sorting 2,400 parcels an hour to 31 distinct destinations.

Westerly

High and Broad Streets

JAMES KNOX TAYLOR – 1914

ERECTED IN 1913 AND 1914, the main facade of this medium-sized post office is dominated by a shallow portico that contains eight fluted stone Doric columns. The building is a blend of colors, with its gray Vermont marble face, granite base and steps, and dull green tile hipped roof set in a Greek pan-and-cover pattern. [*National Register listing 08/12/71*]

Woonsocket

295 Main Street

JAMES KNOX TAYLOR – 1912

CONSTRUCTED BETWEEN 1910 AND 1912, the one-story Beaux-Arts-style post office at Woonsocket has a raised monitor roof over the workroom floor, which gives the odd impression that this structure has more floors than it really has. This raised roof section also shows just how much of the interior of this building was occupied by sorting operations. The building was sympathetically enlarged during the Depression. The postal service moved out of the building in 1975. [*National Register listing 05/30/79*]

VERMONT

Beebe Plain

Canusa Street

UNKNOWN – ABOUT 1782

LOCATED IN A STORE that straddles the international border, half of the Beebe Plain, Vermont, post office building is in the United States and the other half is in Canada. Although the post office occupied a single room at the turn of the century, there were two postmasters, each with his own post office unit located on his respective side of the border. One postmaster was Canadian, the other an American. There were two ways into the store. Over the northerly door to the shop was a sign reading "Beebe Plain, P.Q.," while atop the southerly door was one for "Beebe Plain, Vt." Good neighbors that they were, it was not uncommon for the Canadian postmaster to fill in for his American counterpart, and vice versa, when there was a need to take a long lunch, go visiting, or attend a funeral. Tenants occupied the upper floor of the building. In the upstairs bathroom, someone sitting in the bathtub had his or her head in the United States, while his or her feet were in Canada.

Bennington

118 South Street

JAMES KNOX TAYLOR – 1914

BENNINGTON WAS THE FIRST TOWN in Vermont to have a post office. It was established on November 26, 1783. At that time *The Vermont Gazette* reported: "His Excellency the Governor with the Hon. Council of this State having seen fit to establish a post rider to go weekly from [Bennington] to Albany [New York] the public are hereby informed that the post office business will be transacted at the printing office [of a local newspaper publisher]." Over a century later, Bennington got a new post office, a structure clad in white Vermont marble and combining Greek, Roman, and Tuscan design elements. Among the building's most notable features is its shallow entrance portico supported by six massive Greek Doric columns. The post office vacated the premises in 1967, leading the government to gut the entire interior, destroying most of the interior plaster and mahogany embellishments in the course of converting it into a general federal office building.

[*National Register listing 12/12/76*]

Brattleboro

204 Main Street

OSCAR WENDEROTH – 1916

BRATTLEBORO BEGAN RECEIVING mail in 1784, seven years before Vermont was admitted to the Union, making it one of the oldest communities in the state to have a post office. The first post office was located in the "Old Tavern Inn," an establishment run by John Arms, who served as the town's first postmaster from 1784 to 1792. During the next century the post office moved to a variety of buildings, including a clothing store and the town hall. In 1916, the post office moved to its present location.

Burlington

Main and Church Streets

JAMES KNOX TAYLOR – 1906

ONE OF THE BEST Beaux-Arts-style structures in the state, the Burlington post office is a massive three-story building constructed principally of smooth-dressed marble blocks. The building's most prominent feature is its shallow two-story entrance portico. The overall design features a rectangular first floor and U-shaped upper floors that allow adequate natural light to penetrate into the main post office work room area on the first floor. The building no longer serves as the post office; instead in the 1970s it was turned into the "Smith-Goldberg U.S. Army Reserve Center."

[*National Register listing 11/21/72*]

Plymouth

Coolidge Memorial and Grand View Lodge Road

UNKNOWN – ABOUT 1860

WINNING A PRESIDENTIAL ELECTION is great for the successful candidate and for his hometown, but it is bad news for the local postmaster. It means a great deal more work. The postmaster of Plymouth learned that firsthand following the election of Calvin Coolidge in 1923. Within days of the election, thousands of letters a day began arriving for the President-elect. Many of these were from well-wishers, others were from quacks, and a large percentage were resumés from job seekers.

The old Coolidge store, operated by John C. Coolidge, the President's father, housed the post office in the 1920s. To handle the seasonal influx of mail for the Coolidge summer White House in Vermont, the second floor was converted into a giant workroom for sorting mail. Additional staff also had to be employed to handle the quantity of official mail and public inquiries addressed to Plymouth, especially when the President was in town.

Although he was the proprietor of the country store that housed the post office, John Coolidge was never actually the postmaster. For a time, that job belonged to his wife, Carrie, who served as postmaster from 1903 to 1917.

Later, the post office was moved to the left side of the same structure, relocated into the old carriage house that, when remodeled, provided larger quarters.

President Calvin Coolidge on the front porch of the post office in Plymouth, Vermont, his hometown.

Mid-Atlantic

DELAWARE

Georgetown

Public Square and Bedford Street

JAMES A. WETMORE – 1932

THE APPEARANCE of the Georgetown post office is misleading in that it appears to be a one-story structure, while in reality it's a two-story brick structure with full basement. The upper story windows are partially concealed by the slope of the mansard roof. Other distinguishing features include the entrance portico, which is supported by modified Corinthian columns. Although small, this semicircular entrance portico significantly reduces the building's "governmental" feel. The 9,500 square foot building was constructed by the Garnet-Ryan Company of Philadelphia. Currently, the building is being considered for use in conjunction with the local government.

Kenton

Main Street

FRANCIS GREENWELL – 1881

VERY LITTLE HAS CHANGED about the the Kenton post office, a two-story vernacular frame structure originally built as a store and residence. The structure was constructed in 1881 by Francis Greenwell. The post office occupied the building until the 1900s, at which time it moved elsewhere.

[*National Register listing 06/27/83*]

Kirkwood

Kirkwood and St. George Roads

UNKNOWN – ABOUT 1870

BY THE TIME that this two-story building, with its mansard roof, was completed around 1870, the debates about what to call the village were just about over. The community was originally called Kemp's Corner, which was changed to St. George's Station, and finally was switched to Kirkwood in 1862, in recognition of the contributions of Revolutionary War hero, Cap-

PRECEDING PAGE:

Kenton, Delaware, post office.

tain Robert Kirkwood. Years ago the building, which is the only Second Empire style structure in this immediate area, housed the post office and now a country store. This is a privately owned property.

[*National Register listing 04/08/82*]

Wilmington

Eleventh and Market Streets

ASSOCIATED FEDERAL ARCHITECTS – 1937

DESIGNED BY PRIVATE architects, Associated Federal Architects of Wilmington, between 1933 and 1935, this Art Moderne style federal building, which housed the post office, customs house, and courthouse, was given high marks for the way that it complemented its surroundings. The architects were praised for producing a practical three-story cut-stone structure, one that "kept in mind as of utmost importance the architectural beauty and unity of Rodney Square." Rodney Square was named in honor of Revolutionary War hero Caesar Rodney, who, although seriously ill, rode to Philadelphia in 1776 to cast the deciding vote for the Declaration of Independence. Rodney also served as Delaware's first chief executive.

[*National Register listing 06/14/79*]

DISTRICT OF COLUMBIA

Washington, D.C.—Georgetown

1215 31st Street, N.W.

AMMI B. YOUNG – 1858

TO COMPLY with the Constitution, a ten-mile square area of land, ceded by Maryland and Virginia, was proclaimed the seat of the government by President George Washington in 1791. The post office was established in 1795 and designated "City of Washington, District of Columbia," in 1796. Mail volume greatly increased after Congress moved from Philadelphia in 1800. The pre-District towns of Alexandria and Georgetown became parts of the original Capital City. Alexandria was retroceded to Virginia in 1846.

One of the most touching stories about the Renaissance Revival style Georgetown post office involved an elderly woman who for decades maintained a post office box there. Day after day she visited the box, but never received any mail. Finally a caring postal worker asked her why she continued to make her daily trips to a box she never used. Her reply was wrenching. She sorrowfully said that she initially rented the box before her son went away. In the intervening years she had moved several times, but he knew the box number. Her hope was that someday he would write her—but he never did.

Washington, D.C.

12th Street and Pennsylvania Avenue, N.W.

WILLOUGHBY J. EDBROOKE – 1899

ALTHOUGH GIANT TOWERS and clockworks were a hallmark of Supervising Architect Willoughby J. Edbrooke, the designer of the turn of the century Washington, D.C., post office, they were more for visual effect than for function. In fact, such massive clockworks usually did not work. The Washington, D.C., post office building was a prime example of such imperfect timepieces. The great, four-sided clock suffered repeated cases of paralysis. Two sides worked in spasms of ten-minute intervals, punctuated by comatose intervals of two to three hours. The other sides flatly refused to function.

Local residents took this in stride, but not Postmaster General Albert Burleson. In 1913 he demanded that the builder of the works set them right. Despite the efforts of an army of repairmen, the clock remained insubordinate. Besides, the 250 foot-high clock faces were difficult to see from the ground and even when the mechanisms did fitfully work they were not well known for their accuracy. The large hands were notorious for not keeping good time. They were simply too heavy. They gained time at the start of each hour when they swung down and lost time when they climbed up. Any accumulations of ice or snow only added to their inaccuracy.

As if this were not enough, the clock suffered yet one other shortcoming. In 1956 the steel cable holding the pendulum snapped, sending the weights bowling through to the eighth floor. One office worker was injured in this mishap. The clock was electrified after that.

Pigeons loved the nooks and crannies of this building, but they hated "Old Joe," a baron hawk who ruled the roost. Prior to World War I, the winged pirate kept the pigeon population in check. His skills were so renowned that Postmaster General Frank Hitchcock took pity on the pigeons. According to an account, published in the September 1911 issue of *R.F.D. News*, one day, while sitting at his desk, Hitchcock heard the coo of a young bird. At first he believed the sound was coming from one of the gables over the windows of his office, but upon closer investigation he discovered that it was coming from a nest in the shade of the electric light over his desk. Knowing full well that the hawk would love to get his talons on the young birds, Hitchcock instructed the janitor not to disturb the nest until the little ones were old enough to take care of themselves.

The hawk, who made his winter home in the clocktower, was not content with pigeons. He also committed daily raids on chicken coops around the area. This infuriated the community, which placed a bounty on the poacher. Within a year, the hawk was downed. According to one published account, "A bullet from some unknown source laid him low after the combined efforts of the entire post office staff, including the Postmaster General, to capture him had failed." In the end, Hitchcock finally had his revenge. The bird's remains were carefully preserved by a taxidermist and presented to the Postmaster General like some sort of war trophy, which for several years perched near his desk.

From the beginning many Washingtonians considered this post office to be an architectural monstrosity. Typical of this sentiment, one senator criticized it as "a cross between a cathedral and a cotton mill." Later critics were no less caustic. Historian Gerald Cullinan described it as "one of the most distinguished eyesores in Washington." Many longed for the earliest possible opportunity to be rid of it, which seemed to be close to becoming a reality in 1934, when the headquarters staff of the postal service moved across the street to newer quarters. After that, periodically there was talk of tearing the building down, but nothing much came of it. The idea was repeatedly sidetracked because of the persistent fear that its immense tower might prove indestructible. In the 1970s, supporters kept the building standing and had it converted for mixed use as commercial spaces and offices.

Like any prized gem, this building had a few flaws. Chief among these was that it was taller than it should have been. When you subtract the difference in elevations, its 300 foot-high tower tops the Statue of Freedom which caps the U.S. Capitol building by 28 feet. The nickname for the Romanesque building—"Old Tooth"—reflects the remarkable appearance of the tower.

The building was in use as a postal facility from November 1899 to June 1934. Shortly after it opened city postmaster James P. Willett fell into the shaft of one of the elevators, and was killed almost instantly.

Despite this, the building did have its charms. Architecturally, it embodied a number of "firsts." It was the first building in the Federal City to have its own electric power plant, a system that was capable of illuminating its 3,900 electric lights. It was the first major steel-frame building erected in Washington. And, it was among the largest government buildings constructed prior to the turn of the century. The interior boasted the largest American flag in continuous use. Hung in the building's immense atrium, the 70-by 37-foot flag draped between the third and eighth floors. Each star measured 36 inches and the stripes were a yard wide.

Initially the upper floors of the building housed postal service headquarters, while the lower levels accommodated the city's post office. But, gradually the city office got squeezed out, the victim of the department's need for ever more headquarters space. Local postal operations were relocated in 1914.

From this building a number of innovative postal services were introduced, including Parcel Post, Collect-on-Delivery, Airmail, and Postal Savings.

Washington, D.C.

North Capitol Street and Massachusetts Avenue, N.E.

DANIEL BURNHAM – 1914

THE CAPITAL CITY'S "new" post office harmonized with Washington's "new" Union Station, which was next door. Both structures were designed by Daniel Burnham. Funds for constructing the new city post office, amounting to $3 million, were appropriated in 1911. Burnham's massive white marble structure was considered a model in construction, design, and equipment. Excavating and casting the foundations, which vary from 4 to 12 feet thick, cost $10,000; but the biggest price tag was the building's main corridor, with 64 huge granite pillars, costing $1,000 each, and 72 marble floor lamps with alabaster lenses, each costing $750. Besides its ornate lobby, the postmaster's office, paneled with rare circassian walnut from Imperial Russia, was another of the building's attractive features.

Another prominent point was the building's extensive use of conveyor belts for moving the mail. The conveyor system, known as "the belt line," was installed at a cost of roughly $200,000. This system ensured that little physical effort was needed to transfer mail around the building.

The new post office did a great deal of business. Although unseen by the public, the building's massive cellar vault was another major feature of the place. The vault typically housed approximately $8 million worth of stamps and postal stationery at any given time to accommodate customer needs.

In 1984, following the relocation of postal operations, the Postal Service embarked upon a joint venture with a private developer to redevelop this property, and in so doing produce nearly one million square feet of leasable office and retail space. One portion of this building is occupied by the National Postal Museum. Construction of the 82,000 square foot museum commenced in December 1990. The museum features 32,000 square feet of exhibits, plus a 6,000 square foot research library. The museum's proximity to other important Washington landmarks makes it an ideal facility for both American and international visitors. Close to the United States Capitol, the Supreme Court, and Union Station, the museum is served by a convenient multilevel parking facility and bus and subway lines. The building also houses a museum shop and a philatelic sales area, as well as a full-service post office.

Washington, D.C.

12th Street and Pennsylvania Avenue

WILLIAM A. DELANO – 1934

FROM JUNE 1934 until 1973, Post Office Department headquarters was located in a seven-story neo-classical building. The structure has a limestone exterior and a lizard that would not move. For nearly 15 years post

U.S. Post Office Department headquarters, Washington, D.C., 1934–1973.

office guards tried to dislodge the foot-long lizard from the keystone of the west interior arch of the building's north court by throwing stones, but it would not move. It would not even budge when it sustained a direct hit. That was when the guards realized the lizard was stone. It was put there by architect William A. Delano, who, in 1948, confessed that it was his "symbol." He failed to disclose why he used it and his wife would only acknowledge that its meaning was "private information."

Washington, D.C.

Current Postal Service Headquarters

475 L'Enfant Plaza, S.W.

VLASTIMIL KOUBEK – 1973

SINCE APRIL 1973, the headquarters of the United States Postal Service has been located in a building designed by Vlastimil Koubek, a native of Czechoslovakia who came to the United States following World War II. Koubek's design is compatible with the other adjacent buildings in the L'Enfant office complex, which were designed by I. M. Pei.

Current Postal Service headquarters building, Washington, D.C.

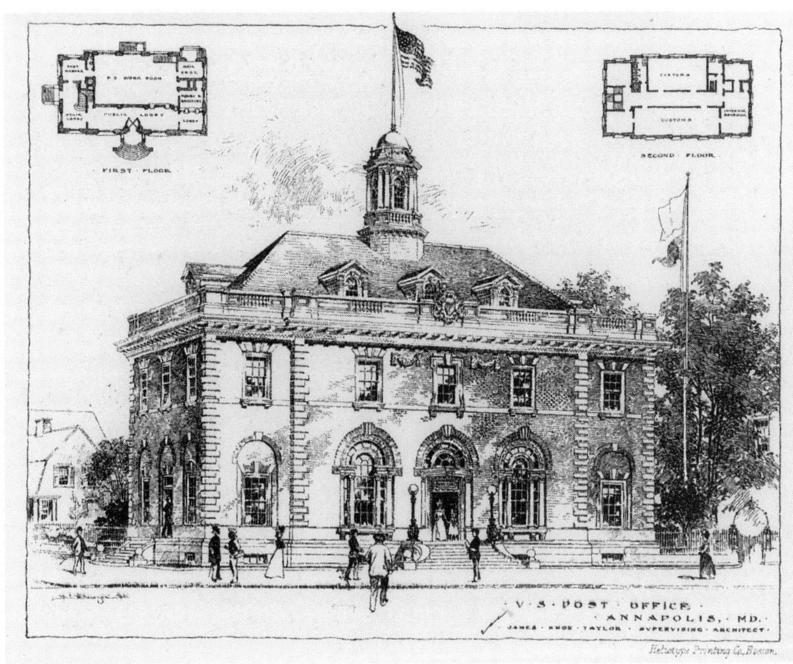

Supervising Architect James Knox Taylor's rendering of the Annapolis, Maryland, post office.

MARYLAND

Annapolis

Church Circle

JAMES KNOX TAYLOR – 1901

SUPERVISING ARCHITECT James Knox Taylor specifically elected to use the Georgian Revival style for the Annapolis post office so that it would be compatible with the city's predominant architecture. The red brick post office particularly complements the nearby Maryland State House, which was built in 1772, and the Governor's Mansion, which was completed in 1869.

Taylor's ability to blend his designs with existing architecture was highly respected. When he retired in 1912 to become the director of the Department of Architecture at the Massachusetts Institute of Technology, his departure from the government was characterized by his contemporaries as "a national calamity." James Knox Taylor died in Tampa, Florida, on August 28, 1929, at age 71.

Baltimore

111 North Calvert Street

JAMES A. WETMORE – 1932

BY THE 1920s, conditions at Baltimore's old post office, constructed in the 1890s, had become unbearable. Hot clouds of dust choked the postal workers' lungs when the windows were closed, and chilling drafts made workers sick when the windows were left open. The tower, a worthless structure, was only good for the view it afforded and as a place for storing musty old ledgers.

On May 29, 1928, the last day of the Congressional session, legislation was passed to build a new post office at Baltimore, located on the same site as the old post office. Postal workers vacated the premises on January 1, 1930, taking up temporary quarters in the city's Parcel Post annex on Lombard Street. In April, 1930, a contract was awarded to N. P. Saverin of Chicago to build the $3.3 million structure within 900 days. The building was fully completed on June 4, 1932, substantially ahead of schedule.

Main postal operations for Baltimore were moved to a 13-acre site in Shot Tower Industrial Park in May 1972. A major rehabilitation effort quickly took place, beginning in the autumn of 1972. ⟦ *National Register listing 03/25/77* ⟧

Hyattsville

4325 Gallatin Street

LOUIS A. SIMON – 1935

HYATTSVILLE'S ONE-STORY brick post office owes much of its existence to the fact that the Fourth Assistant Postmaster General at the time, Smith W. Purdum, was a resident of Hyattsville, and he watched over nearly every aspect of its construction. As Fourth Assistant Postmaster General, Purdum was responsible for the agency's Division of Engineering and Research. Purdum was among the dignitaries who laid the cornerstone for the building on June 19, 1935.

The interior mural, painted by Eugene Kingman in 1937, is also attributable to Purdum, who was an avid horseman. The artist was advised to consider horses, having been told "in view of the fact that this is the home of the Fourth Assistant Postmaster General who is an enthusiast about horses I hope that your subject matter will be able to include some horses in the design." This may have been an attempt to placate Purdum, who was upset by the Supervising Architect's refusal to replace the arrow on the weather vane with a trotting horse. As it was, Purdum strongly suggested that the artist consult with a leading resident, Mrs. J. Enos Ray of Hyattsville, on the mural's design, which was done. At this point, Purdum still stayed very active in the mural's creation, reviewing of the painting from time to time, suggesting that the ears of the foremost horse be raised, instead of remaining lowered, as the artist had originally painted them. ⟦ *National Register listing 07/24/86* ⟧

Westminster

83 East Main Street

LEWIS NEWMAN – 1933

IT IS AMAZING that the Westminster post office was ever built, given all the general contractors that were ultimately involved. Initially, a construction contract was awarded in April 1931 to the Quaker City Masonry Company, but that firm promptly withdrew its bid, prompting the government to award the work to the Brooklyn and Queens Screen Manufacturing

This photograph of the Westminster, Maryland, post office was taken on May 2, 1933, while the building was still under construction.

Company of Mitchell Field, Long Island. By September 1931, the Long Island firm was in receivership, and the work was ultimately assumed by the bondsman, the National Surety Bonding Company of New York City. Work resumed under the oversight of the bonding company reaching a point where the structure was under roof and the plaster work was nearly finished, before the bonding company went into receivership. A contract was awarded on March 5, 1933, to the Fred Comb Company of Minnesota, which completed the building in August 1933 at a cost of $22,505.

With all of these changes, the structure, basically a one-story building of two-story height with a full basement, built principally of "beaver dam," marble, and brick, was still completed well below the $120,000 amount authorized by Congress in 1931. The post office, which measured 80 by 72 feet overall, of which about 70 percent was workroom space, was occupied on September 1, 1934.

NEW JERSEY

Blawenburg

Routes 518 and 601

UNKNOWN – 1832

THIS VILLAGE POST OFFICE has not moved around much in over 150 years, in fact it has not moved more than a couple of hundred feet throughout its entire history. The original post office, established in March 1832, was housed in the front of a small country store located at the southeast intersection of the Georgetown-Franklin Turnpike and Blawenburg-Belle Mead Road, where it remained until about 1948. It then briefly moved across the street to another general store, and subsequently moved back across the street to a small structure behind the original 1832 general store, where it remained until the 1960s. It was moved for the last time about 1964, this time about 200 feet south of the 1832 general store to its present location. The current post office originally served as a one-vehicle garage that housed the community's first fire engine. When the fire department outgrew the building, it was turned into a post office.

Jersey City

Washington and Montgomery Streets

JAMES KNOX TAYLOR – 1913

ALTHOUGH THE ORIGINAL PLANS for the Jersey City post office were approved in March 1912, construction was not far enough along to inaugurate Parcel Post from this site, when that service was inaugurated nationwide on January 1, 1913. During the first week of Parcel Post Service, Jersey City became the country's sixth largest parcel mailing center, handling over 60,000 packages. The volume surpassed Detroit, Baltimore, Cincinnati, and San Francisco. Postal officials were elated by these statistics.

To handle the tremendous demand, the postal service ordered a fleet of gasoline-powered trucks. According to the January 18, 1913 issue of *R.F.D. News*, "In arranging for bids, the [Post Office] Department announced its purpose of procuring several classes of the vehicles, but in each case to adopt the standard type that will be used generally throughout the country. All vehicles will be painted red in accordance with the plan to keep this color for post office equipment in general." Each of the nation's major mail centers, including Jersey City, received a portion of this truck order.

In November 1913, when the new post office opened, Jersey City was one of the nation's principal distribution hubs for trans-Atlantic mail.

Jersey City's Beaux-Arts-style post office was expanded during the Great

The Jersey City, New Jersey, post office during construction.

Depression. The plans for the extension and remodeling, principally affecting the rear of the building, were completed in April 1932 by a local firm, William Neumann & Sons. The renovation, carried out to match the original style of the building, significantly expanded the general workroom floor, enlarging it by about 30 percent, and provided separate rooms for Collect-on-Delivery business and for Special Delivery Service. Other changes included a threefold expansion of the office of the superintendent of mails, opening up the Money Order section on the south side of the building, and enclosing the Parcel Post drop-off windows and the lockbox areas that fronted onto the building's main public lobby.

Paterson

Hamilton and Ward Streets

WILLIAM MARTIN AIKEN – 1899

PATERSON'S POST OFFICE in the 1890s was a case where drawings betrayed words. In his 1897 *Annual Report*, Supervising Architect William Martin Aiken states his practice in designing government buildings: "In the drawings and specifications of all buildings, since April, 1895, the prime consideration has been thorough but simple construction, using the most substantial and fireproof materials permissible within the limits of appropriation, elaboration of design being of secondary importance." Paterson's post office, however, was far from simple.

Constructed between 1897 and 1899, the post office Aiken designed featured elaborately stepped brick Flemish-Revival-style gables, steep pitched roof, and ornately rounded window arches. The design was probably used because of Patterson's large Dutch population, attracted to the city because of its thriving silk industry in the last century. Although the design is quite spectacular to behold, what is even more remarkable is that it did not sustain any awkward additions over the years. Today, the building serves as an annex to the Passaic County courthouse.

NEW YORK

Albany

Broadway and State Street

WILLIAM POTTER AND JAMES HILL – 1884

IN THE CASE of the Albany post office, two minds were indeed better than one. While the basic footprint and plan of the asymmetrical structure, as designed by Supervising Architect William Potter, were retained, the towers and roofline were drastically shortened by his successor, James Hill. The

Two Supervising Architects, William Potter and James Hill, had a hand in designing the Albany, New York, post office.

result was a much improved hybrid design, one that was necessary to cut costs. The changes reduced the overall estimate of the project from $750,000 to about $623,500, which was roughly the ultimate amount provided by Congress. Among the changes, Hill turned away from Potter's Gothic details, opting instead in favor of an Italian Renaissance treatment.

Construction of the building, on land donated by the citizens of Albany, started in June 1877, and was completed late in 1884. In advance of its final completion, the building was partially occupied on January 1, 1884. While the first floor was principally occupied by the postal service, other government tenants included the internal revenue service, weather bureau service, pension bureau, federal court, and the steamboat inspection service. The building now serves only as a courthouse.

Buffalo

121 Ellicott Street

JEREMIAH O'ROURKE, WILLIAM AIKEN,
AND JAMES KNOX TAYLOR – 1901

ALTHOUGH ITS cathedral-like characteristics, including an oversize 244-foot-tall pinnacle tower decorated with crockets, prominent gable finials, and an abundance of ridgeline embellishments, gave the old Buffalo post office a highly criticized exterior that was like few other postal facilities, it was the building's five-story-tall skylight above the central workroom floor that seems to have created the most trouble for the postal workers who had to work the mail there. One oldtime postal clerk later recalled how "the light, filtering through the dust-laden skylights, was so poor that the clerks became as myopic as the Prisoner of Zenda as they sorted letters."

This problem aside, nothing about this building was cheap or without controversy. Even before the plans for this building were on paper, it was the focus of the raging national dispute over the implementation of the Tarney Act of 1893, which required that federal buildings be designed as a result of architectural competitions. While giving public assurances that the Buffalo post office would be the first federal project to be competitively designed, behind the scenes Treasury Secretary Henry G. Carlisle, who was responsible for the Supervising Architects office, ordered Supervising Architect Jeremiah O'Rourke to begin work on the plans. O'Rourke's design was approved in 1894, setting off a firestorm of protests. O'Rourke's original design was immediately branded "inferior and unworthy for the purpose." Despite such protests, O'Rourke's Gothic design, modified by his successors, William Aiken and James Knox Taylor, was largely completed as planned.

The site for the old Buffalo post office was acquired on February 6, 1892 for the princely sum of $476,250, and excavation started late in 1894. Constructed principally of pinkish granite quarried at Jonesboro, Maine, it cost over $1.5 million. The interior corridors and lobbies were finished in polished white marble, enameled brick wainscots, and terrazzo and mosaic floors. The groined ceilings extend from marble columns and pilasters.

In 1963 the post office moved out of the building and the departure set off a running debate over the fate of the building. Some wanted the building to be torn down, while others argued to have to designated as one of the state's historic landmarks. One of those who wanted it razed called it "a mongrel structure," claiming that it was "dungeon-like in its aspect, repellent to the visitor and lacking in the conveniences suitable for habitation." Luckily, the building survived and was renovated between 1979 and 1981 at a cost of about $18 million. As part of the Erie County Community College's city campus, the building incorporates a library, auditorium, cafeteria, and lounge, all within the confines of the old workroom floor, which was transformed into a spacious 120 by 140 foot atrium. [*National Register listing 03/16/72*]

Gilbertsville

1 Commercial Street

UNKNOWN – 1889

ALTHOUGH GILBERTSVILLE'S one-story post office has been located in the same building for more than a century, the exterior appearance of the building has been significantly changed and the location is different. The original building, which measured 16 by 30 feet, was moved to its present location after the town suffered a major fire in 1893 that miraculously spared the post office. The structure's facade, which featured splendid Victorian gingerbread, was remodeled in 1929, providing it with the Greek Revival exterior seen today. An addition was added in 1953. Despite the fact that the exterior has changed over time, the interior still appears much as it did in 1889, including the original triangular oak screenline unit, manufactured by the Kayless Lock Company of Indianapolis, that was acquired for about $500.

Since 1946 the building, which is on the National Register of Historic Places, has been the property of the Village Improvement Society, which rents the building to the Postal Service.

Hyde Park

East Market Street and U.S. Route 9

LOUIS A. SIMON – 1940

IN 1939, DURING the dedication ceremony at the Rhinebeck, New York, post office, a few miles from the President's home at Hyde Park, Franklin D. Roosevelt chided his Treasury Secretary, Henry Morgenthau, Jr., and his Postmaster General, James A. Farley, that if they wanted to keep their jobs they had better locate the next post office constructed in Dutchess County at his hometown, Hyde Park. Roosevelt knew that it was a safe bet that this would be the case, since work was already underway on the Hyde Park post office, a Dutch Colonial style structure that was dedicated in 1940.

[*National Register listing 05/11/89*]

New York City

Eighth Avenue between 31st and 33rd Streets

MCKIM, MEAD, AND WHITE – 1914

The New York City post office is among the world's busiest postal facilities.

ONE OF THE GREAT disappointments for William Mitchell Kendall, the principal architect for the New York City post office, and a member of the staff of McKim, Mead, and White, was that the structure was never really finished. According to Kendall's original plan, a large sculpture was to be incorporated in the niches of the corner pavilions facing Eighth Avenue. For years after the post office opened to the public, the aging Kendall would make the same plea to each newly installed postmaster: "Please finish the

post office," and each time he was ignored. His last opportunity to beg an incoming postmaster came shortly before his death, when he begged to see the statuary started while he was still alive. No statues were ever installed.

It also pained Kendall to see the inscription chiseled above the frieze, a rather free rendering of the original words of Herodotus, become commercialized and paraphrased. Many readers have come to accept these words—"Neither Snow, Nor Rain, Nor Heat, Nor Gloom of Night Stays These Couriers from the Swift Completion of Their Appointed Rounds"—as the official motto of the postal system; however, the United States Postal Service does not actually have a motto. The son of an instructor of classical languages, the idea of using Herodotus came to William Kendall one night while he was reading Greek for pleasure.

Kendall's building is a massive five-story, pink granite structure, one that *Popular Mechanics* hailed as "the greatest building of its kind in the world." Construction of the 400,000 square foot space, built at a cost of $6 million, consumed 165,000 cubic feet of granite, 18,000 tons of steel, and 7 million bricks. The window areas consist of approximately 200,000 square feet of glass. The building's main lobby corridor, produced with a palette of buff marble, white plaster, and glass, runs the length of the two-block-long exterior colonnade. The ceiling of the two-story lobby area, which measures 29 feet wide by 280 feet long, is adorned with the coats of arms of ten nations: Belgium, The Netherlands, Italy, France, England, Germany, Russia, Spain, Austro-Hungary, and the United States.

An addition to the New York City post office, known as the "Annex," was dedicated in December 1935. One of the stunning exterior highlights of this addition is a sculptured grouping by Charles Keck in the center of the Ninth Avenue facade. The flanking figures represent "Night" and "Day," symbolic of the fact that the postal service works both day and night, while a central figure represents the Seal of the United States.

Originally known as the "Pennsylvania Terminal" in 1914, and later as the "General Post Office" after 1918, in 1982 the name of the New York City post office building was legislatively changed, renamed in honor of New York native James A. Farley, Franklin Roosevelt's first postmaster general and the 53rd Postmaster General of the United States. [*National Register listing 01/29/73*]

Poughkeepsie

55 Mansion Street

ERIC KEBBON – 1938

AN OUTSTANDING EXAMPLE of the Colonial Revival style, the Poughkeepsie was the first of five New Deal era post offices constructed in Dutchess County. The post office was built between 1937 and 1938 by Silberblatt and Lasker, Inc., at a cost of $330,000. The construction documents consisted of 218 pages.

A native of Dutchess County, President Franklin Roosevelt took a particular interest in this project, offering countless design suggestions such as the use of regional stone for the exterior walls. The President also participated in the cornerstone-laying ceremony on October 13, 1937, and the

The Poughkeepsie, New York, post office at night.

building's formal dedication on December 5, 1938.

According to Joyce Ghee, an historian for Dutchess County, the stone carvers involved with this project were the highest-paid workers, receiving a minimum wage of $1.62 an hour. Iron workers received a minimum of $1.50, while plasterers and bricklayers earned a minimum of $1.37. Laborers were the lowest-paid workers, receiving a minimum of 50 cent an hour.

The original post office building contained 32,900 square feet, and housed offices for other government agencies, such as the Agriculture Department, the FBI, and the Navy, Army, and Marines. [*National Register listing 05/15/89*]

Rhinebeck

14 Mill Street

LOUIS A. SIMON – 1939

A SHORT DISTANCE north of Poughkeepsie, the Rhinebeck post office was another of Franklin Roosevelt's personal favorite New Deal era projects, in fact he was so involved in the design and construction of this particular post office in the late 1930s that the local press called him "the nation's No. 1 'unlicensed architect.'" Eleanor Roosevelt characterized the President's involvement by observing that "I never knew anyone to take as much interest in the public buildings of the neighborhood as my husband. He has watched every step ... of the building in Rhinebeck; he is off this morning to discuss that."

The First Lady had her own opinion of the post office: "As you drive up Market Street from the south, the road is not absolutely straight and, therefore, the cupola looks a little bit out of line. However, I don't suppose anyone else will ever be bothered by such a detail, tho I'd like the road changed."

FDR, who particularly liked the Dutch Colonial style because it was so common in that part of New York State, relished the fact that this particular building, dedicated on May 1, 1939, was a replica of the first Dutch style stone house of any consequence built in the region. The post office actually was constructed from some of the stones from the ruins of the original farmhouse, erected in 1700 by Hendrick Kip. Attending the dedication ceremonies in 1939 along with FDR were the Crown Prince and Princess of Denmark and Iceland. [*National Register listing 05/11/89*]

PENNSYLVANIA

Dillsburg

National Postal Museum, Washington, D.C.

UNKNOWN – 1913

PROVIDING SERVICE for a community of under 5,000 residents, the Dillsburg post office occupied about half of the first floor of this three-story building from 1913 to 1971. Several telltale objects help to identify this as a governmental institution: the American flag, the mailbox, and the marine recruitment poster. In the 1960s the interior of the building was dismantled and shipped to the Smithsonian Institution in Washington, D.C. Today the interior serves as a portion of the "customers and communities" exhibit at the National Postal Museum.

The "screenline" unit from the Dillsburg, Pennsylvania, post office, now on display at the National Postal Museum.

Erie

617 State Street

MIFFLIN BELL – 1887

THE HANDIWORK of Supervising Architect Mifflin E. Bell, the Erie federal building was completed late in 1887 at a cost of slightly over $250,000. Two years in the making, the entire first floor was dedicated to postal business. The upper floors were taken up by federal offices of the Weather Bureau, Internal Revenue Service, courthouse, marine hospital, and pension examiner. Two different stones were used to construct this building: granite for the basement and sandstone for the upper exterior walls.

Johnstown

131 Market Street

JAMES KNOX TAYLOR – 1914

THE DESIGN OF THE BUILDING, considered Greek Revival in appearance, was approved on May 1, 1911, and construction was carried out between 1912 and 1914. The principal contractor for the project, which was completed for $121,503, was W. H. Fissell of New York City.

After the post office vacated this building, its space was taken over by the other tenants of the building, which included the Veterans Administration, Internal Revenue Service, Bureau of Mines, Selective Service, and the Works Projects Administration. In the 1960s the building was purchased by Crown America Corporation for use as its headquarters, the corporation paying about the same amount as it cost to build the structure a half century before. When Crown America later moved its headquarters elsewhere, the building once again took on a new life, serving as the offices for a variety of nonprofit organizations.

When a committee was established to select the site for a replacement building in Johnstown in the 1903os specifically designed to accommodate only the postal service, they originally wanted the highest elevation possible because of the town's history with floods. No high ground was available in the business section of town, however, so the group had to settle on a site at Franklin and Locust Streets.

The original use of six revolving doors (three on the Franklin Street side and three on Locust Street) proved to be a deadly detail for one of the building's first patrons, an elderly man who was critically injured in 1938 when one of the revolving doors facing Locust Street spun out of control. As a result of this fatality, the government removed the spinning doors.

Warren

Liberty and Third Streets

D. K. DEAN – 1883

ONE OF WARREN'S leading citizens in the 1880s, Thomas Struthers, agreed to pay for the construction of a much-needed library building if his neighbors were willing to buy the land for the site. True to Struthers' word, groundbreaking ceremonies took place on June 20, 1882, only five days after the land was purchased by the members of the Warren Library Association. The excavation, foundation stonework, and exterior wall building were hastily started in the hope of enclosing the building before winter set in, but construction was halted on December 5, due to foul weather, leaving the structure with only a few feet of walls. Work resumed in the spring, and the building was completed that winter.

The finished building was a striking example of mixed use. The library's main reading room occupied a 57 by 45 foot space, with a 20-foot high ceiling; the public auditorium measured 67 by 64 feet, with a 39-foot ceiling above the stage; and the Masonic Hall dominated the third floor. Two storefronts also were available on the street level.

Part of Thomas Struthers' original concept for the community building called for the income from renting out the structure's auditorium, plus the rent from its two storefronts and the income from the Masonic Hall, to go toward the maintenance of the library. One of the two original storefronts, an elegant space trimmed with ash woodwork, housed the post office. Approximately $3,000 was spent to furnish the post office lobby. However, by 1902 it was clear that the post office needed more space. To accommodate the town's growing postal operations, the entire front of the building was dedicated to the post office.

One drawback to the building in the 1900s was that it had no loading dock. Mailbags and employees alike came and went through the side door. At that time, iron bars and steel grates were added to the first floor windows to increase security for the post office. By 1917 it was evident that the post office had totally outgrown the available space in the Struthers Library Building, prompting the postmaster to relocate elsewhere.

Between 1883 and 1918 the residents of Warren, and those in the surrounding countryside, began receiving a number of new mail services from the Struthers Library Building, including City Delivery Service, which was inaugurated in Warren in 1887, and Rural Free Delivery, which began in 1903.

Now a landmark in Warren, the Struthers Library Building was returned to much of its original appearance by 1983, in time for its 100th birthday.

VIRGINIA

Big Stone Gap

U.S. Route 58

JAMES KNOX TAYLOR – 1913

IN 1908 CONGRESS approved $15,000 for the purchase of the site for the post office at Big Stone Gap, and by 1910 authorized the use of up to

$100,000 for the building. The initial design for the structure was prepared under the supervision of James Knox Taylor, whose plans were carried out by his successor.

The builder of this impressive three-story Second Renaissance Revival structure was the Plowman Construction Company, which completed the project for $94,000.

The main facade is dominated by a Tuscan portico that includes four pairs of coupled, unfluted columns that shield the building's three principal entrances. Over the years the first floor, the principal level used by the postal service, was extensively remodeled to accommodate new innovations in mail processing. In the 1970s the Postal Service announced plans to demolish the building, but public reaction to this was swift and loud, and the building still stands. [*National Register listing 12/23/75*]

Bristol

Piedmont and Cumberland Streets

ALGERNON BLAIR – 1933

POLITICS AND GEOGRAPHY have made this a unique post office. Residents of Bristol, Tennessee, had all the benefits of a big-town post office, but Bristol, Virginia, did not. The two Bristols were literally a stone's throw apart, separated only by the main street, which was in fact the state line. The Virginia residents wanted their own post office. Although the Postmaster General at the time, Frank Hitchcock, opposed the idea of creating a separate post office for Bristol, Virginia, he was overruled by President William Howard Taft. In only a few months, however, the Bristol, Virginia, office was ordered closed by incoming Postmaster General Albert Burleson on July 31, 1913. A swarm of strong community protests ensued, and by October 4, thanks to the intervention of Virginia's two U.S. Senators, President Woodrow Wilson got Burleson to relent, allowing Bristol to keeps its post office.

During the 1930s Bristol received this two-story brick post office constructed by Algernon Blair of Montgomery, Alabama, which currently stands vacant.

The post office at Bristol, Virginia.

James Store

Routes 14 and 602

UNKNOWN – 1925

WHEN IT CAME to naming the post office, Edward W. Jones could not quite make up his mind. When he applied for the office in 1879 his application initially bore the name "James Store." On second thought he crossed that out before mailing it, and replaced it with "Brick Store." Upon further consideration he reversed himself once more, crossing out that name too. In the end he went back to "James Store," squeezing it in once again on top of the other two entries.

The former James Store post office before it was closed.

Over the years most towns with "Store" in their names have dropped that designation, but not this community. It fits. Its post office has been in one store or another since that 1879 beginning. Until recently, the post office was in Willis Cox's general store and gas station. This site is currently vacant.

Richmond

100 East Main Street

AMMI B. YOUNG – 1858

THE SITE FOR RICHMOND'S current post office was purchased in 1854 and construction commenced the following year. The original three-story granite building, constructed to house the post office, revenue service, federal courts, and customs service, was finished in 1858 at a cost of $250,000. When Richmond became the capital of the Confederacy, the post office was evicted and relocated to the Spottswood Hotel, where it remained until 1865, while the original building housed the offices of President Jefferson Davis and the Confederate cabinet, as well as the Confederate Treasury Department.

At the end of the war the Renaissance Revival style federal building escaped the disastrous fire that consumed much of the city following the evacuation of the Southern government in April 1865. The original handwritten order to evacuate the records of the Confederate Post Office Department, dated April 2, 1865, is part of the collection of the National Postal Museum. The order, to C. G. Addison, states "You are hereby ordered to accompany the books, records, [etc.] of this office to Charlotte [North Carolina] and remain there until further orders." Ironically, after the war the building was the site of the indictment proceedings and trial against Jefferson Davis on charges of treason against the United States. Ultimately, the charges were dropped on February 15, 1869, after several

Post-Civil-War rendering of the Richmond post office.

postponements by the government. After the Civil War a number of extensions and renovations have been made to the building, beginning in 1888 with the addition of two wings on the Main Street front and an extension on the Bank Street side. The total cost of these alterations, completed in 1889, was $183,000. A second expansion occurred shortly before World War I. This time the remodeling cost $800,000 and included an extension of the building along 10th Street, plus the addition of another story. A $1 million annex for Parcel Post was added during the Depression, giving the building it present configuration.

[*National Register listing 06/04/69*]

The Plains

4314 Fauquier Avenue, just off Main Street

UNKNOWN – 1933

HOUSED IN THE SAME PLACE for over six decades, this vernacular stucco post office has changed little as far as its architecture goes. According to the postmaster, Susan Jones, "The building was built, or at least equipped, especially for the post office in 1933 and most of the furniture still used is the oak cabinets from that time." The heating system has been modernized, though. In the old days the coal furnace in the basement required constant attention. The task of shoveling coal was shared by employees, as was responsibility for cleaning the office and washing the windows.

WEST VIRGINIA

Elkhorn

Main Street and Route 52

UNKNOWN – 1888

UNLIKE THE POST OFFICES in many other Appalachian coal mining towns, the one at Elkhorn was not incorporated into the coal company's store or mine office. It is a freestanding frame structure that measures 30 by 16 feet overall. Time has not affected its appearance very much. According to postmaster Joan Semonco, "Elkhorn's post office looks virtually the

The handicapped accessibility ramp, an essential alteration, is almost longer than this post office, located in Elkhorn, West Virginia.

same today, inside and out, as it did on March 7, 1888, the day it opened to the public," the only exception being the handicapped accessibility ramp that was recently added.

Fairmont

Fairmont Avenue and Second Street

LOUIS A. SIMON – 1940

SEVERAL YEARS BEFORE the current post office opened, Fairmont experienced an unheard of labor action when 25 employees of the post office, the entire workforce, went out on strike at the height of the Christmas mailing season following the dismissal of four of their colleagues. Postal workers were rushed in from surrounding post offices to keep the mail moving and postal inspectors were dispatched to make arrests. Within a week of the stoppage, all of the striking employees were behind bars on charges of conspiracy to delay the mails. Although the mail was being expeditiously processed, Congress called for a full investigation.

The current post office is a multistory New Deal era Starved-Classical style structure.

The post office at Fairmont, West Virginia.

This photograph of the Headsville, West Virginia, post office was taken before it was dismantled and transported to the National Museum of American History in Washington, D.C.

Headsville

National Museum of American History, Washington, D.C.

HENRY HEAD – 1861

TYPICAL OF COUNTLESS post offices that served crossroad communities in agrarian regions of the country in the mid-19th century, the post office at Headsville, West Virginia, now serves as an exhibit and a working post office in Washington, D.C. Henry Head, builder of this country store-post office in 1861, served as the postmaster of the Headsville post office until 1880, remaining a loyal Union supporter during the Civil War. Various postmasters followed Head, operating from the original store; however, when John Staggs became postmaster in 1914 he moved postal operations to his own store. In 1971 Henry Head's store was dismantled piece by piece and transported to Washington, D.C., where it was rebuilt inside the Smithsonian Institution's National Museum of American History.

St. Albans

202 Sixth Avenue

LOUIS A. SIMON – 1937

THE ONE-STORY post office at St. Albans was classified as a "Class D" operation, which meant that its annual postal receipts amounted to less than $15,000. Under a plan devised by federal government in 1915, this designation also determined how much money the federal government would normally be willing to spend on the construction of the town's new post office. Under the government's 1915 formula, devised under the direction of Treasury Secretary William McAdoo, a Class D operation was worth a brick building, with very little or no stonework or terra cotta, and that is precisely what was built in 1937 to serve the town's 3,200 residents. This structure, the only example of a Class D post office in the Kanawha Valley region, continued to serve the postal needs of the community until 1986.

[*National Register listing 11/04/94*]

Wheeling

1528 Market Street

AMMI B. YOUNG – 1859

DESCRIBED BY Ammi B. Young as being "Italian, with Greek details," a new concoction for Young in the mid-1850s, the style of the Wheeling federal building is now described as Renaissance Revival. This building, one of 35 such Renaissance Revival federal buildings designed by Ammi B. Young during 1855 and 1856, is also important because of the cast-iron columns and iron framing, used as a fireproofing technique. This framing includes nine-inch rolled structural I beams, making this one of the earliest surviving examples of large rolled wrought-iron floor beams; however, in the strictest sense, this is not a true iron skeletal structure since the masonry walls are load-bearing. Heavy cast-iron double front doors, plus iron shutters, also afforded a degree of fire protection. The use of such fireproof elements was the result of the catastrophic fires that had taken place in countless major American cities throughout the 19th century.

The three-story symmetrical sandstone structure acquired national prominence during the Civil War. To protect it from being taken over by secessionist forces, citizens of the town occupied the building, turning it into a pro-Union stronghold. It also served as the site of the first constitutional convention for West Virginia, which became the 35th state on June 20, 1863.

Since the building opened in the spring of 1859, few of the architectural changes made over the years, including the addition of a fourth floor and the removal of Young's original sandstone chimneys, have been allowed to remain to diminish the building's original appearance. The fourth floor was removed and replica chimneys have been reinstalled. Today, the building, which is known as "Independence Hall" and is also called the "birthplace of West Virginia," reflect's Young's design wherever possible.

South

ALABAMA

Atmore

North Main Street

LOUIS A. SIMON – 1935

ALTHOUGH THE POST OFFICE at Atmore is typical of many other Depression-era post offices in most respects, it has one distinction that many of the other surviving examples of the small-town Starved-Classical-style government buildings do not possess; up until 1996 it had a fully equipped air-raid shelter in the basement. As a result of the Cuban missile crisis, thousands of sites nationwide, including post offices and other federal buildings, were designated as Civil Defense shelters. Atmore received thousands of pounds of supplies in 1963, including 50 barrels of water, each containing 15 gallons; 25 tins of hermetically sealed crackers; and 10 boxes of medical supplies, plus radiological monitoring instruments. These were all stored in the basement of the post office, which was set up as a fallout shelter capable of accommodating 224 people. Over the years these Civil Defense stockpiles in other locations have been discarded, but not the supplies at Atmore.

Atmore is located about midway between the Pensacola, Florida, Naval Air Station and the Air Force base at Mobile, Alabama. The post office was originally selected as the site of the Civil Defense shelter because it was the only building in town with a basement. According to Atmore postal supervisor Betty Coker in 1994, "We have been located in this building since 1935, and I guess that is the reason why the [Civil Defense] things in the basement have never been removed."

Birmingham

1800 Fifth Avenue, North

JAMES A. WETMORE – 1921

THE PROPERTY FOR THIS post office was acquired a few years before the design was completed in 1916, but the building's construction was interrupted by World War I, awaiting completion until 1921. The original federal building at Birmingham is a massive marble-clad structure

PRECEDING PAGE:

The Magnolia Springs post office in 1905, top, which is now a private residence, bottom.

that extends 375 feet along Fifth Avenue, its principal facade, and 165 feet along its sides. Securing such a large structure is a attributable to the powerful intervention of Representative, later Senator, Oscar W. Underwood, who championed this project in the Congress. Classified as a two-story structure (the third story, which was incorporated into the design after World War I, as were the end wings, was treated as an attic level), the building's two principal entrance pavilions flank a central colonnade that consists of 14 freestanding, unfluted Ionic columns. Each entrance is accessed by a broad flight of stone steps and is highlighted by engaged Ionic columns that match those of the main colonnade. The building has undergone several changes, including a remodeling in 1927 that affected the attic spaces. In 1940, considerable remodeling was done to the judicial sections of the building. In 1972-1973 the post office spaces were converted into additional offices for the federal court.

[*National Register listing 06/03/76*]

Clopton

Highway 105 and County Road 68

UNKNOWN – 1853

IT APPEARS AS THOUGH the post office did not move around much in Clopton, certainly much less often than in most other places, having been in only three locations in the past 140 years. The first post office was established in 1853 in a small country store. Although no longer used as a post office, or anything else for that matter, the original wood frame building is still standing after roughly 140 years. The post office moved across the street in 1912 to its second location. The current post office, located across the street from the second site, is in a grocery store. The

Clopton's post office was housed in this building between 1853 and 1912.

Some alterations have affected the appearance of the Fairfield, Alabama, Depression era post office.

three buildings are situated so close together that visitors to Clopton can see all three post offices without turning their heads.

Originally an important stopping place for wagons traveling from Ozark to Abbeville, the community now is small, according to its postmaster, Betty Deloney: "Clopton's biggest asset is the community spirit which binds its members together for projects and always shows the warmth and hospitality of days gone by."

Fairfield

45th Street and Lloyd Nolan Parkway

LOUIS A. SIMON – 1937

FAIRFIELD DESPERATELY NEEDED a new post office in the 1920s and the town's postmaster, Ada Burks, was bound and determined to get one. She spearheaded the drive to convince her local congressman and postal officials of the need. She described the existing site as "old, dirty, and in need of repairs and the lessor very disagreeable and slow in providing the necessary repairs and upkeep. The ventilation is poor, and the lighting such that all distribution of mail by clerks and carriers, as well as most of the window work must be done under artificial light." Despite the fact that her campaign took 12 years, Burks never gave up, and her efforts finally paid off. Supervising Architect Louis A. Simon was authorized to design a new post office in the 1930s.

Originally, the design called for a stucco structure, but the town objected, citing that such a treatment "would be completely out of harmony with the surrounding buildings." The citizens wanted something more traditional, and they got their way. The cornerstone for a more expensive brick building was laid in 1936. Despite the passage of time, the people of Fairfield continue to be proud of their "new" post office.

Magnolia Springs

14577 Oak Street

UNKNOWN – 1905

THE BUILDING THAT SERVED as Magnolia Spring's post office from the 1900s to the 1940s is now a private residence, but other aspects of the postal service in this town remain unchanged. When patrons can't conveniently come to the post office the mail typically has to come to them. That is the way it has been at Magnolia Springs since 1916.

For more than three-quarters of a century, residents along a roughly 25-mile stretch of the Magnolia and Fish Rivers have gotten their mail by boat. This novel type of service was instigated in 1916 by the town's postmaster at the time, William B. Thomas, who is seen here in the doorway of his one-story office. Thomas' tenure as postmaster spanned from 1905 to 1919, while his wife, Grace, served from 1919 to 1941. As in any good-sized community, today mail delivery is made six days a week, but here it comes by boat.

Selma

908 Alabama Avenue

JOHN KNOX TAYLOR – 1909

SYMBOLICALLY PLACED across from the Dallas County courthouse, the three-story Federal building serves as an imposing statement of the federal presence at Selma. In 1909 a "Memorial Arch" was erected on the sidewalk in front of the Alabama Avenue entrance to the brick and stone federal building. That was the year the federal building was completed, and the arch is dedicated to the memories of two Alabama senators, John Tyler Morgan (1824-1907) and Edmund Winston Pettus (1821-1907).

Other than a one-story addition to the south of the building in 1928, the exterior is basically unaltered. The same cannot be said of the interior, which has been significantly remodeled in the process of converting the first floor spaces to offices. [*National Register listing 03/26/76*]

ARKANSAS

Little Rock

Second and Spring Streets

ALFRED B. MULLETT – 1881

CONSTRUCTED IN 1881, largely of sandstone on a pink Indiana granite base in an Italianate Renaissance style, the symmetrical Little Rock post office and custom house possesses elegant proportions. It also housed one

This historic postcard view reflects the way the current post office building at Little Rock appears today, except that the road in front is now paved.

of the first elevators installed in the state. Two wings were subsequently added to either end of the building. The post office vacated the property in 1932. Since then it has been used by other government agencies, including the armed forces, which used it as an induction station.

[*National Register listing 05/07/73*]

Mena

520 North Mena Street

JAMES A. WETMORE – 1917

THIS TWO-STORY BRICK BUILDING now serves as the Mena City Hall. The original structure was the result of the efforts of Congressman Ben Cravens, who secured passage of the necessary initial legislation for the project in 1910. On February 21, 1917 the government called for bids on the project, receiving a winning quote of $40,700 from the Richardson Engineering Company of Bainbridge, Georgia. Excavation work began on May 16 and the cornerstone was laid on October 10. Public enthusiasm ran high throughout the construction process, yet it ended with something of a letdown, a disappointment over the differences that existed between the original sketches of the building and the final product. The drawings were far more elaborate, depicting a much larger structure. This difference should not have come as so much of a shock. A great deal changed between 1910, when the project was proposed, and 1917, when it was finished. Construction projects around the country were being toned down because of economy and the First World War. This building also reflects the implementation of Treasury Secretary William MacAdoo's standardization and classification scheme, which was introduced in 1915.

[*National Register listing 06/05/91*]

Prescott

207 East Elm Street

JAMES A. WETMORE – 1927

BEFORE THIS FEDERALLY OWNED post office was opened in 1927, the unhappy postmaster described his duties this way:

> I open my office at 7 a.m. I handle the mail that the three [rural] carriers handle and nearly as much more, write money orders, attend to the general delivery, keep books, carry all the responsibility, hear all complaints from both office and rural patrons, furnish the building and all office fixtures and work about 12 to 14 hours per day. All for about $700 per year. No vacation or holiday, not even Sunday.

The new post office, with different hours and a larger staff, was built for about $50,000 by W. D. Lowell of Minneapolis, Minnesota.

FLORIDA

The Key West, Florida, federal building was the site of the Court of Inquiry into the sinking of the ship the U.S.S. Maine.

Key West

Front Street and Clinton Square

WILLIAM A. FRERET – 1891

THE KEY WEST POST OFFICE served as one of the primary post offices during the Spanish American War, serving sailors aboard 104 naval vessels and troops sent to Cuba and Puerto Rico, but in some respects it is

a wonder that it was ever built at all. The project began well enough, with Congress authorizing the construction of the post office and custom house in 1885 on a site that was described as "the coolest, prettiest, healthiest and pleasantest [sic] place in town."

Although the site was thought to be perfect, the construction process was anything but ideal. Bids for the excavation work were awarded to McDermott and Higgs of Key West, on January 30, 1888. This aspect of the project, worth $10,647, was to be completed in three months, but took much longer. McDermott and Higgs was also the successful bidder for the rest of the construction, with a quote of $72,555, but, almost immediately the project was thrown into controversy because of McDermott's excessive drinking and his questionable judgment. While on a trip to New York City to acquire materials for the project, McDermott reportedly got drunk, squandered the company's funds, and offered part of the post office contract to the owner of a dance hall. Higgs offered to complete the project, but was forced to stop because of the financial losses caused by McDermott.

The next group of contractors, principally cigar manufacturers, knew little about construction and fared only slightly better. There were disputes over nearly every aspect of the project, including the fact that the bricks were highly alkaline and of poor color and the window sills were defaced in transit.

In desperation, in May 1889, William Kerr was sworn in as the superintendent of buildings in Key West with a specific charge that he clean up the mess surrounding this project, which by then was well behind schedule. One of the things that Kerr could not control was yellow fever, which played havoc on the project.

Slated to open in January, 1891, the building opened to the public in stages, with the postal service finally taking possession of its portion of the building on April 1, 1891. The customs service moved in next, on July 1, 1891, followed by the federal court, which occupied the second floor on January 25, 1892, over a year behind schedule.

In all fairness, not all of the delays were the contractor's fault. A number of questions were raised over aspects of the design. William Freret's original plan called for the installation of fireplaces, which prompted a court judge to remind Freret that the building was in southernmost Florida. "We need protection against heat rather than cold," he told the Supervising Architect. The same judge also complained about the fact that apparently no provisions were made for urinals and water closets.

The project did include several novel touches, including a lawn. Grass was uncommon in Key West, and a protective iron fence was requested in 1895 to keep pedestrians from trampling the grass.

The federal court room on the second floor served as the site for the February 1898 Court of Inquiry appointed by President McKinley to investigate the sinking of the *U.S.S. Maine* in Havana Harbor. In 1933 the post office was relocated to a new building, leaving the federal court as one of the last government tenants of this Richardsonian Romanesque style brick, brownstone, and terra cotta structure. The four-story building was placed on the National Register of Historic Places in 1973. Twenty-one years later, in 1994, a 99-year lease to the property was awarded to the Key West Art and Historical Society. [*National Register listing 09/20/73*]

Miami

300 Northeast First Avenue

JAMES A. WETMORE AND LOUIS A. SIMON – 1933

THE SPANISH-MEDITERRANEAN style of architecture was largely introduced in Florida in the late 1880s in response to the development of winter resorts. Such resorts became particularly popular during World War I, when wealthy Americans found that they could not travel abroad. By the 1930s this was an established architectural type in Florida, finding uses in a wide variety of residential and commercial applications, including the city's three-story, gray coquina stone federal building, which included the U.S. district court and the post office.

The most spectacular aspect of this building is its central open courtyard, which is embellished with a marble writing table supported by griffin-like legs. A hexagonal fountain highlighted the courtyard until the 1950s, when it was unfortunately removed. [*National Register listing 10/14/83*]

Miami Beach

1300 Washington Avenue

UNKNOWN – 1935

MIAMI BEACH IS KNOWN for its exceptional concentration of Art Deco buildings, and the Miami Beach post office, built in the 1930s as a federal Works Project Administration project, is a stunning example of this architectural style. One of the building's outstanding features is its cylindrical rotunda, the interior of which is covered with a Depression-era mural.

The Miami Beach, Florida, post office is a stunning example of the Art Deco style.

Ochopee

Highway 41

Ochopee, Florida, is believed to be the nation's smallest post office.

UNKNOWN

SIZE CONSTITUTED a raging debate in the 1950s. The pressing question was which was the nation's smallest freestanding post office. *Postal News*, the Post Office Department's employee publication at that time, asked for the names and dimensions of possible contenders. Among the finalists were LaBlanca, Texas (192 square feet); Gober, Texas (168 square feet); Bokeeli, Florida (150 square feet); Farnhurst, Delaware (105 square feet); and Diehlstadt, Mississippi (100 square feet). The winner, though, was the Ochopee post office, which measured in at slightly over 60 square feet.

Palm Beach

95 North County Road

LOUIS A. SIMON – 1937

AN OUTSIDE ARCHITECT was asked to design the post office at Palm Beach, but when the construction estimate was presented, the government changed its mind. The projected cost of the building, estimated at $200,000, was far too expensive. Instead, the Office of the Supervising Architect designed a Spanish Colonial Revival style structure, described as "very different from the others designed by the Government in that it is much more ornate and presents a 'richer' look so that it conforms with the exclusive atmosphere of Palm Beach." Built by a Florida contractor, Watt and Sinclair, it certainly had a hefty price tag even when it was designed by the government's architects, costing $164,400.

[*National Register listing 07/21/83*]

Pensacola

North Palafox and East Chase Streets

RUDOLPH STANLEY-BROWN – 1939

PENSACOLA IS NOTEWORTHY for at least two reasons: the Mission style post office constructed there during the Depression, and a most unusual "parcel" mailed from there in 1915. The precious "little" package was mailed from Pensacola to Christiansburg, Virginia. Wearing a placard bearing her name and destination, a six-year-old girl was shipped by mail. The child's parents were separated. Her mother, who had fallen on hard times, was in Florida, and her father was in Virginia. A Florida probation officer, who temporarily had custody of the youngster, could not afford the train fare for the youth and an adult traveling companion so he entrusted her to Uncle Sam. According to a contemporary newspaper account, the cost of sending her to her father by Parcel Post was 15-cents.

Years later, between 1938 and 1939, the town's new federal building, which housed the courthouse and post office, was constructed. The 52,958 square foot building is faced with Oolitic limestone and the front portion of the building is capped with a red clay, Mission tile, hipped roof. Among the outstanding features of the building, which now serves as the federal court house at Pensacola, is its shallow balcony, with a remarkable wrought-iron railing, that runs nearly the entire width of front facade.

St. Augustine

Corners of Cathedral Place, St. George, and King Streets

MELLEN C. GREELEY – 1936
REMODELING OF 16TH CENTURY SITE

FROM 1834 UNTIL 1965 the federal post office was located on one of the most historic properties in St. Augustine: "Government House," a leading administrative center since at least 1598. The site has been the location of the Spanish governors' residence, the federal building, and, since 1966, the main offices of the Historical St. Augustine Preservation Board.

Over the years the buildings that have occupied this site have been significantly remodeled, yet with each successive renovation segments of the earlier structures have been successfully incorporated into the new buildings. The last significant reconstruction occurred in 1936 to accommodate the needs of the postal service. Thankfully, the project's architect, Mellen C. Greeley, took great pains to preserve aspects of the building's original appearance. His plan, reminiscent of the Spanish styling of the building in 1764, incorporated remnants of three of the old exterior walls, including the north wall, constructed about 1834; the east wall, built in 1713 and reconstructed in 1786; and almost all of the south wall, constructed in 1713. All of the holdover exterior walls are clearly discernible in Greeley's renovation.

The location of the governors' residence on this site reflected a Royal decree that mandated that all Spanish towns have a central plaza for gatherings and processions that was outlined by the community's important buildings, such as the church, market place, and government offices. In this case, the house built for Governor Gonzalo Mendez de Canzo fronted onto the west end of the St. Augustine plaza.

GEORGIA

Atlanta

76 Forsyth Street

JAMES KNOX TAYLOR – 1911

TO QUELL A NATIONWIDE rampage of lawlessness in 1926, the Post Office Department ordered a batch of armored mail trucks and received a contingent of a few thousand Marines. The armored trucks were assigned to cities with Federal Reserve Banks and small detachments of the leathernecks were briefly placed on guard duty at 108 of the nation's largest post offices, including Atlanta, which received 30 Marines. Armed guards escorted many mail shipments and Marines with fixed bayonets marched to and fro in mail facilities until they were relieved of the guard duty toward the end of 1927.

The post office moved out of its Second Renaissance Revival style five-story building about 15 years ago, leaving it all to the federal courts.

[*National Register listing 05/02/74*]

Carrollton

402 Newnan Street

JAMES KNOX TAYLOR AND OSCAR WENDEROTH – 1914

THE ONE-STORY red brick post office, designed under James Knox Taylor's supervision, but constructed under Oscar Wenderoth's, was created as a result of the political influence of Carrollton attorney and U.S. Representative William Charles Adamson, perhaps best known for his authorship of the Adamson Eight Hour Law, which restricted workers to an eight-hour day. The building was constructed at a cost of about $60,000. In 1967 the building was turned over to the Carroll County Board of Education.

[*National Register listing 04/18/83*]

Cassville

1813 Cassville Road

JOHN C. MCTIER – ABOUT 1889

NOW PRIVATE PROPERTY, the old post office at Cassville exemplifies a type of structure that was common throughout Georgia during the late 19th century, small commercial buildings that served dual purposes. In this case the building, a one-story wood-frame structure, measures about 14 by 25 feet. The back portion served as the residence of the postmaster, Sallie L. Bruce, while the front functioned as the post office until her death in 1915, when it was used as a general store. The post office was built by Mrs. Bruce's brother, John C. McTier. Twice after 1915 the building was again used as the post office, serving as such from 1921 to 1934 and again from 1935 to 1989. The building now serves as a gift shop.

[*National Register listing 08/31/92*]

Macon

475 Mulberry Street

JAMES KNOX TAYLOR – 1908

THE EXTERIOR OF THIS three-story federal building is Georgia marble, as are the four pairs of double Ionic columns over the main entrance area of this T-shaped building. The construction was carried out by the Mankin Construction Company of Richmond, Virginia, between 1905 and 1908. A sizable wing was added to the rear of the building in 1917. A new federal building was constructed in 1964 on College Hill.

[*National Register listing 01/20/72*]

The hipped roof of the tower of the post office at Savanna today, far right, does not match the original design prepared by William Martin Aike.

Savannah

127 Bull Street

JEREMIAH O'ROURKE, WILLIAM MARTIN AIKEN,
AND JAMES KNOX TAYLOR – 1899

THE CITIZENS OF SAVANNAH objected to the government's initial idea of placing the federal building at the corner of York and Abercon Streets in 1889, urging Congress to compel the Treasury Department to build "a more suitable" structure elsewhere. Congress sided with the citizens, authorizing additional funds for a new government building. Construction of the federal building at the Wright Square location began in the summer of 1894. Because of the relatively short tenures of the Supervising Architects during the 1890s, three would have a hand in the completion of the building.

The three-story structure is dominated by its central tower, extending well above the original U-shaped building. The building you see today is twice the size of the original structure completed in 1899. The major alteration occurred in the 1930s. The building no longer serves as the main city post office, but continues to function as a postal station. [*National Register listing 07/07/74*]

KENTUCKY

Belleview

6256 Main Street

UNKNOWN – ABOUT 1880

CURRENTLY A PRIVATELY OWNED building, this Gothic Revival style structure was built for Jonas Clore in about 1880, and served a variety of different purposes between 1880 and 1920, including housing a basket shop and a doctor's office, before becoming the post office in the early 1920s. This one-and-one-half-story frame structure continued to house the post office until 1970. [*National Register listing 06/14/90*]

Covington

700 Scott Boulevard

THOMAS HARLAN ELLETT – 1941

THE DESIGN FOR THE COVINGTON post office was produced in conjunction with a 1939 nationwide design competition among private architects, sponsored by the Treasury Department, a design contest that attracted over 650 submissions. The winning designer, Thomas Harlan

The Covington, Kentucky, post office was designed by a private architect, Thomas Harlan Ellett.

Ellett of New York, received $4,500 for his design, and another $4,500 for preparing the necessary working drawings for the project.

Ellett's design incorporated two striking limestone carved lintels above the two entrances that front onto Scott Boulevard. These artistic enhancements were not crafted as part of any make-work program for starving artists, but were part of a calculated expenditure, amounting to one percent of the total cost of the building, that allowed works to be produced under an anonymous competition sponsored by the Treasury Department's Section of Fine Arts. The two lintels, designed by New York City sculptor, Carl L. Schmitz, are devoted to Kentucky themes: "Horsebreeding" and "Tobacco," and were carved by Reinhold Hirlund. The interior features another artwork funded under the same federal program, a bronze statue by Clement J. Barnhorn of a female figure with up-stretched arms. Construction of the federal building commenced in January 1940, one month after the construction contract was awarded. The work was slated for completion within one calendar year, but the construction actually consumed 13 months, with the formal dedication taking place on February 22, 1941. Overall, the building has changed little since then.

Harrodsburg

105 North Main Street

JAMES A. WETMORE – 1932

IN MANY RESPECTS, the styling of the Harrodsburg post office was unlike other facilities built during the Depression. It was far fancier than most structures built between 1932 and 1940, thanks largely to the fact that it was designed and constructed before the full reality of the nation's economic woes set in. That is not to say that there were not problems with this project, not the least of which was that it was a long time in coming.

The government purchased the property for the post office before World War I, paying about $9,000 to Jesse E. Cogar, but because of the war, earlier buildings on the site were not torn down until the late 1920s. A representative for the Supervising Architect's office visited Harrodsburg in 1930, seeking design ideas from the local citizens. The resulting design, said to have come out of that local consultation, was adapted from "The Wick," an 18th century structure at Richmond Hill in Surrey, England.

The construction contract for the Georgian Colonial style building was awarded to a North Carolina firm on October 30, 1930, but before the exterior walls were completed the contractor went bankrupt. The work was completed by the Estrupp Company, which was engaged by the original contractor's bonding company.

The building was dedicated on February 12, 1932, a date that was selected in commemoration of the birthday of Abraham Lincoln, who was born in Kentucky.

[*National Register listing 03/01/89*]

Louisville

300-314 West Liberty

ATTRIBUTED TO AMMI B. YOUNG – 1858

THIS POST OFFICE IS THOUGHT by some to have been designed by Ammi B. Young, who had a distinguished career, designing buildings for Dartmouth College as well as the Vermont State Capitol Building, before he became the government's chief architect in 1852. If the attribution to Young is correct, this structure would have been designed during the latter portion of his tenure as the nation's principal architect. Another possible claimant for credit as the building's architect is Elias E. Williams, a local architect who lived between 1798 and 1874.

The original building, a villa-like design, has been somewhat buried beneath later substantial alterations. No elements of the original interior remain.

The building housed the customs house and post office until the mid-1890s, when a new government building was completed. The property was then acquired by Walter H. Haldeman to house the printing operations and offices for his newspaper, the *Courier-Journal.* An additional floor was added to the structure for this purpose, and the floors in the rest of the building were reinforced to accommodate the eight huge printing presses. By the early 1900s the building had become intertwined with a storage company operation, giving the building its current historic name, the "Old U.S. Customshouse and Post Office and Fireproof Storage Company Warehouse."

[*National Register listing 05/31/80*]

South Union

399 South Union Road

UNKNOWN – 1917

A COMMUNAL VILLAGE organized by "Shakers" in 1807, South Union was granted a post office in 1826. By that time it was one of the five largest Shaker communities in the country. Known locally as "Shakertown," the first post office was in a small log cabin presided over by Shaker David Smith.

Over the years other sites have housed the post office. Since 1917 it has been located in the Shaker store at the railroad depot. According to Tommy Hines, director of the Shaker Museum at South Union: "The current building has the distinction of being the last building constructed by the South Union Shakers before their community disbanded in 1922." This site is also important because it is the last of the 19 Shaker-constructed post offices to survive in the United States.

LOUISIANA

Baton Rouge

355 North Boulevard

WILLIAM MARTIN AIKEN – 1895

LOCATED NEAR THE CENTER of downtown Baton Rouge, the exterior of the old federal building, a three-story structure constructed of heavy masonry with buff Baltimore brick and terra cotta facings, features northern Italian Renaissance Revival styling. This is considered to be one of the finest, and most pretentious, examples of a turn-of-the-century Renaissance Revival architecture in the State of Louisiana, a building that is credited with contributing significantly to the architectural development of the state.

The main entrance, a five-bay Ionic portico with massive corner posts and heavy parapet, is one of the building's striking features. Another prominent feature of the building is that it is surmounted by an elaborate terra cotta balustrade with urns and a central cartouche. The interior of the building has been substantially remodeled over the years, except for the old courtroom, with its two-story coffered ceiling and round arched windows, which remains relatively intact.

This building served as the post office from the mid-1890s until 1933, when it became the city hall. Since 1957 the building has housed the "City Club." A recent addition at the rear of the structure does not degrade the overall appearance of the building, as seen from North Boulevard.

[*National Register listing 06/09/80*]

Bogalusa

305 Avenue B

JAMES A. WETMORE – 1931

CONSIDERED A "HIGH STYLE" of the "Starved-Classical" architecture of Depression era post offices, this two-story brick building, with basement, has undergone very few changes since it was completed in 1931. The only major addition, principally an extension of the first floor and basement and the addition of a mailing vestibule and loading platform to the rear of the facility, was completed in 1962. [*National Register listing 01/27/83*]

Morgan City

First and Everett Streets

JAMES A. WETMORE – 1928

TO ENSURE THAT MORGAN CITY would get a post office, the mayor at the time, M. E. Norman, went to Washington in 1928 to consult with President Calvin Coolidge and Representative W. P. Martin. The president and congressional leaders were receptive, but it was suggested that the decision might be easier to make if the local community showed its support for the project by purchasing the site. Local businessmen hastily contributed the money necessary to acquire land for the post office. The government selected Algernon Blair of Montgomery, Alabama, as the general contractor for this two-story structure.

The building is described as an odd combination of a Beaux-Arts elements, such as the grand arcade and a dormered mansard roof that is partially hidden by a balustrade; and Georgian details, including the main entrance, which has been described as being "overblown" and "out of place." The entire blend has been called "adequate and not jarring."

[*National Register listing 12/17/82*]

New Orleans

600 Camp Street

J. GAMBLE ROGERS – 1915

MARK TWAIN PROBABLY would have thought that New Orleans did not really get a good post office until this three-story eclectic style Italian Renaissance building, constructed at a cost of $2.5 million, was dedicated in 1914. This is not to say that New Orleans has not had a rich and colorful postal history; on the contrary, its past has probably been more colorful than that of most other post offices.

For example, in a span of about two years the New Orleans post office

The sculptures on the end pavillions of the New Orleans, Louisiana, post office are clearly visible in this illustration.

was run by three different governments. Louisiana operated it as an independent republic from January 26 to February 3, 1861; it was part of the Confederate States of America until May of 1862; and it then returned to federal control following the federal occupation of the city. A detachment of Marines took possession of the post office and customs house building on April 25, 1862. The building was in a sorry state. The structure had been under construction before the war and was still only partially complete. A hostile mob confronted the Marines, forcing the outnumbered unit to withdraw. The crowd ransacked the unsecured building. They tore down the American flag, rifled the mail and destroyed much of the usable furnishings. A larger contingent of federal troops soon hastily returned to suppress such public demonstrations.

Mark Twain's opinion of New Orleans architecture, and especially its post office, wasn't very flattering. His general view was that "to speak in broad, general terms, there is no architecture in New Orleans, except in the cemeteries." Concerning the post office, he was more blunt. His opinion was that:

> There is a huge granite United States custom-house (and post office) — costly enough, genuine enough, but as to decoration it is inferior to a gasometer. It looks like a state prison. But it was built before the war. Architecture in America may be said to have been born since the war. New Orleans, I believe, has had the good luck — and in a sense the bad luck — to have had no great fire in late years. It must be so. If the opposite had been the case, I think one would be able to tell the "burnt district" by the radical improvement in its architecture over the old forms.

That all changed with the completion of the town's white marble building fronting onto Lafayette Square. Work on this structure began in 1909 and was completed in 1915. Among the more notable features of the structure are the two 25-foot high copper and bronze sculptures that consist of globes supported by four female figures representing history, industry, commerces, and the arts. The main post office remained in this building until 1963.

St. Martinville

Main and Port Streets

EUGENE DUCHAMP DE CHASTAIGNIER – 1876

ORIGINALLY BUILT as a fine residence by Eugene Duchamp De Chastaignier, one that would reflect Louisiana's French influences, the post office at St. Martinville has a shallow basement, typical of structures in low-lying areas that are prone to flooding, and a large attic, where the valuable "stuff" usually consigned to the basement could go for posterity. Another characteristic that reflects the climate is the fact that the building contains 36 openings, essential for achieving adequate air circulation. The building, constructed of handmade brick and ancient red cypress, did not become the post office until the late 1930s. It still retains much of the original "household" charm, interspersed with practical details, such as the inclusion of a boiler room in what was once the outside kitchen and servants' quarters. ❘ *National Register listing 04/05/72* ❘

MISSISSIPPI

Aberdeen

201 West Commerce Street

MIFFLIN E. BELL – 1888

THE LAND FOR THE ABERDEEN post office was purchased in 1885 for $4,000 under a government appropriation for $75,000 that was expected to pay for the new federal building. The drawings and specifications for this Romanesque Revival style federal building, a rare type of architecture in Mississippi, were prepared by Supervising Architect Mifflin Bell and were approved in September 1886.

Photograph of the former Aberdeen, Mississippi, post office, circa 1925.

Construction of the red brick and grey stone trimmed building, with terra cotta decorations, commenced late in 1886. Two years later the 230,000 cubic foot structure was finished. Although the total been of the original project was to have been $75,000, the final total was significantly higher, amounting to $90,000.

An annex was constructed during the Depression, and interior remodeling was carried out in the early 1960s, but in both cases the alterations were reasonably sympathetic to the original design.

The entrance area is striking, consisting of a five-bay arcade supported by stone pilasters and double columns.

In 1975 the building was purchased by the Monroe Country Board of Supervisors for $75,000, the amount that was originally appropriated by Congress to build the structure back in 1885. Funds for the renovation, amounting to twice the 1975 purchase price, were provided under a grant from the American Revolution Bicentennial Administration. Since 1977, the building has been known locally as the "Monroe County Chancery Building."

[*National Register listing 09/29/76*]

Bay Saint Louis

Main and Second Streets

LOUIS A. SIMON – 1936

THE FORMER BAY SAINT LOUIS post office is perhaps the hungriest example of the Starved-Classical style. However, despite the fact that it lacks even the simplest embellishments, as far as many residents are concerned, the post office is the conduit to the federal government. Believing this to be the case, one patron of the Bay Saint Louis post office, a building that was constructed by Dye and Mullings of Columbia, Mississippi, wrote to the postmaster general many years ago asking that he replace the $1 bill that was all but destroyed by her dog. While the Post Office Department was not responsible for this sort of thing, the postmaster general knew that the Treasury Department was responsible for mutilated currency and so he forwarded the lady's request, along with several small remnants of the bill, to the Secretary of the Treasury. In due course, the dollar was replaced. Like the $1 bill, this New-Deal–era building, now vacant, also has been replaced by a new post office.

Biloxi

216 Laneuse Street

JAMES KNOX TAYLOR – 1908

THE MAIN ELEVATION of this three-story building appears today exactly as Supervising Architect James Knox Taylor originally intended, although it no longer functions as the federal post office, customs house, and courthouse. the current owner is the City of Biloxi, which uses the building as the city hall. The city took over the building about 40 years ago.

The building was constructed on property acquired in 1901 from Mrs. C. F. Theobald for $8,000. The general contractor was the Standard Construction Company of Chicago, which was awarded the project based upon its $90,770 bid. The building was to have been completed by May 1905, but work was delayed for a number of reasons, including several hurricanes and an outbreak of yellow fever. The structure was completely turned over to the government in 1908.

Hurricane Elena did extensive damage in 1985, prompting the City of Biloxi to renovate the structure, returning it to much of its original appearance.

Gulfport

2421 13th Street

JAMES KNOX TAYLOR – 1910

CONSIDERED ONE OF THE best-preserved structures in Gulfport, this post office is also the finest example of Second Renaissance Revival architecture in Mississippi. Its main facade features a stunning porch arcade with round arches supported by Doric columns.

Basically a symmetrical two-story structure with single-story wings, the construction was carried out by George E. Moore and Sons of Nashville, Tennessee. [*National Register listing 08/19/84*]

Vicksburg

Walnut and Crawford Streets

WILL A. FRERET, JAMES H. WINDRIM, WILLOUGHBY J. EDBROOKE, AND JEREMIAH O'ROURKE – 1894

ORIGINALLY THE POST OFFICE and customs house, since 1944

Now the home of the Mississippi River Commission, the Vicksburg post office was completed in 1894.

this Romanesque-style building has housed, the Mississippi River Commission, a part of the Army Corps of Engineers that is responsible for correcting and deepening the channel of the Mississippi River and protecting its banks.

In the years before this building was turned over to the Mississippi River Commission, it was known for its lack of liquids of another kind. In many dry states the gurgle of liquor bottles became a familiar sound following the introduction of Parcel Post, but liquor sales disrupted the profitability of many post offices when more and more states, including Mississippi, began "going dry." The small post offices across from Vicksburg, on the other hand, went from small-time operations to thriving offices because of liquor sales. Liquor was mailed to these offices and picked up by thirsty Mississippi residents across the river. Out-of-state post offices did so much business that they often had to employ several additional clerks and acquire adding machines to keep track of business.

NORTH CAROLINA

Belmont

115 North Main Street

LOUIS A. SIMON – 1939

NOW THE CITY HALL, this building housed Belmont's post office until 1970. The one-story brick structure was purchased by the city in conjunction with a 1971 grant from the Lineberger Foundation. The building was rededicated on April 10, 1973.

The somewhat unusual appearance of the otherwise common building type probably owes as much to the opinions of the Right Reverend Vincent G. Taylor as to anything else. Father Taylor, the head of Belmont Abbey, was unimpressed with other small post office designs and was not shy about sharing his thoughts. He wanted Belmont to have "a building somewhat better than those that have been erected in the small towns of this vicinity." In response, Supervising Architect Louis A. Simon advised Father Taylor that his office had:

> Secured considerable data and photographs indicating the character of the more important buildings in the town including the Abbey and College group and in developing the preliminary drawings for the proposed Post Office every possible consideration will be given leading to the design of a building appropriate to its surrounding.

Eight different bids were received to construct the building, the lowest of which was submitted by L. B. Gillimore of Greensboro, North Carolina, with a quote of $40,900. The building was dedicated on December 4, 1939. As with many other Depression-era post office projects, one percent of the overall cost was set aside for murals or sculpture. In this case the set-aside amounted to $730, which was used to create a lobby mural painted by Peter DeAnna, at the time a teenage artist from Washington, D.C.

[*National Register listing 11/29/95*]

Fayetteville

301 Hay Street

JAMES KNOX TAYLOR – 1911

THIS ONE-STORY post office, built between 1909 and 1911, is one of only three structures in Fayetteville constructed in this style. Principally of brick with granite and limestone enhancements, the building's construction was slowed by the use of inferior materials, particularly the brick, stone, and mortar, and by bad weather. The post office took possession of the property on April, 4, 1911.

The south wing of the building was a later addition, added in the mid-1930s. Two decades later the postal system began looking for a bigger home. In the 1950s the local library was allowed to take up some space, gradually using more and more of the building, which by the mid-1960s was almost entirely taken up by what is now the "Frances Brooks Stein Branch" of the Cumberland County Library System. [*National Register listing 07/07/83*]

Raleigh

300 Fayetteville Street

ALFRED B. MULLETT – 1877

IF THIS LISTING HAD TWO VIEWS, one of the building as it originally appeared, the other it appears today, you would be able to judge the true extent of the extensive revisions that have taken place as a result of three major renovations. While the current building still offers a

Architect's rendering of the Raleigh, North Carolina, federal building.

glimpse of the original elegance shown here, it has been described by one state historical officer as a building that "recants the original Second Empire styling and places the emphasis on the horizontality of the structure."

The original building itself was a long time in coming. Congress first appropriated money for Raleigh's federal building in 1857. Out of these funds the government expended $7,700 to acquire a portion of the property in January 1861. However, with the outbreak of the Civil War, the project was dropped. The project was given a second thought in 1873. This time, the city donated the adjacent land to the government. This represented one of the first federal post offices built in the south following the Civil War. The cornerstone was laid in 1874 and the project was completed three years later.

The original structure was a three-story granite-faced brick building, with the telltale mansard roof typical of Second-Empire styling. The three central bays of the east facade originally formed a projecting pavilion. The original building was five bays deep and had an entrance in the center of each three-story section of the east facade. An elaborate roof treatment provided added emphasis to the entrance pavilion. The overall cost of the original construction was approximately $400,000.

In 1913 the building underwent extensive renovations. The changes included the addition of four more bays and a triple dormer, as well as the elimination of the chimneys on the east facade. The rear of the building was also extended. Additional changes were made in 1937 and 1938, this time including the addition of four bays on the west facade and the simplification of the dormers. The interior of the building was almost entirely redone at this time.

Salvo

State Route 12 South of Park Road

LAFAYETTE DOUGLAS – ABOUT 1910

CONSIDERED TO BE THE NATION'S oldest portable post office, and one of the smallest post office structures in the country, measuring about 8 by 12 feet, the Salvo post office served this Hatteras Island community for about 80 years. The only smaller post office is at Ochopee, Florida. Salvo is prone to violent Atlantic storms and hurricanes, and one of the notable features of this building are the "flood holes" that were drilled into the floor at the time of its construction so that storm water could easily drain out.

When it was built, the wood-sheathed building was located in the postmaster's front yard and served the entire Salvo community, which in 1910 consisted of about 75 residents. Reportedly, the post office has been moved three times because of the appointment of new postmasters. Each new postmaster purchased the building and moved it to his or her own property. Despite its diminutive size, the structure is divided into two equal portions, the post office lobby and the postmaster's workroom.

The building was in continuous use until October 7, 1992, at which time it looked basically the same as it had in 1910. It sustained significant fire damage in 1992, however, due to arson. With funds raised by the local community, the building was restored in 1993.

⟦ *National Register listing* 09/23/93 ⟧

Winston-Salem

Liberty and Fifth Streets

JAMES KNOX TAYLOR – 1907

THE OLD FEDERAL BUILDING at Winston-Salem was initially completed in 1907 and was enlarged substantially in 1914. The building was extensively enlarged again in the late 1930s at a cost of about $250,000, with the addition of over 13,000 square feet. The result was a building that was nearly twice its original size. All of this space would constitute a problem for one of the town's postmasters many years later.

From time to time postmasters have had to act as real-estate agents. When other government agencies moved out of the Winston-Salem post office, the postmaster began looking for new tenants. Unfortunately, not all of the office spaces were rentable. According to a 1977 Postal Service report, "The old FBI offices had peepholes in the triple locked doors, electronic burglar alarms were everywhere, and sensor wires ran up and down the walls at six-inch intervals." The U.S. Marshall's offices were not much better. They had a five- by eight-foot steel-plated vault and spacious holding cells. Then there was the wood-paneled courtroom with 30-foot ceilings.

The Postal Service moved from the building in 1991 to a new facility at 1500 Patterson Avenue. The original building was later sold to the Millennium Group and was rented out to the public as a cultural arts center.

SOUTH CAROLINA

Beaufort

302 Carteret Street

JAMES A. WETMORE – 1917

AT A TIME WHEN OTHER MEMBERS of Congress were generating an array of "pork barrel" bills for federal post offices, one of South Carolina's congressmen in 1909 showed great restraint. Only one appropriations bill was sponsored by Representative J. O. Patterson, and that was a comparatively modest amount, $125,000, for the post office at Beaufort. Work on the two-story brick building, considered "a standard Treasury Department building form" of Georgian Revival influence, was not immediately started; in fact it was not completed until 1917. The post office remained at this location until the 1970s, when the structure was acquired by the City of Beaufort for use as its city hall.

Charleston

122 East Bay Street

WILLIAM RIGBY NAYLOR – 1771

THE EXCHANGE BUILDING, the oldest post office building in the Carolinas, has played a role in Charleston's mail service since 1771. George Ropell, who took over as postmaster when his predecessor, Peter

The Charleston Exchange Building as it appears today.

Delancey, was killed in a duel, was the first to conduct business in the building. A few years later, when Charleston fell to the British in 1780, the Exchange Building served as a prison. Among the captives held in its dungeon were two former postmasters and a future postmaster. Other sites housed the post office before and after 1800. Thomas Bacot, who was appointed postmaster by George Washington in 1791, moved the post office back to the Exchange Building in 1815.

Upon his death in 1834, Bacot was succeeded by Alfred Huger. A year later Huger, armed with a double-barrel shotgun, single-handedly faced down an angry mob on the steps of the Exchange Building. The mob had gathered in response to abolitionist mailings from the North. The angry citizens demanded that the abolitionist mail be burned. Although Huger temporarily managed to hold the crowd off throughout the day, later that night the disgruntled citizens entered the post office, seized the unwanted pamphlets, and set them on fire outside the building.

During the Civil War the Union bombardment of Charleston severely damaged the Exchange Building, prompting the post office to relocate until repairs were completed in 1875. An earthquake heavily damaged the building in 1886, prompting the post office to move again, this time to a new building, erected in 1896 on the site of the ruins of the police station destroyed by the earthquake. The Exchange Building continued to house other government agencies after the post office moved out, including the U.S. Lighthouse Department. In 1981 the building was dedicated as an historical memorial.

Columbia

Main and Laurel Streets

ALFRED B. MULLETT – 1874

CONGRESS INITIALLY AUTHORIZED $50,000 to construct a post office in Columbia in 1857, but the money was never spent due to South Carolina's secession from the Union. After the Civil War, Congress reauthorized funds for a new federal building, but insisted that the land be given to the government. Thirty-five residents banded together to come up with the $2,500 that was necessary to purchase a suitable plot, which was donated to the government on April 8, 1870. Supervising Architect Alfred B. Mullett prepared the designs for the granite-faced facility. Construction commenced during the summer of 1871, and the project was completed in 1874. The current owner of the property is the City of Columbia, which uses the building as the City Hall.

Florence

Irby and West Evan Streets

JAMES KNOX TAYLOR – ABOUT 1906

THIS THREE-STORY Second Renaissance Revival style building served as the center for the federal government in Florence for more than 70 years, housing the U.S. District Court, the post office, and even the local congressional office for members of the U.S. House of Representatives. Among the more eye-catching of its features are the extended eaves and the circular "eye of a bull" dormers that accentuate its hipped roof. The first floor of the exterior is principally clad in sandstone, while the upper floors are tan brick. A three-story addition was added to the rear of the building in the 1930s. The Postal Service moved out of the building in 1975. [*National Register listing 12/21/77*]

Moore

Junction of County Roads S-42, 86, and 199

THOMAS PRICE – ABOUT 1793

LOCATED SOUTHEAST of Moore is "Price's Post Office," also known as "Price House." This attractive symmetrical two-story brick structure served as the home of its builder, Thomas Price. The building includes a characteristic unusual this far south, a Dutch gambrel roof with a steep lower slope. This type of roof was far more common in the Middle Atlantic states. Price's plantation property included a general store and slave quarters. The site is now owned by the Spartanburg County Historical Preservation Commission. [*National Register listing 10/28/69*]

Rock Hill

102 Main Street

LOUIS A. SIMON – 1932

THE EXTERIOR of the three-story federal building at Rock Hill consists of a pink granite base, topped by a rusticated limestone shell on the first floor, with yellow brick used for the second and third levels. This is capped off by an ornate limestone balustrade. This building owes its existence to Congressman William F. Stevenson, who in the mid-1920s sponsored the legislation that secured the necessary funding for a building of this style and size. Congress allocated up to $300,000 for this combination post office and courthouse. Because times were tough, only two South Carolina cities were approved for post offices during the years immediately before the onset of the Great Depression. Only about $176,000 was actually needed to build the structure. The work was carried out by the Batson-Cook Company of West Point, Georgia, one of 21 firms interested in securing the construction contract. The building was occupied on November 28, 1932. The postal system continued to occupy the property until the mid-1980s, when the site was acquired by the City of Rock Hill for $280,000 to house the local convention and visitor's bureau and the community's arts council and Congressional delegation. [*National Register listing 01/21/88*]

TENNESSEE

Braden

189 Highway 59

J. W. MCCRAW – 1909

SINCE 1886 ALL OF BRADEN'S postmasters have been McCraws. Charles T. McCraw, the great uncle of the current postmaster, served from 1886 until 1916. It was he who first used about one-half of the current family store to house the local post office. Harris L. McCraw took over in 1916 and served until 1962, when operations were turned over to his son, the current postmaster, Harris L. McCraw, Jr.

Chattanooga

East 11th and Lindsay Streets

WILLOUGHBY J. EDBROOKE AND JEREMIAH O'ROURKE – 1893

BEGUN IN 1891, the Romanesque style federal building at Chattanooga is a large three-and-one-half-story structure that combines contrasting smooth and rough stone surfaces. Also notable is the use of elaborately carved arched stone window transoms over top of straight-topped windows. Alterations over the years have included the addition of one wing, constructed between 1905 and 1910, and a major change in the roof line, reducing its original steep pitch. The post office continued to occupy the site until 1933, when postal operations were moved to a different location. In the 1970s the building was taken over by the Tennessee Valley Authority for offices. *National Register listing 04/13/73*

Clarksville

Commerce and Second Streets

WILLIAM MARTIN AIKEN – 1898

GERMANIC STYLES, in the original design for the Clarksville post office, were preferred by Supervising Architect William Martin Aiken, but the local citizens initially had some reservations about this rendering. The common view, expressed in the summer of 1897, was "that Clarksville does not propose to accept the crazy plans that have been submitted from the architects' office for this building." Citizens called the design "an absurdity and a public laughing stock."

Despite such harsh public opinion, the government went ahead with Aiken's design, using it for bidding purposes. Fourteen bids were received by August 4, 1897, the lowest of which was a quote from Charles A. Moses for $32,243, which was accepted, despite the fact that the price did not include the cost of the heating system. Although the groundbreaking ceremony took place on September 1, 1897, and the cornerstone was laid on December 1, the community, which had not given up the fight to have the design changed, succeeded in gaining a "stop work order" thanks to some help from its congressional delegation.

By January 1898, Aiken was no longer Supervising Architect, having been replaced by James Knox Taylor, who was all too willing to modify Aiken's design for the building. Taylor's alternative plan kept the first floor intact, but eliminated the soaring tower and steeply pitched hipped roof, with its 20 gables and 4 guardian eagles, replacing it with a full second story with four arcaded windows set into a low-pitched hipped roof.

Taylor's changes were criticized too, called extremely conservative and "almost dull compared to the first plan." This time the community's reaction prompted the local newspaper to express the view that, given the proposed revisions, the "old post office plans are deemed the most acceptable," giving Aiken's original design a second chance.

The building was completed largely according to Aiken's plan in November 1898, and continued as the post office until 1936, when it was subsequently sold to the city for $50,000. The Clarksville department of electricity began using the building in 1938, remaining until 1982. In 1984 the Clarksville-Montgomery County Historical Museum opened in the building, renovating some of the additions made after 1898 for exhibition and work-related spaces. ‖ *National Register listing 03/08/78* ‖

Jellico

Main and Second Streets

OSCAR WENDEROTH – 1915

IN 1909 CONGRESS initially considered an appropriation of $60,000 to acquire the land for a new post office building at Jellico. Five years later, about the time construction on the cut limestone building by W. H. Fissell & Company finally commenced, this was one of two sites in the coal regions of Virginia and Tennessee that was designated as a mine rescue station. Besides serving as a site for periodic mine safety reviews and a command center in the event of a mining disaster, the rescue station, located on the second floor, housed emergency equipment that

Post office and mine rescue station, Jellico, Tennessee.

could be used to help extract trapped or injured miners. The other mine-safety station established in the Appalachia coal-mining area was at Norton, Virginia.

The original design for this Beaux-Arts-style structure was prepared under the direction of Supervising Architect James Knox Taylor, who was replaced by Oscar Wenderoth before this building was finally dedicated.

[*National Register listing 02/10/84*]

Memphis

1 North Front Street

JAMES G. HILL, JAMES KNOX TAYLOR, AND JAMES A. WETMORE – 1885/1903/1929-1930

VISITORS LOOKING FOR THE BUILDING pictured here will not be able to find it. That is because what is left of the original 1885 structure has been obliterated by subsequent facelifts. The original three-story stone post office, flanked by two towers rising over 100 feet on the north and south ends, was begun in 1876 and completed in 1885. However, the current appearance of the Memphis post office does not bear any resemblance to its original Italian Renaissance design devised by James G. Hill. In effect, the current building is really three buildings in one: incorporating elements of Hill's original design from 1876, a major addition done in 1903 under the supervision of James Knox Taylor, and the final remodeling carried out in 1929-1930 under the direction of James A. Wetmore. Taylor's revisions were modest compared with those by Wetmore, whose radical changes cost $1.5 million and included the demolition of the towers and other alterations that totally reconfigured the structure.

[*National Register listing 06/30/80*]

The Memphis, Tennessee, post office as it originally appeared, about 1909.

Nashville

901 Broadway

WILLIAM A. POTTER – 1882

RESEMBLING A EUROPEAN TOWN HALL, and typical of what can happen when price is no object, the Nashville post office was Supervising Architect William A. Potter's most expensive federal project. First introduced with his Nashville design in 1875, the telltale high central tower became a repetitive enhancement used by Potter on larger government buildings. Although in this particular case the tower appears labored, weighted by oppressive-looking arches, corbeled balconies, and embellishments, towers such as this became synonymous with the federal image. The design was criticized at the time by some who observed "the central tower, with a good deal of elegance, is inadequate for these corner-masses; the group of pinnacles and balconies which belt it round, is not yet quite satisfactorily harmonized." To the contemporary view, there was one saving grace, "The triple porch is decidedly rich and effective."

The cornerstone was laid in 1877 by President Rutherford B. Hayes, and the building was first occupied in 1882, providing facilities for customs, the Internal Revenue Service, and the post office. Two additions were added in later years, including one to the rear of the building in 1903 and another in 1916. The Post Office Department remained in the building until 1934 when a new office was constructed two doors down on Broadway.

Many things entered the mail stream from this building when Parcel Post Service was started in 1913, and not all of them were pleasant. A near riot erupted when a can of fertilizer burst open. According to one newspaper account: "There was a near-mutiny among the office force who were handling the package." [*National Register listing 11/15/84*]

The old post office at Nashville possesses all of the characteristics of a European town hall.

Midwest

ILLINOIS

Cairo

Poplar and 14th Street

ALFRED B. MULLETT – 1872

ALTHOUGH CONGRESS approved funds for the Cairo federal building in 1857, the project took nine years to get started, the delay caused by the Civil War. Situated on an irregularly shaped plot, which is said to have been selected by Stephen A. Douglas, the property was donated to the government in 1866 by the city. The first $50,000 in funding for the post office project was made available in 1866, prompting construction on the site to commence in 1867. Indiana freestone was used for the exterior walls. Work on the structure, which cost $281,044, was completed during the summer of 1872.

Because of its strategic location, Cairo's federal building was considered to be one of the most important government facilities in the country when it was built, principally housing the post office, federal courts, customs service, and weather bureau. The post office continued to operate from this Second Empire style building until 1942, when operations were moved to the current building. The Cairo police department used the building between 1956 and 1975.

In recent years various federal and local grants have enabled the building to be preserved, especially the courtrooms; and efforts to convert other portions of the building into a museum are being continued by volunteers as funds becomes available. Among the items on display on the first floor of the building is the desk that General Ulysses S. Grant used while he was stationed at Cairo, a scale model of the Civil War era federal gunboat *U.S.S Cairo,* and a fire pumper used in Cairo during 1865.

Champaign

Randolph and Church Streets

JAMES KNOX TAYLOR – 1905

IN ITS ORIGINAL FORM, this one-story brick and limestone building, with a raised basement, was an exceptional example of what could be done with prefabricated terra cotta ornamentation modules, including

PRECEDING PAGE:

Alfred B. Mullett's rendering of the Cairo, Illinois, post office.

deeply fluted and banded Ionic pilaster capitals embellished with tassels and rosettes. In 1929 an addition was made that, while it lacked the character of the original structure, did add substantially to its overall size, increasing it by one-half and adding about two-thirds to the height of the original building's west side. A further addition, carried out in the 1930s, altered the north and south facades, and to a smaller extent, the eastern face of the building. [*National Register listing 08/17/76*]

Chicago

433 West Van Buren Street

GRAHMAN, ANDERSON, PROST, AND WHITE – 1933

CHICAGO'S MAIN POST OFFICE is a massive structure, a mail processing factory that contains over 2.2 million square feet of space. Begun in 1931 and completed the following year, the building includes 20 freight elevators, 35 elevators for passengers, and 48 different locker rooms that have personal-storage capabilities for nearly 10,000 postal workers.

Eldorado

900 South 4th Street

LOUIS A. SIMON – 1936

THE POST OFFICE AT ELDORADO has been in 12 different locations since it was established in 1858, and moving time was a prime time to pilfer. Years ago, just before the post office moved to a new location in 1913, burglars struck; however, in anticipation of the move the mail had been placed in locked bags and the stamps were nicely packaged. The place was piled high with sacks, crates, and packages. The burglars rifled as many sacks and ripped open as many parcels as possible, but those they ransacked contained nothing of value. No money, mail, or stamps were taken.

This was one of a rash of Illinois post office robberies that occurred at the same time, including breaks at Riverton and Woodlawn.

The last move in Eldorado was made in 1936, when the post office arrived at its present location. The move into that building, on property that had been purchased in 1934 for $4,000, was made without incident. The plain brick Depression era post office was constructed under a government appropriation of $71,000. According to one local publication, printed shortly after this building opened, "With the erection of a government-owned building... moving days are over for the Eldorado post office, unless some calamity strikes and the modern brick structure is destroyed."

Galena

110 Green Street

AMMI B. YOUNG – 1859

ONE OF THE OLDEST SURVIVING government-owned post office

buildings, the Galena post office still possesses all of its original Renaissance Revival charms, including a lobby area with magnificent mahogany counters with arched postal windows and a magnificent wrought- and cast-iron stairway that is further enhanced by a solid-mahogany handrail. The physical layout of the building is basically the same as it was when it was constructed, allowing visitors to experience the illusion of stepping back in time. The *Weekly Northwestern Gazette* predicted in 1859 that the 5,947 square foot federal building, built principally of limestone at a cost of $61,372, would last a thousand years. In making that prediction, the publication observed that only two things were likely to destroy the structure: an earthquake or an angry mob. Neither ever materialized. Still used as the post office, the building shows no signs of any structural weaknesses. The first floor was designed for the post office, while the second story served the customs house. The second floor is just as spectacular as the first level, with 12 foot oak doors and 7 working fireplaces with marble mantles. The upstairs area was used for lavish social gatherings during much of the building's early history.

Joliet

150 North Scott Street

JAMES KNOX TAYLOR – 1903

ORIGINALLY BUILT between August 1901 and June 1903 by Adam Groth, a local contractor in Joliet, the two-story light-colored limestone post office underwent renovations several times to keep pace with expanding mail volumes. The first of these renovations occurred prior to 1930 and involved the construction of additional space on the loading docks, while the second round of renovations were made in 1931 and 1932, when the workroom area was significantly enlarged. Since these changes were made more than a half-century ago, few other alterations have taken place. [*National Register listing 08/20/81*]

Leaf River

104 West Second Street

RALPH BLAIR – 1952

SIZE AND SERVICE are not synonymous. The patrons of this third-class post office knew that all along, but they were even more impressed with the level of service when the postmaster's husband installed a drive-in window, making this the first postal facility to offer such a thing. This was a boon for local businesses, especially on rainy days. The need for such a feature grew out of the common complaint that customers were unable to find suitable parking. Many patrons were frustrated at having to search for as much as ten minutes for a parking spot, only to have to settle for one several blocks away from the post office. It was not the walk that bothered such customers, it was the disappointment that came from discovering that after all that they did not have any mail. The postmaster's husband, Ralph Blair, who was in the carpentry trade, actually did the work in his spare time, creating the drive-in window over the course of about three months. The drive-in window opened on July 28, 1952.

New Salem

Lincoln's New Salem State Historic Site

JOSEPH BOOTON – RECONSTRUCTION, 1932-1933

KNOWN AS THE "Second Berry-Lincoln Store" because of the partnership between William Berry and Abraham Lincoln in the early 1830s, this building is a replica of post office and store where Lincoln served as postmaster. He was appointed on May 7, 1833 because, it is said, his predecessor spent most of his time selling whiskey, instead of serving his postal customers. This re-creation was based upon extensive research and upon descriptions of the place by such people as Daniel Green Burner, who clerked for Lincoln. Burner described the store as "a frame building, not very large, one story in height, and constructed of two rooms." The building was described in 1896 as 18 feet long by 12 feet wide, by 10 feet high at the ridge line, with black walnut weather boarding. To minimize the risk of break-ins such village stores typically had only one entrance, the front door; although based upon at least one 1835 account, Lincoln was somewhat cavalier when it came to using such precautions. According to the letter, "The Post Master Mr. Lincoln is very careless about leaving his office open & unlocked during the day. Half the time I go in and get my papers etc. without anyone being there as was the case yesterday." A covered porch was another typical architectural feature common among such backwoods stores, one that encouraged congregating, but the original reconstruction lacked a porch because of evidence that suggested that Lincoln's original store had a large oak tree immediately in front that might well have provided ample alternative cover.

Plainfield

Route 59 and Main Street

UNKNOWN – 1834

BUILT ORIGINALLY AS a one-story tavern in the early 1830s, "Halfway House" was located at the halfway point on the Chicago and Ottawa Trail, a 70-mile mail route. There, fresh horses were hitched and mail for nearby Joliet was dispatched. No nails were used in forming the frame for the house, which consists largely of massive walnut supports. Instead, all of the joints were mortised and tenoned together using wooden pegs. The exterior siding also is largely comprised of black walnut. The structure, locally considered to be "very restrained Greek Revival" in styling, is the oldest surviving post office site in Will County. The side porch is a later addition, being added sometime during World War I. The building is on the National Register of Historic Places. Joliet's postmaster in the late 1830s is said to have typically transported the mail to and from Plainfield in his hat. The proprietor of the local tavern maintained the post office in a back wing of the house until 1845.

INDIANA

Brazil

100 East National Avenue

JAMES KNOX TAYLOR – 1913

CONSIDERED THE BEST example of this style of architecture in Clay County, this two-story masonry Beaux-Arts-style structure, resting on a raised granite-faced basement, was begun in 1911. Supervising Architect James Knox Taylor's original plan called for the exterior to be clad in limestone, but local residents expressed their opposition to this plan on the grounds that a locally produced alternative was easily available, and the purchase would be good for the local economy. As a compromise, the exterior walls consist of buff brick manufactured by the Hydraulic Press Brick Company in Brazil at a cost of $16.70 per 1,000 bricks. The main portico, consisting of seven bays, of which five comprise a "blind" colonnade, are marked by six Tuscan columns of Indiana limestone that reflect Taylor's original intentions.

Taylor's design did include one flaw. The original main stairs at the front were found to be far too narrow. A replacement design, more elaborate than Taylor's, was prepared by his successor, Oscar Wenderoth. The new stairs, completed in October 1915, were constructed by J. P. Van Fossen of Rockville, Indiana, using Vermont granite.

In 1977 the building was purchased at auction by the Clay County Historical Society for $31,175.50. Following extensive repairs and renovations, the building was opened as a county museum in 1980.

[*National Register listing 09/08/94*]

Evansville

Second and Sycamore Streets

WILLIAM A. POTTER – 1879

CONSIDERED BY MANY to be William A. Potter's most stunning federal building, the Evansville custom house and post office, built between 1875 and 1879, was designed in a style that suggests a French chateau influence, and contains a profusion of colors: buff limestone walls,

William A. Potter's rendering for the Evansville, Indiana, post office.

brown sandstone trim, blue and red slate roofing, and red granite columns. Potter's interpretations of this architectural form typically combined the use of such colors to their maximum affect. Arcade porticoes were another treatment commonly employed by Potter.

This building, constructed between 1876 and 1879 at a cost of $350,000, was characterized as the most magnificent post office in the Midwest. In addition to the post office, the building housed the customs service, internal revenue service, pension examiners offices, weather bureau, and the offices of the inspector of maritime boilers and hulls.

The post office left the building in the late 1960s. Since that time the building has housed the offices of the local chamber of commerce, a restaurant, and an art gallery. [*National Register listing 07/02/71*]

Indianapolis

46 East Ohio Street

JOHN HALL RANKIN AND THOMAS W. KELLOG – 1905

SHEATHED IN INDIANA LIMESTONE, this Italian Renaissance style building is a four-story structure designed by John Hall Rankin and Thomas W. Kellog of Philadelphia and constructed by the John Pierce Company of New York, which submitted the lowest construction bid for the project, with a quote of $1,267,530. The main entrances, located at either end of the south facade, are adorned by pairs of heroic statues by John Massey Rhinde. An additional $1.5 million was spent in the 1930s to expand the building. [*National Register listing 01/11/74*]

Terre Haute

Seventh and Cherry Streets

MILLER AND YEAGER – 1932

AN EXCELLENT EXAMPLE of the Art Deco style of building adapted for government use, this symmetrical structure, principally dressed in a limestone veneer and designed by the local architectural firm of Miller and Yeager, incorporates an assortment of Art Deco treatments, such as stylized American eagles, Egyptian floral motifs, and modern metal grillwork. This building has not undergone any significant alterations and, except for the tasteful inclusion of handicapped access ramps, appears just as it did in 1932. [*National Register listing 08/13/84*]

IOWA

Cedar Rapids

305 Second Avenue

WILLIAM MARTIN AIKEN – 1897

CONSTRUCTED AT A COST of about $100,000, this three-story Romanesque Revival structure served a community of about 27,500 residents. The original appearance, which included turrets and a tower with a pyramidal roof, was changed within a decade of its construction. The remodeling, carried out under the supervision of James Knox Taylor at a cost of about $215,000, resulted in the current configuration. The post office remained at this site until a new federal building was constructed in the 1930s. The former post office was purchased in 1936 by Weaver Witner, who transformed much of the space into a grocery and converted the remaining areas into commercial office spaces. The county acquired the structure in 1979, following Mr. Witner's death.

[*National Register listing 11/10/82*]

Des Moines

Second and Walnut Streets

JAMES KNOX TAYLOR – 1910

INTENDED AS ONE of the key components of a government complex that was constructed on the banks of the Des Moines River, this post office is considered the finest surviving example of classical architecture in central Iowa. The original design was completed in 1908. A major expansion occurred in the 1930s, principally involving the addition of two floors and a garage to the south section of the building. The addition is discernable because of the lack of striated tooling on the stone and the simplified overall style that was employed. [*National Register listing 11/19/74*]

Iowa Falls

401 Main Street

OSCAR WENDEROTH – 1914

THERE ARE TWO UNUSUAL things about this listing, neither of which is architectural, but affected the design and construction of the building The first has to do with the peonies that liven up the south lawn of this site. The plants are older than the building itself. They were planted between 1864 and 1909 by the original owner of the property and were kept as an element of the overall landscaping plan.

Another unusual thing about this post office is that it was built at all. Typically buildings like this were reserved for county seats. Luckily for Iowa Falls, it had a larger population than Eldor, the seat of government of Hardin County. Hence this post office was built in Iowa Falls, while Eldor did not receive a federally constructed post office until 1939.

The dark-red-brick post office at Iowa Falls, measuring 44 by 80 feet, with its main entrance on the long Main Street side, was designed by Oscar Wenderoth and constructed by Thayer and Thayer Builders between 1913 and 1914. About the only complaint that the local community voiced concerning Wenderoth's design was that the four monumental Doric columns that support the main portico were constructed of wood, not made from stone.

Wenderoth, a native of Philadelphia, joined the staff of the Office of the Supervising Architect in 1897, rising to the post of chief draftsman, an appointment he received in 1907. Wenderoth was selected to head the Supervising Architects office in 1912, remaining until his resignation in 1929. He died in 1938. [*National Register listing 01/05/94*]

Keokuk

25 North Seventh Street

MIFFLIN E. BELL – 1888

MIFFLIN BELL DESIGNED this red brick structure with limestone trim in a somewhat Romanesque style, but his original plan included one apparent flaw: the five-story clock tower. Some critics contended it was not tall enough to let residents see the time. Others judged it to be out of proportion with the overall shape of the building. Some leveled both complaints. In any event, Bell's successor, James Windrim, had the tower extended an additional 25 feet at a cost of $9,000. This alteration required the top of the original tower to be taken down and rebuilt exactly as designed after the extension was inserted at the fourth-floor level. The clock chimes became so much a part of the local community that, when the mechanism was stopped for infrequent repairs and the chimes did not sound at the quarter-hour intervals, the whole community was said to be been "disrupted and off schedule." [*National Register listing 01/24/74*]

The limestone for the Atchison, Kansas, post office came from Cottonwood, in the same state.

KANSAS

Atchison

621 Kansas Avenue

WILLOUGHBY J. EDBROOKE AND JEREMIAH O'ROURKE – 1894

THE TOWN OF ATCHISON has the distinction of being named after a person who may briefly have served as President of the United States. Many believe that David Rice Atchison was President for a day. This resulted from the fact that Zachary Taylor's original inauguration date fell on a Sunday. Because of the Sabbath, the swearing-in ceremony was postponed till Monday, allowing Atchison, who was president pro tem of the Senate, to assume the presidency.

Another noteworthy fact about Atchison is that its Romanesque-style post office has been in continuous use for more than a century. As a result of legislation sponsored by Kansas Senator John J. Ingalls, the funds for the building were authorized on May 16, 1890. The government purchased the property for the post office for $14,500 and awarded a construction contract to a Topeka firm for $60,878.17. The contract contained the provision that limestone from Cottonwood, Kansas, be largely used for the structure. It also called for the completion of the building within nine months, with the application of a $20 penalty for each day of delay. The project took over a year to complete, the postal service occupying the building on March 15, 1894.

The appearance of the building is deceiving. Although it appears to have two floors, there is only one. The second story windows were designed to illuminate the workroom floor, which dominates the 13,644 square foot structure. Over the years there have been repeated calls to build a new post office, but each time the subject came up, the community took a second look at the historic building it had, and decided to keep it. The building underwent a major renovation in the early 1950s, and again in 1993. Because of those efforts, one comment that was made in 1894—"The new Atchison post office is one of the handsomest structures in the States"—remains true today.

[*National Register listing 03/16/72*]

Council Grove

Main Street and Highway 56

GOD – ABOUT 1600

PIONEERS ON THE SANTA FE TRAIL could send letters home at an unusual drop-off point, known affectionately as the "Post Office Oak." The tree is located in Council Grove, Kansas, and was in use as an exchange point between 1825 and 1847. Wagon masters heading in the direction of the addressee were obliged to convey messages found at the base of the tree. A trading post, set up in 1847, served as the community's first formal post office. The tree fell victim to a devastating windstorm in 1980. As a result, it was severely trimmed back, leaving little more than the trunk.

Dodge City

700 Central Avenue

JAMES A. WETMORE – 1932

HERMAN J. FRINGER BUILT the first frame structure in Dodge City in 1872. It was a drugstore fronting onto the Atchison, Topeka, and Santa Fe Railroad tracks. Fringer was one of the 12 signers of the city's charter in 1872. Originally the town wanted to be called "Buffalo City," but the name "Buffalo" was already taken. Because of its proximity to Fort Dodge, "Dodge City" was a reasonable alternative. Although it was not his principal business, Fringer's drugstore doubled as the post office from 1872 until 1881. His first concerns were reflected in one of his early advertisements, which read: Herman J. Fringer Dealer in Drugs, Medicines, Notions, Perfumery, Stationery, Paints, Oils, Dyes, Stuffs, &c., &c., &c." In 1932 a new $112,500 two-story brick post office was dedicated. Like Herman Fringer's original post office, this Depression-era building is a short distance from the railroad tracks.

Kanorado

202 Main Street

UNKNOWN – 1905

KANORADO STRADDLES the Kansas/Colorado state line, which is the derivation of the town's name. When townsfolk applied for a post office in 1888, they were advised by the postal service that another town already had a similar name. Kanorado would have to go. While this was okay with the residents, who hastily switched the name to Lamborn in honor of Millard F. Lamborn, a local merchant and the town's first postmaster, the switch wasn't all right with the railway that ran through town. The railroad would not go along. It kept the old name on its depot. This created a great deal of confusion, which was finally resolved in 1903 when the Post Office Department relented, allowing the old name to be used. In 1934 the post ofice moved to its current location, a brick building constructed in 1905 for use by the Kanorado State Bank.

Topeka

424 South Kansas Avenue

JAMES I. BARNES – 1933

A FEW YEARS BEFORE this post office opened, and despite the fact that it could not be done, local officials tried to tax the Topeka post office. They even went so far as to inform the federal government that the post office was going to be sold a public auction for nonpayment of its taxes. The Treasury Department advised the local postmaster to notify the local authorities of the law and to shoo them off if they tried something silly. Oddly enough the announcement of the pending tax sale attracted at least one serious bidder. A woman inquired about the prospects of buying her own "perfectly good federal post office."

The post office building that opened in 1933 stood on the site of the untaxable earlier structure, and was an even better post office. The demolition of the earlier one, which had been completed and occupied in 1884, was carried out by James I. Barnes, the same general contractor who was responsible for building the town's New Deal era post office. The new post office required more property and additional land was purchased in 1931 for $105,000. The three-story building itself, finished in Bedford limestone and St. Genevieve golden vein marble, was dedicated on December 11, 1933, at a cost of $615,512. Despite the fact that this building was constructed during the early part of the Depression, this post office was not actually built as a federal employment project, having been conceived before the Depression, largely because of the efforts of Vice President Charles Curtis, who was from Topeka.

Weskan

108 Main Street

UNKNOWN – 1914

ORIGINALLY KNOWN as "Montero," this town was forced to change its name in order to get a post office. According to postal officials, this was essential to avoid being confused with "Monteno." Located in western Kansas, the acronym "Weskan" was coined by the town's first postmaster, Edward Carter, in 1887 to reflect the fact that the town was the last one on old U.S. Route 40 before the road crossed the state line into Colorado. Over the years the post office has been housed in a country

Two rural letter carriers about to leave C. E. Swanson's post office in Weskan, Kansas. The building is now an electrician's shop.

store, garage, the Union Pacific depot, and ultimately in 1920 in a second-hand bank building that was built in 1914. Because of its original tenant, the post office at Weskan has an exceptionally large walk-in bank vault, an unusual feature for an office of its size.

Up until the 1930s, when the post office was upgraded from a fourth-class to a third-class office, Postmaster Clarence E. Swanson had to do other things to simply make ends meet. Besides running the post office, he operated a cream-buying station a short distance away from the post office building, and did odd clerical work for others around town so that he could pay his bills. Clarence Swanson's store is still standing, although in recent years it has served as an electrician's shop.

Wichita

401 North Market

JAMES A. WETMORE – 1936

WICHITA'S LOCAL PRESS was tickled pink over the prospects of the town's new post office, a three- and four-story Art Deco building. They called it "A Thing of Beauty" and editorialized that "Those who designed the Post Office and Court House for Wichita have not committed a single sin against simplicity." The opinion of the *Wichita Eagle* was that this included only those ornaments that were absolutely necessary. "Every inclination to delirium in decoration was summarily ditched in the architect's office down in Washington, and entire reliance placed in the incomparable charm found only in straight lines kept in symmetrical proportion." Representing an exceptional example of a Class A federal building under the Treasury Department's formula for federal projects in large metropolitan areas adopted before World War I, this limestone-sheathed building cost of $1.2 million to complete.

[*National Register listing 07/18/89*]

MICHIGAN

Ann Arbor

220 North Main Street

C. HOERTZ AND SON – 1909

ALTHOUGH THE ORIGINAL authorization for the construction of this building was secured in 1903, the actual work on the one-story gray limestone building by C. Hoertz and Son of Grand Rapids wasn't begun until 1906. The first federally owned building constructed in Ann Arbor, the structure was slightly enlarged in 1926 to accommodate a growing volume of Parcel Post. This was followed by an even greater expansion between 1932 and 1933, carried out by the Rice Construction Company of Chicago, Illinois, that was appropriately in keeping with the style of the original structure. [*National Register listing 05/22/78*]

Battle Creek

67 East Michigan Avenue

ALBERT KAHN – 1904

ONE OF THE FIRST BUILDINGS to be designed by Albert Kahn, this Second Renaissance Revival style structure was funded under a 1904 appropriation championed by Battle Creek's Congressman, Washington Gardner, that initially set aside $110,000 for the project. The sum subsequently had to be increased by $20,000 to see the project through. Among the noteworthy architectural features of Kahn's design are the stone entryway, the stone quoins in the corners, and the lavish use of blue and white marble for the interior. A major addition, which matches the original section fairly well, was added in 1907.

[*National Register listing 08/21/72*]

Climax

107 North Main Street

WILLIS L. LAWRENCE – 1931

THE POST OFFICE AT CLIMAX is a one-man memorial to Willis L. Lawrence, one of Michigan's first rural letter carriers. Lawrence, who began carrying mail in 1896, gathered field stones, each selected for its size and shape, from each farm along his mail route. Seventy-three loads were required to construct the building. Work on the 30 foot long by 20 foot wide structure began in May 1931, with Lawrence doing a great deal of the carpentry work. Dedicated on September 26, 1931, three years before Lawrence's death, the sturdy stone structure is in keeping with Willis Lawrence's vision; "I wanted to build high on the sands of time so the waves could not wash away the structure." Today, the stone post office serves as the Lawrence Memorial Library.

Detroit

Detroit River

UNKNOWN – 1895

A NOVEL FORM OF MAIL SERVICE was started in 1895 to serve the 4,000 vessels operating on the Great Lakes. At that time the freshwater seamen employed on the ships equaled the population of a reasonably large city, but they received inadequate service. The key funnel point was Detroit, where ships navigated the Detroit River at a rate of one every four minutes. Because the steamers could not afford to stop or even slow down for mail, an innovative system was devised so mail could be exchanged in a bucket stretched between the passing steamer and a briefly tethered rowboat. During the first year of service only 500 letters a day were delivered by the "Detroit Marine Delivery Service." In recent years the mail volume has reached approximately a million pieces a year. Although a bucket is still used, the deadly little rowboat was discarded long ago in favor of a much more powerful and larger powerboat.

Grand Rapids

Ionia and Pearl Streets

JAMES KNOX TAYLOR – 1910

ALICE ROOSEVELT LONGWORTH, Theodore Roosevelt's daughter, traveled to Grand Rapids to lay the cornerstone for this three-and-one-half-story monumental structure on February 12, 1909. Her participation heightened interest in the ceremony, and added to its memorable qualities, largely, some said, because of the "smoke tendrils from the lady's cigarette!" An amazingly witty character, who apparently loved juicy gossip, Longworth reportedly placed a small embroidered pillow beside her favorite chair that contained a message to the effect that: "If you don't have something nice to say about someone... come sit next to me."

The building, constructed at a cost of about $500,000, is one of the finest structures of its kind in the Midwest. Although the Civil Defense shelter sign fastened beside one of the arched stone entranceways is out-of-character, one face of the building, with its window balcony, would be just superb as a stage set for a movie depicting European royalty waving to a flock of admiring peasants below. ‖ *National Register listing 07/10/74* ‖

Jackson

Rear of 125 North Jackson Street

JOSEPH G.R. BLACKWELL – 1839

BUILT IN 1839 to house the post office, a general store, and one of the city's first newspapers, this time-worn two-story sandstone structure is one of the first permanent buildings constructed in Jackson. Initially it fronted onto a public square, but it has since become largely hidden from view by other buildings that were subsequently constructed around it. In 1894 the post office was relocated into a government-owned building. This old structure survived on its merits as a warehouse over the years, miraculously escaping destruction. [*National Register listing 03/16/72*]

Niles

322 East Main Street

JAMES KNOX TAYLOR – 1910

THE APPROPRIATION for this one-story buff brick and limestone Classical Revival building, with full basement, was secured by Congressman Edward LaRue Hamilton, who was extremely pleased when the project was completed under budget. Of the $60,000 set aside for the building, the total cost of construction, carried out by Max Stock, a Michigan contractor, was $48,500. An addition to the east end of the building, which largely matches the scale, style, and materials used earlier, was made in 1937, and a further enlargement that doubled the size of the structure, constructed in a more contemporary styling with architectural detailing that sets this addition apart from the other, was made in 1956. The post office relocated in 1982, enabling the building to be acquired by the City of Niles. [*National Register listing 09/12/85*]

Saginaw

500 Federal Avenue

WILLIAM MARTIN AIKEN – 1898

ALEXIS DE TOCQUEVILLE formed many impressions of America, and it is thought by some that he left many behind. The French political historian once visited Saginaw and in honor of his brief stay the original east side of the town's post office was said to have been designed by Supervising Architect William Martin Aiken as a replica of de Tocqueville's ancestral home in Menou, France. Although this is a great story, there appears to be no basis in fact for this tale. Congress authorized $100,000 for the site and

The Saginaw, Michigan, post office resembles a French chateau.

construction of the building. Aiken completed the drawings and specifications for the chateau style building by 1896.

By the 1970s the building was obsolete. The Postal Service had vacated the premises, moving to larger quarters, leaving the fate of the structure uncertain. The local historical society took up the challenge of saving the building as an important national architectural landmark. It now serves as a regional museum.

MINNESOTA

Alexandria

625 Broadway Street

EARL AND AITON – 1910

DESIGNED BY Earl and Aiton and constructed between 1909 and 1910 at a cost of $40,358, primarily of brick and stone, the front facade of this one-story Second Renaissance Revival style building is dominated by a portico entrance that includes a pair of Roman Doric columns on either side of the arched entrance. The post office remained at this location until 1977. When departed, the building was declared government surplus, and in 1977 it was acquired by Crown Reality, Inc., for use as offices.

[*National Register listing 04/16/79*]

Anoka

300 East Main Street

JAMES KNOX TAYLOR – 1916

A LARGE-SCALE Georgian Revival building constructed in 1916, the Anoka post office is covered with a veneer of light-colored brick. Its low pitched hipped roof contains three dormers on the front and rear sides, plus a tall brick chimney on the west slope. Three semicircular arches, which enclose the main entrance flanked by two window units, define the building's main facade. Following the relocation of the post office, the building was subsequently acquired for commercial and office use by Counselor Reality.

[*National Register listing 12/31/79*]

Fort Snelling

1 Fort Drive

UNKNOWN – ABOUT 1820

THE NORTHWESTERNMOST military post in the United States in

the early 1820s, the massive diamond-shaped limestone fort at the junction of the Mississippi and Minnesota Rivers has at one time or another been in Michigan, Iowa, Wisconsin, and Minnesota Territories, as well as twice in unorganized territories, before finally becoming part of the state of Minnesota. During this time Fort Snelling became a major trading center as well as an important gateway to the northwestern frontier.

Mankato

401 South Second Street

WILLIAM MARTIN AIKEN – 1896

THIS POST OFFICE WAS BUILT to budget and basically completed in 1896. Congress had authorized $100,000 toward the cost of acquiring the site and constructing the building, including fireproof vaults, heating and ventilating apparatus, and elevators. Even though some slight details remained to be completed, expenditures after occupancy amounted to $99,860.49.

The building is principally rock-faced buff-colored Mankato stone. A tall, square, flat-roofed clock tower originally dominated the main entrance, but this feature was subsequntly removed. Other alterations include a major addition in the 1930s, supervised by James A. Wetmore, which doubled the overall size of the building, changing to a more horizontal structure. A further enlargement was carried out in the mid-1960s. [*National Register listing 06/17/80*]

Minneapolis

100 South First Street

LOUIS A. SIMON – 1935

THE LARGEST POST OFFICE building in Minnesota, this structure conforms to the Treasury Department's 1915 classification for a first-class postal facility with $800,000 or more in annual receipts. These guidelines, established under the Public Buildings Commission, designate this as a "Class A" post office, meaning that its exterior was to be covered with either marble or granite and that monumental proportions and

The rear of the Minneapolis, Minnesota, post office faced the Mississippi River before the 1989 extension to the back section of the building was completed.

detailing were to be used. The site of a "Class A" facility also was important in that such structures were to be on prime property, land essential to the city's economic and cultural development.

Art Deco in appearance, the Minneapolis general mail facility contained a number of first-class innovations in keeping with its elevated status. When it was completed in 1935 the building included: air-conditioning, one of the first public buildings to have this sort of creature comfort; a 25-yard long firing range, used by the postal inspectors and sports-minded postal employees; and one of the nation's longest lighting fixtures, a 350-foot tall, 20-ton bronze chandelier with neon lighting. (The neon was eliminated in the 1950s.)

The four-story building, clad in Mankato granite and Minnesota dolomite and costing about $5 million, was so large that at one point it was suggested that the flat roof be transformed into a landing field for airmail planes. Thankfully this harebrained scheme never materialized.

Several major changes have affected the building over the years, including a somewhat unpopular $7 million seven-story parking garage that was constructed in the 1970s. A much-needed major $52 million expansion plan, designed by a Minneapolis architectural firm, Hammel, Green, and Abrahamson, was begun in 1989, and ultimately doubled the size of the original building.

Moorehead

521 Main Avenue

OSCAR WENDEROTH – 1915

NOW PRINCIPALLY USED to house the Plains Art Museum, the Moorehead federal building, which once housed the post office and the U.S. district court, was initially planned in 1903, but actual construction of the brick and stone two-story structure, with a raised stone basement, did not commence until about 1911. The main entrance is highlighted by a portico supported by six Ionic columns. [*National Register listing 05/07/80*]

New Ulm

Center Street and Broadway

JAMES KNOX TAYLOR – 1910

THE DESIGN OF THE NEW ULM post office matched the ethnic origins of most of the town's early residents, settlers that came to Minnesota from Würtemberg, Bohemia, and Bavaria in Germany. In this case the Germanic flavor is attained by an arresting blend of alternating deep red rough bricks and gray-white concrete, steep slate roof, scroll-shaped window gables, and stepped gable and dormer ends topped with long blunt finials that extend well above the roof ridge in a European Renaisance style. Congress approved the initial funds for the post office in 1906, allowing $30,000 for the project, but when the inital plans were shown to local residents there was a vigorous protest over its "lack of architectural beauty." With the addition of $20,000 more, and the development of a new approach, one that has been described as "brutally dramatic," the community was well satisfied. Construction, carried out by Steward and Hager of Janesville, Wisconsin, was completed in 1910.

[*National Register listing 04/28/70*]

St. Paul

109 West Fifth Street

WILLOUGHBY J. EDBROOKE – 1901

IN THE 1890s Postmaster General John Wanamaker believed that many older post offices were "dank, dingy, overcrowded and unhealthy, if not actually dangerous." To Wanamaker's way of thinking, these older buildings needed to be replaced, but not particularly with the kind of structure that was constructed at St. Paul. Wanamaker favored smaller post offices, with fewer stories, two or three at most. His goal was to enable more sunlight to penetrate into the workroom floors. Wanamaker also hated the idea of sharing space with the Justice and Treasury Departments. His position was the "The great need is [for] small buildings wholly [devoted to] postal purposes." The town fathers of St. Paul and Minnesota's federal legislators did not share Wanamaker's opinion, so in the end, St. Paul received a giant brownish-gray granite Romanesque-style structure, built between 1894 and 1901 at a cost of about $2.5 million. Among its outstanding features are its two massive clock towers. The 150-foot tall south tower was erected in accordance with the plans devised in 1894, while the 296-feet tall north tower, with its 46-square-foot base, was incorporated into the design in 1899. In 1972 the building was purchased by the city of St. Paul for $1.

[*National Register listing 03/24/69*]

MISSOURI

Berger

211 Market Street

UNKNOWN – ABOUT 1880

FIFTEEN THOUSAND of the nation's post offices in 1956 were in facilities provided by the postmaster. Another 25,000 were in leased or federally owned buildings. The quaint brick post office at Berger was in the leased category. The post office occupies the lower-front portion of the building. From time to time the upper floor has been rented out to individual tenants.

Apartments occupy the upstairs of the Berger, Missouri, post office building.

Carrollton

101 North Folger Street

JAMES KNOX TAYLOR – 1912

CONSTRUCTED AT A COST of $60,000 between 1910 and 1912 by the Hiram Lloyd Building and Construction Company of St. Louis, Missouri, on property that was purchased for $8,500, this two-story Second Renaissance Revival style building, constructed principally of Missouri limestone, has had few alterations since it was completed in 1912. The possibility of enlarging the structure's workroom space was raised in 1966, but no action was taken.

Among the prominent features of this early 20th century federal building are its low-hipped red-tile roof with exceptionally deep overhang and round, arched attic dormers. One of its greatest distractions is its large masonry chimney, with a copper shield, that seemed to dominate the north portion of the roof. [*National Register listing 05/12/77*]

A view of the front of the Louisiana, Missouri, post office taken shortly before it was completed in 1906.

Louisiana

522 Georgia Street

JAMES KNOX TAYLOR – 1906

INCLUDED AS PART of an omnibus appropriation, $40,000 was approved by Congress for the acquisition of this site and construction of the Louisiana post office shortly after the turn of the century. Supervising Architect James Knox Taylor designed the building in a typical one-story Beaux-Arts style in 1903. Construction of the brick building by the R. W. Menke Stone and Lime Company was completed in

1906. Still in use, the post office was remodeled and extended in 1935, and it was further improved in 1978 with the addition of handicapped ramps.

Notch

Southeast of Reeds Spring

LEVI MORRILL – 1893

"UNCLE IKE," WHOSE REAL NAME was Levi Morrill, built and operated the post office at Notch from 1893 until his death in 1926. At the time of his death at 89, Morrill was among the nation's oldest living postmasters. During his tenure, the Notch post office was housed in a single room of this roughly 12- by 14-foot unpainted clapboard building, with an uncovered front porch. Built entirely of native materials, the post office building is one of five structures that comprise the Levi Morrill "Homestead." The structures have remained virtually unchanged, and this cabin still holds the handmade sorting case and desk that served as Morrill's office.

Morrill became famous as a result of *The Shepherd of the Hills*, a popular melodramatic novel by Harold Bell Wright in which Morrill was cast as the secondary character, Uncle Ike. The post office run by this character was said to occupy "a commanding position in the north-east corner of Uncle Ike's cabin, covering an area not less than four feet square." The description of the interior was about as flattering as this photograph:

> The fittings were in excellent taste, and the equipment fully adequate to the needs of the service: an old table, on legs somewhat rickety; upon the table, a rude box, set on end and divided roughly into eight pigeon holes, duly numbered; in the table, a drawer, filled a little with stamps and stationery, filled mostly with scraps of leaf tobacco, and an odd company of veteran cob pipes, now on the retired list, or home on furlough; before the table, a little old chair, wrought in some fearful and wonderful fashion from hickory sticks from which the bark had not been removed.

"Uncle Ike" in front of his post office at Notch, Missouri.

Following Levi Morrill's death, his wife, Jennie, succeed him as postmaster, serving until the mid-1930s. [*National Register listing 04/03/79*]

Powersite

1885 State Highway VV

RESIDENTS OF POWERSITE – 1929

RESIDENTS WORKED OFF THEIR DEBT at a rate of 20 cents an hour enlarging the Powersite post office, which in 1929 was in postmaster Ted Magness's general store. Many of the townsfolk owed money to Magness for groceries and were more than willing to lend a hand to reduce their accounts. They dug and poured foundations, hauled and laid stone, and built the roof. Since then there have been other postmasters, but only one site for the post office. The Powersite post office was remodeled in the 1990s.

St. Louis

Eighth and Olive Streets

ALFRED B. MULLETT – 1884

ELEVEN YEARS IN THE MAKING, the old St. Louis post office was literally built like a fortress. Fearing both fire and an attack on the building, not because of the post office, but because it also housed the city's customs house where an average of $2 million was collected annually on river traffic, the structure was built to withstand a siege that never materialized. Over a decade in the making, everything about the original structure was fortress-like, including the 25-foot deep dry moat that surrounded the exterior. The massive foundation walls, constructed of Missouri red granite blocks, were laid to a thickness of ten feet; the upper-story walls, gray granite quarried on Hurricane Island, Maine, were about four feet thick, and iron shutters that pull out from the walls

The old post office at St. Louis, Missouri, is the only large Second Empire style post office designed by Alfred Mullett that remains.

could be closed over the doors and windows in the event of an attack or an inferno. These coverings included gun ports. Fire-resistant materials were used throughout the building, including iron beams and cast-iron columns. The building also included a well in the basement, and ice boxes for provisions to last through any siege. The building has seven chimneys, each with three to six flues.

Among the building's most striking elements are the magnificent allegorical statues by Daniel Chester French that adorn the pavilion. These depict "America at War" and "America at Peace," flanking a stunning American bald eagle with outstretched wings. Visitors to the old St. Louis post office can now see these works up close by touring the inside of the building.

The St. Louis post office is the last surviving example of Supervising Architect Alfred Mullett's massive French Empire style of building, grand structures that once included the post offices at Boston, New York, and Chicago. Fortunately, smaller examples of his Second Empire style of post offices survive elsewhere around the country.

[*National Register listing 11/22/68*]

St. Louis

329 South 18th Street

EAMES AND YOUNG – 1904

KNOWN AS THE "Union Station Post Office Annex," this red brick structure was used to expedite incoming and outgoing mail transported aboard railway mail trains. The work in this building was so efficient, with over 25,000 pounds of mail processed daily, that it was said that any letter handled at this facility could be delivered one day earlier than if it were processed anywhere else in the country. This is principally a service structure situated within the St. Louis Union Station rail yards, a giant, multifloor work space with no formal entrance. The style reflects a Second Renaissance Revival composition. The building had deteriorated significantly over time, its slate roof and interior wood working having been heavily damaged by a fire in 1979. The roofing was subsequently replaced by asphalt shingling. [*National Register listing 09/26/85*]

Washington

123 Lafayette Street

JAMES A. WETMORE – 1925

THIS TOWN'S POST OFFICES have almost always been built of brick. Settled predominantly by German immigrants who established a large number of brickyards, Washington was known prior to the Civil War, as the "bricktown of Missouri." This town is said to have originally had more brick structures than Chicago. In the 1850s the post office moved to the Gregory House Hotel, a brick structure built in 1853. Other post offices over the years have also been brick structures. The current post office, constructed in 1925, is also built of brick.

NEBRASKA

Fremont

605 North Broad Street

WILLOUGHBY J. EDBROOKE – 1895

THE FREMONT POST OFFICE was one of the projects completed under appropriation bills passed in the late 1880s during what has been called the "Billion-Dollar Congress," an unflattering label that denotes its massive "pork barrel" spending. The post office was built of rusticated sandstone from Warrensburg, Missouri, and granite from St. Cloud, Minnesota, between 1893 and 1895. The design reflects Supervising Architect Willoughby J. Edbrooke's favorite style, Romanesque. The arched entrance to the original one-story federal building, which measured 75 by 46 feet, was located in an central pavilion on the east side of the structure. The hipped roof includes gabled dormers.

Two additions have taken place since the 1890s. One that was carried out between 1910 and 1911, and nearly doubled the size of the original structure, while the other, accomplished at a cost of about $73,000, occurred between 1936 and 1937. Both additions principally affected the rear of the structure. The building now is privately owned and is used for commercial purposes.

[*National Register listing 02/29/96*]

Nebraska City

202 South Eighth Street

MIFFLIN BELL – 1889

FUNDING FOR THIS COMBINATION courthouse and post office was approved during the 1885-1886 Congress, with a construction contract awarded in the summer of 1886. Supervising Architect Mifflin Bell's design, reflecting his preferred Romanesque Revival style, is one of the few of this type surviving in the Nebraska. Architecturally, it is almost unaltered. This building reportedly is the oldest government-owned structure in the state. It consists of a three-story fired red brick building, with full basement. The four corners are dominated by extended turrets above the first floor.

[*National Register listing 09/03/71*]

Scottsbluff

120 East 16th Street

JAMES A. WETMORE – 1931

THIS TWO-STORY masonry structure was originally designed before the Great Depression to be much grander and far larger. The actual construction, carried out between May 1930 and June 1931, reflected the economic realities of the times. Despite the fact that it is smaller, less expensive, and less ornate than initially planned, the main stone facade of the rectangular building, comprised of five bays divided by six monumental pilasters, still conveys the designer's original intentions. The post office vacated the property in September 1987. [*National Register listing 10/05/89*]

NORTH DAKOTA

Bismarck

304 East Broadway

JAMES KNOX TAYLOR – 1913

BISMARCK'S FEDERAL BUILDING was one of Supervising Architect James Knox Taylor's last post office projects. He resigned about halfway through the construction phase to assume the post of director of the School of Architecture at the Massachusetts Institute of Technology. The massive three-story Second Renaissance Revival style stone structure, with full basement, was stylistically unlike any other building in town. Another outstanding characteristic is its red tile roof, which causes it to stand out from other neighboring structures. [*National Register listing 06/23/76*]

Grassy Butte

Off U.S. Route 85

CARL JAGOL, JOHN MARUCHEK, AND JOHN HUFFMAN – 1916

THIS POST OFFICE was constructed by immigrants who settled at Grassy Butte, part of an enclave with strong Eastern European ties. The building is one of the last surviving Ukrainian-type log, milled lath, and native clay and straw plaster structures in North Dakota. The exterior construction technique, wattle and daub over log, represents a significant style of vernacular ethnic architecture. The building housed the post office for nearly a half century. The property has been taken over by the McKenzie County Historical Society. [*National Register listing 11/26/80*]

Rugby

205 Southeast Second Stret

LOUIS A. SIMON – 1940

ONE OF TWO FEDERAL projects announced for North Dakoata in 1938, the Rugby post office was allotted $85,000. Four bids were received during the summer of 1938, the lowest of which was $55,377 from Minecke-Johnson of Fargo. The beginning of construction was delayed 15 months, until May 1940, because of questions over the title to the site. The project, a "Starved-Classical" building similiar to countless others, including five in North Dakota (Oakes, Langdon, Hettinger, New Rockford, and Lisbon), was completed in December 1940. This is one of only three post offices in North Dakota to have a Depression-era mural sponsored under the Treasury Department's Fine Arts Section. The other murals are at New Rockford and Langdon.

[*National Register listing 11/01/89*]

Williston

322 Main Avenue

OSCAR WENDEROTH – 1915

IN 1909 NORTH DAKOTA'S Congressional delegation sponsored an array of "pork barrel" appropriation bills to create many new post offices, each with a $100,000 price tag. Besides the post office at Williston, sites and buildings were also authorized for Mandan, Jamestown, Dickinson, and Valley City. This limestone-clad building served as the post office until 1969, as well as housing other government functions, such as the Navy recruiting center, soil conservation office, and Internal Revenue Service. The two-story structure has been taken over by the city of Williston for use as office space.

[*National Register listing 10/22/79*]

OHIO

Akron

70 East Market Street

WILLIAM MARTIN AIKEN – 1895

CONSTRUCTED OF DEEP-RED brick and reflecting an Italian-Renaissance flavor, the two-story turn-of-the-century federal building at Akron features exceptionally wide overhanging eaves for its low-pitched roof line, tall and massive brick chimney tower, and a three-arched limestone-trimmed main entrance area. Accentuating the unique contours of the site, which slopes significantly, the design incorporated a high limestone base course that wraps around the entire structure at the first-floor windowsill level.

[*National Register listing 05/26/83*]

Cincinnati

1624 Pasadena Avenue

UNKNOWN – 1840

ORIGINALLY CONSTRUCTED as a single-story frame structure in 1840, this was the first post office in the community of College Hill. The second floor, added in the last half of the 19th century incorporates decorative brackets at the overhang of the roof and the porch embellishments, such as the lacelike cut-out rail panels, giving the rectangular building a simple Italianate appearance. [*National Register listing 06/16/76*]

Cleveland

201 Superior Avenue

ARNOLD W. BRUNNER – 1905

UNABLE TO CONSTRUCT the main post office over railway tracks, postal officials located structures, such as this, within the boundary formed by several rail terminals to minimize on-street transportation time and costs. The corners of this five-story building were enhanced by two magnificent freestanding groups of sculpture by Daniel Chester French symbolizing "Jurisprudence" and "Commerce." "Jurisprudence" consists of a calm and serene figure of "Justice," flanked by a mother clasping her baby, indicating that laws exist for the protection of the family on the left, while a felon, crouching in chains, appears to the right. "Commerce" is a more modern presentation consisting of a figure representing "Commerce" in the center, flanked by "Electricity" on the right and "Steam," represented by a male figure grasping a wheel, on the left.

The American eagles and shields that surmount each corner of the Cleveland, Ohio, federal building are equally as impressive as Daniel Chester French's massive statues of "Jurisprudence" and "Commerce."

During the 20th century, post office design provided exceptional oppor-

tunities for sculptors, muralists, and architects. The original occupants of the Cleveland federal building included the post office, federal courts, custom house, steamboat inspection offices, immigration and pension bureaus, geologic survey, hydrographic offices, and Civil Service Commission. The building was designed by New York architect Arnold W. Brunner and constructed of granite over a five-year period, from 1905 to 1910, at a cost of $3.3 million. The postal service vacated the property in 1937.

[*National Register listing 05/03/74*]

Dayton

West Third and Wilkinson Streets

JAMES KNOX TAYLOR – 1915

ON MARCH 25, 1913, Wolf Creek, a tributary of the Great Miami River, overflowed its banks, flooding Dayton. The post office then in use there was inundated with more than five feet of water. The flood marooned 50 postal employees and 36 patrons for several days in the upper floors of the building. For the first day, the stranded party had nothing to eat and only rain water to drink. On the second day, a line was strung across to a nearby building and bread was hoisted into the post office. The following day cheese and canned foods were hauled in. By March 29, the flood waters had subsided and cleanup operations began. Mud and slime were everywhere; the carcass of a drowned horse was found in the mail room. Undaunted by these conditions, postal workers began delivering and collecting mail on March 31, even though many street letterboxes had been swept away by the floodwater.

That flood also caused work on Dayton's new post office, this Neo-classical structure being built for $417,581 by the McCaul Company of Philadelphia, the builder of other noteworthy federal building such as the United States Mint at Philadelphia, to be significantly delayed. The project was finally completed on January 1, 1915, nearly five years after initially funding for this federal building was approved by Congress.

[*National Register listing 03/10/75*]

Franklin

Fifth and River Streets

UNKNOWN – ABOUT 1802

THE OLDEST SURVIVING structure in Franklin, and believed to have housed the first post office, this two-story log building, measuring about 18 by 22 feet, was relocated in 1974 about a block from its original site on the east side of River Street to keep it from being destroyed because of the desire to build an apartment complex on the property. Today, the cabin that once served as the principal trading post and post office between Dayton and Cincinnati is situated in a public park on the bank of the Great Miami River. Later additions have been removed, leaving it as it was in the early 19th century.

[*National Register listing 03/17/76*]

Marion

169 East Church Street

JAMES KNOX TAYLOR – 1910

CONGRESS INITIALLY APPROPRIATED $75,000 for the federal building at Marion in 1906, but had to add another $20,000 before the project was completed in December 1910. Built by John W. Uncafer, principally of limestone on a granite base, this is one of two significant Neoclassical structures in Marion (the other is the Warren G. Harding Memorial Tomb that was built in 1926). The post office building is situated on a plateaulike site that rises well above surrounding properties. The entrance portico, with six fluted 20 foot tall limestone columns with Ionic capitals, dominates the main facade. The mansard style roof, which rises 15 feet above the walls, is covered with red-orange clay tiles. Two alterations have taken place over the years, including the construction of an addition to the south side of the structure that was carried out in 1924 at a cost of $20,000, and a further renovation in 1937 at a cost of nearly $50,000. The post office was relocated in 1988. [*National Register listing 11/28/90*]

Toledo

13th Street and Madison Avenue

JAMES KNOX TAYLOR – 1911

THE PROPERTY FOR the Toledo post office was purchased in 1907 for $135,000 and the building was constructed between 1909 and 1911 at a cost of $550,000. Highlights of the 302 foot by 146 foot original structure include Doric columns that frame either side of the two principal entrances and accentuate the main facade and a copper roof that is ornamented with anthemia. The post office used this building from December 11, 1911 until 1965, when it was declared surplus federal property. In 1966 the building was donated to the Toledo public school system, which converted the structure into a vocational rehabilitation center. [*National Register listing 02/23/72*]

The former Toledo, Ohio, post office now belongs to the local Board of Education.

SOUTH DAKOTA

Provo

State Highway 471

UNKNOWN – 1942

ACCORDING TO PHILATELIC LORE, the world's first stamp collector was a young lady who advertised in a British newspaper for used postage stamps. She did not actually want to collect them; she wanted to wallpaper a room with canceled copies of Great Britain's first postage stamps, issued in 1840. The former Provo post office looks like that young lady's dressing room must have when she was finished. Three walls of the post office lobby are wallpapered with approximately 150,000 canceled stamps. The project took about ten years and required roughly 25 bottles of glue to complete. Now privately owned, at one time the Provo post office was a thriving place, serving up to 5,000 people, most of whom were employed by the Black Hills Army Depot at Igloo, South Dakota, a name which was derived from the igloo shape of the Depot's concrete and earth-covered munitions bunkers. The former post office building now stands vacant, an unnecessary feature in a town that has only about five families remaining. The structure reportedly is in the process of being moved.

Volin

Route 1

CHRISTIAN MARINDAHL – ABOUT 1870

KNOWN AS THE "Marindahl post office" in honor of its builder, Christian Marindahl, this one-and-one-half-story log building with shed addition was constructed on a rubble foundation and faced in beveled wood siding. It is recognized as the first nonmilitary post office in South Dakota. [*National Register listing 04/16/80*]

Watertown

26 South Broadway

JAMES KNOX TAYLOR – 1909

CONSTRUCTED OF TWO different colors of cut limestone, the symmetrical two-story Second Renaissance Revival federal building at Watertown, which housed the post office and the offices of the U.S. Department of Agriculture, is purely a James Knox Taylor product, right down to the massive American eagle with outstretched wings that peers down at visitors from the balustraded roof line. Like so many older federal buildings, the building was enlarged in the 1930s. In the

1970s there was talk that the building would be razed, but local support rallied to save the structure so that its importance to the development of Watertown could be properly recognized.

[*National Register listing 12/12/76*]

WISCONSIN

Ashland

Second Street and Sixth Avenue West

WILLOUGHBY J. EDBROOKE – 1893

LOCALLY QUARRIED cut brownstone was used for Ashland's post office, considered one of the finest Romanesque buildings in northern Wisconsin. It was constructed in 1892 and 1893 by Foster and Smith of Sault Ste. Marie, Michigan. A four-story square tower with pyramidal roof dominates the north end of the building. Because of its commanding view of Chequamegon Bay, the upper level of the tower was used as an observation platform and signal post. Although hard to detect at first glance, a well-designed addition to the north end of the building was completed early on; the work was so tastefully done that the demarcation between the old and new portions is hardly distinguishable. Only the contours of the windows differ. The building continued to serve as the post office until the late 1930s. When the post office vacated the premises in the 1930s, the property reverted back to the city.

[*National Register listing 01/21/74*]

Eau Claire

500 South Barstow Commons

JAMES KNOX TAYLOR – 1909

THE MOST STRIKING THING about this three-story post office, constructed between 1907 and 1909, is not that the light-tan brick and smooth-faced limestone used by James Knox Taylor complement each other so well, although they clearly do: Instead, it is the giant carved limestone American eagle with outstretched wings that seems to grab the viewer's attention. The eagle ornaments the main entrance portico like a Christmas-tree angel. The portico also includes four massive limestone Corinthian columns, which rise from the second to the third floor and delineate the portico's three bays. The portico is further embellished by three stone wreaths in the decorative panels that define the second floor windows. The building was substantially enlarged during the Depression.

[*National Register listing 07/25/91*]

Kaukauna

112 Main Avenue

LOUIS A. SIMON – 1937

THIS IS A PRIME EXAMPLE of the smallest of the "one-man" Depression-era post offices, a label that signifies that the postmaster had no other paid assistants to help run the place.

Located on Island Number 4 in the lower Fox River where it runs through the center of Kaukauna, this very simple and symmetrical brick post office was constructed between 1934 and 1937 by Charles Bloss and Sons of Ashland, Wisconsin. Its main facade is dominated by an arched double doorway, a thin stone band of scrolls and rosettes, and raised capstones above the main entrance. These dominant features, sparse though they are, tend to give the illusion that the building has a main pavilion, when in reality the entire front plane is basically flat. In the interests of ecomony, Louis Simon used this technique, and this design, elsewere around the country.

[*National Register listing 01/22/92*]

Menasha

84 Racine Street

JAMES A. WETMORE – 1931

IN KEEPING WITH the government's desire to duplicate designs and floor plans whenever possible, this structure possesses all of the trappings of a "Class C" Federal Building constructed in accordance with the government's 1915 building standards, which meant that it includes a brick facing, stone trim, and marble interior finish, and it was replicated elsewhere around the country during the 1930s. The two-story post office, constructed by Vincent Chibai, is an unexpected blend of styles that combines colonial features with a mansard roof with dormers.

[*National Register listing 08/22/86*]

Neenah

307 South Commercial Street

JAMES A. WETMORE – 1918

CONGRESS APPROVED THE FUNDS to construct the post office at Neenah in 1916 and the two-story masonry structure, with its hipped roof containing three hipped dormers and its front entry trimmed in limestone, was built by C. W. Grindele Company between 1916 and 1918. Other than the addition of a loading dock in the mid-1950s, and the installation of an exterior basement entrance in the 1970s, the overall exterior appearance of this Georgian Revival structure has not changed significantly. The building's use and interior plan has changed, however, largely as a result of the relocation of the post office in 1967 and the subsequent extensive modifications of the building in the 1970s to accommodate the structure's conversion into a restaurant and discotheque.

[*National Register listing 11/08/90*]

Oconto

141 Congress Street

JAMES A. WETMORE – 1922

IT SHOULD NOT BE HARD to discover this post office, since it reportedly "clearly stands out among other buildings [in Oconto] as having the distinct typical Government architecture of the early part of the twentieth century." This is perhaps as it should be, considering the fact that this is the first and only federal building constructed there. The structure is extremely simple one, consisting of a two-story brick boxlike building with little architectural detailing. [*National Register listing 08/22/80*]

Racine

603 Main Street

JAMES A. WETMORE – 1930

UNLIKE MANY OTHER large-scale buildings constructed in the years around the start the Great Depression, the main entrance of the Racine post office dominates the short side of this rectangular structure, which is built of Indiana limestone and measures 89 feet wide by 160 feet long. This placement was dictated by the size and shape of the property, the slope of the side streets, and the availability of the short frontage onto Main Street. While James A. Wetmore normally tended to place the principal entrance at one end or in the center of the longest span of a building, in this particular case he could not use either of those approaches. The result, however, is a well-proportioned main facade that is dominated by only six fluted Corinthian columns and pilasters that are 22 feet tall. The contractor responsible for executing Wetmore's design was Mads Madsen Company of Minneapolis, Minnesota. [*National Register listing 05/08/85*]

Waukesha

235 West Broadway Avenue

OSCAR WENDEROTH – 1913

THE FIRST FEDERALLY CONSTRUCTED building in town, and one of the best remaining examples of Classical Revival architecture in Waukesha, this post office featured a triangular design, which was ideal for the wedged-shaped site. It was constructed in 1913 and operated as a post office until 1962. Among the building's most striking exterior features are the drum and shallow copper-clad dome that caps the main entrance. The interior lobby space, which consists of a circular colonnade of red marble columns with gold Corinthian capitals that focus on the coffered dome and stained glass skylight, is a extremely attractive space. The building was taken over by a local bank in the mid-1960s.

[*National Register listing 10/28/83*]

West

ALASKA

Barrow

3220 Brower Street

CHARLES BROWER – 1898

THE U.S. POST OFFICE at Barrow, Alaska, has served as the northernmost U.S. postal facility for much of Alaska's history. The oldest surviving building that served as the post office, the Cape Smythe Whaling and Trading Station, was built by Charles Brower, who also served as the community's first postmaster. During the Alaskan gold rush, mail was brought from Kotzebue over a 600-mile route traversed entirely by dog sleds. Only two round trips were attempted each winter. Mail was dispatched as often as possible during the summer season aboard revenue cutters or other vessels. The post office moved into new quarters in 1975. Charles Brower's building is now a cafe.

Cooper Landing

Mile 49, Sterling Highway

FRANK YOUNG – 1900

NAMED IN HONOR OF JAMES M. COOPER, the first American to discover gold in the region, the town of Cooper Landing has a chalet-style log "A-frame" post office. It was built by Frank Young in 1900, and is considered the oldest building in the community. The structure initially served as a mail runner's cabin in the days when mail was moved by dogsleds, before becoming a store and post office in the 1930s. Postal operations are now conducted in the oldest portion of the building, a section known as the "Jack Lean Wing." [*National Register listing 05/23/78*]

Cordova

Second Street

JAMES A. WETMORE – 1924

COMPLETED IN JULY 1924, Cordova's federal building is a three-story

PRECEDING PAGE:

Remnants of the post office at Craig, Alaska, after the 1931 fire.

building that housed the postal system, federal court, and state court. The exterior is reinforced cast concrete. The local community praised the structure, calling it "the best and finest post office building erected north of Bellingham, Washington, and in fact there is no better in the U.S. for a town the size of Cordova." The principal tenant now is the U.S. Forest Service. [*National Register listing 08/02/77*]

Craig

National Postal Museum, Washington, D.C.

UNKNOWN

FIRES HAVE ALWAYS PLAGUED the Postal Service. When communications with this post office abruptly stopped on March 19, 1931, a postal inspector was promptly dispatched to investigate. The inspector soon discovered the cause, but wasn't certain if he needed proof of the disappearance of the post office. Using a rake, the inspector gathered up as much of the charred remnants as possible and placed them in a canning jar, which he included in his investigative report. The remains of the Craig, Alaska, post office are now part of the National Postal Museum's collections.

Fairbanks

Second Avenue and Cushman Street

GEORGE N. RAY – 1932

ALMOST IMMEDIATELY after this Art Deco style reinforced cast concrete building was completed, a rotating beacon was installed on the roof as a navigational aid for pilots. The beacon, which was visible for about 60 miles, remained in place here until the early 1950s. A weather balloon release station was operated on the roof of this building. Designed by Washington, D.C., architect George N. Ray, the federal building at Fairbanks was relatively expensive for its size, costing about $420,000 to complete. The exterior makes extensive use of aluminum, a popular Art Deco material, including cast decorative panels between the windows and parapets and aluminum doors. The grillwork above the main entrance was formed in the shape of an American eagle with outstretched wings. The federal government vacated the property in the late-1970s. The vacant property, which was claimed under the Alaska Native Claims Settlement Act, was rehabilitated and transformed into rentable spaces for shops and other commercial ventures.

ARIZONA

Nogales

Hudgin Street and Morley Avenue

JAMES A. WETMORE – 1924

ONE OF THE FEW post offices constructed in the Southwest during the austere economic climate between 1920 and 1926, the Nogales post office was a holdover from earlier federal building appropriations passed in 1913. Of the 75 post offices built nationwide between 1920 and 1926, only six were constructed in the West. This two-and-one-half-story stucco building with full basement was constructed by Devault and Deitrick of Canton, Ohio, which was awarded a construction contract worth about $91,000. The building was opened on July 1, 1924.

[*National Register listing 12/03/85*]

Oracle

Five miles southeast of Oracle

UNKNOWN – 1880

THIS ONE-STORY ADOBE building, considered one of the oldest surviving territorial post office structures in the state, served as the mining headquarters for the American Flag Mines, as well as the local post office, from 1880 until postal operations were transferred to the town of Oracle, five miles to the north, in July 1890. Since 1910 the property has been owned by the U.S. Forest Service, which has leased it out for grazing.

Located about halfway between Tucson and the copper mining region to the north, Oracle was named after the ship that transported one of the town's founding fathers around the Horn in 1873. Oracle became a popular health resort in the Santa Catalina mountains in the early 1900s. Around the turn of the century, John W. Estill moved his arthritic wife to Oracle because of its beneficial climate. After growing tired of commuting back and forth from Ohio to see her, he relocated there too, and in 1901 he opened the town's first general store and took on the job as postmaster. The post office was housed in Estill's store for several decades until the building was destroyed by fire.

[*National Register listing 06/20/79*]

Prescott

101 West Goodwin Avenue

LOUIS A. SIMON – 1931

CONGRESS APPROPRIATED the expenditure of $7,500 to acquire the site for the Prescott post office in 1914 and the property was purchased in 1915; however, it did not authorize construction funds until 1929, with an appropriation of $235,000. The building was designed in 1929, with 12 firms bidding for the construction. The lowest bid, received from Robert McKee of El Paso, Texas, was accepted, with construction commencing on September 17, 1930. While local residents were elated over the thought of getting a new post office, they were not pleased to learn that it would be constructed with out-of-state stone, including limestone from Indiana and granite from Minnesota. The public was placated when it became clear that, while native blue granite from Yavapai Hills was available, it could not be economically quarried.

Almost half of the town turned out for the cornerstone laying ceremony, which took place in February 1931, and was prematurely halted by a snow storm. The following November the post office occupied the new building, which has been described as "strongly conservative," possessing a rigid symmetry that makes this a significant example of a late Beaux-Arts style building. According to the paperwork prepared in conjunction with its nomination for inclusion on the National Register of Historic Places:

> The building ante-dates building activity of the Public Works Administration and was built under the Public Building Act of 1926. Given its date [completed in 1931], this was one of the last post office buildings to be constructed before the change in design and construction techniques heralded by the onset of the Depression.

Because this three-story structure's original configuration and interior ornamentation have remained largely unchanged, it is a rare surviving example of the 1930s Beaux-Arts style post office. [*National Register listing 12/03/85*]

Tucson

555 East Broadway

JAMES A. WETMORE – 1930

CONSIDERED TUCSON'S most refined and best preserved Depression-era building, this four-story tall structure, which originally housed the post office and the U.S. district court, is a simple rectangular brick block with a Mission-tiled hipped roof. Its three secondary sides are largely unadorned, leaving the main facade, with its striking central two-tier colonnade comprised of glazed terra cotta embellishments, to convey its architectural character. The lack of landscaping and architectural detailing on all but the East Broadway side were largely dictated by the size of the site and available funding.

Like so many other building constructed in the early years of the Great Depression, the efforts to initiate construction began well before, in this case starting about 1910. World War I and the nation's postwar frugality delayed this and other such worthwhile projects until an enormous federal building program was undertaken by Congress during the Hoover administration in the late 1920s and early 1930s. To connect this building with a new court house constructed across the street, an enclosed walkway over Broadway was constructed after 1930. [*National Register listing 02/10/83*]

Wickenburg

144 North Frontier

UNKNOWN – 1915

THE ONE-STORY "OLD BRICK POST OFFICE" at Wickenburg, constructed between 1909 and 1915, also housed a grocery store and the offices of the *Arizona State Miner,* as well as the local post office. Few other buildings constructed during the 1910s survive in Wickenburg, making this one even more of a rarity. [*National Register listing 07/10/86*]

Yuma

370 West Third Street

ROY PLACE – 1933

ORIGINALLY THE MAIN city post office, this federal building now serves as an annex to a new post office. The design by Roy Place reflects a Spanish Colonial Revival influence. This particular style was popular between the 1890s and 1920s, making this a late interpretation of this architectural style. Place utilized this style during this portion of his career. The front elevation of this two-story building, constructed of native Arizona stone, is dramatic, with six smooth columns with Corinthian capitals, balcony rails and window grills of wrought iron, decorative stone arches over the entrance portico, bas-relief stylized eagles, and Spanish roof tiles.

Place, who was born in San Diego, California, on December 17, 1877, established a practice in Tucson. He designed a significant portion of the buildings on the University of Arizona campus, as well as other Arizona landmarks, before his death in 1950.

This building was constructed by the Bannister Field Company of Los Angeles, which had submitted a winning bid of $129,00. Although the government may well have wanted to use a different type of stone, it appears that Senator Carl Hayden was influential in gaining the use of Arizona tufa, mined at the Wickenburg quarry. Hayden's ability to get the government to make such a concession did not sit well with the citizens of Prescott, who had tried to get their post office built with local materials, but were rebuffed by officials in Washington, D.C. The building was opened on April 16, 1934. [*National Register listing 12/03/85*]

Roy Place served as the architect for the Yuma, Arizona, post office constructed in the early 1930s.

CALIFORNIA

Cassel

Cassell Road

UNKNOWN – ABOUT 1909

IN THE 1970S the United States Postal Service required a posted fire emergency plan for all facilities. The mandatory "Fire Emergency Plan" for the former post office at Cassel pretty much summarized the condition of this weathered wooden tinderbox, built about 1909: "If fire should occur in this building, God help you. Save yourself, run like Hell!!!" A new post office, housed in a leased facility built at a cost of $98,204, was established in 1981.

Harmony

Highway 1

UNKNOWN

HARMONY'S POST OFFICE is a secondhand 19th century structure, a facility that serves a surrounding population of about 18 people. The hand-me-down post office once housed "The Harmony Creamery Association," a cooperative where publisher William Randolph Hearst frequently stopped for milk and cheese on his way to his famed "Castle." For several decades, until the mid-1950s when the dairy industry relocated to other portions of the state, The Harmony Valley Creamery Association produced quality butter and cheese from milk furnished from about 20 dairy farmers that once operated in the region. Since the mid-1950s it has functioned as the town's post office, although traces of its past, such as the rusted impressions made by the bottoms of milk cans, remain long after dairy operations ended. The entire town, all two square miles of it, including the post office building, was purchased by Jim and Kay Lawrence in 1981 for $650,000. At the time of the sale, the only phone in town was in the post office, and that was a pay phone.

Long Beach

300 Long Beach Boulevard

JAMES A. WETMORE AND LOUIS A. SIMON – 1934

THE FIRST LARGE-SCALE PWA Moderne style federal structure built in California was one of the few buildings to survive the 1933 earthquake that was responsible for leveling many of Long Beach's older structures. The ornamentation of the seven-story Long Beach post office is basically Art Deco in flavor. Begun in 1932 and completed in 1934, the first two floors of the reinforced site-poured concrete structure form a rectangle that measures 202 feet long by 135 feet wide. Rising from the center of the rectangular two-story base, which was largely devoted to workroom space for mail processing, is a stepped square central tower that rises another five stories. [*National Register listing 01/11/85*]

Merced

401 West Eighteenth Street

ALLISON AND ALLISON – 1933

ACCORDING TO THE DESCRIPTION of the Merced post office that appears on the nomination form for the National Register of Historic Places, "Like the Post Office for Beverly Hills [California], executed by Allison and Allison at the same time as this building, the stylistic expression is neither avant garde nor strictly classical. It is a well-preserved and locally prominent example of its genre—a small public building of the early 1930s."

While all that is true, it omits a couple of other features that make this one-story symmetrical building significant: It was designed by a Los Angeles architectural firm, rather than by the Office of the Supervising Architect, and it was the first federally constructed building to be erected in the town of Merced, a community that calls itself the "Gateway to the Yosemite Valley."

The use of Allison and Allison for the design of this post office was justified under the Public Building Acts of 1926 and 1930. This legislation gave the government the option of either commissioning private architects for federal projects or using the Supervising Architect's office. The Supervising Architect's staff was increased from 432 in 1929 to 750 in 1932, partly to accommodate the increasing workload and partly to help stave off such outside threats.

Congress approved $180,000 for the Merced post office in 1931, and work commenced the following year. The building was dedicated on November 23, 1933, and continued to serve as the community's main post office until 1965. The building is now a branch post office, designated as the "Bell Station" in tribute to one of Merced's longtime postal employees, Thomas V. Bell, who retired from the postal system after nearly a half-century of service.

[*National Register listing 02/10/83*]

Modesto

Twelfth and I Streets

JAMES A. WETMORE – 1933

CONSTRUCTION OF the Modesto post office, like that of so many other "pork barrel" projects frantically approved before World War I, was postponed because of the war. When construction finally began it featured a significantly reduced pricetag and proceeded at a much slower pace than originally publicized. The Modesto federal building received its initial okay in 1913 with a Congressional authorization to purchase the site for the post office, property that was acquired for

Modesto, California, post office.

$17,000 in December 1916; but further action on the project was delayed until the late 1920s. At this point the project got bogged down in the debate over whether such projects should be farmed out to private architects or retained by the Office of the Supervising Architect. Such arguments only added to the frustration level of the local population, who wanted the project to proceed as quickly as possible, prompting residents to counter the dawdling by applying pressure to political leaders in Washington, D.C.

When the project was finally back on track in the early 1930s, James A. Wetmore opted to use one of his preexisting floorplans for expedience, reusing the details and specifications he had previously employed at Erie, Pennsylvania, and Crockett, Texas. A construction contract was awarded on November 9, 1932 to Murch Brothers Construction Company, a St. Louis firm that had already successfully constructed post offices in several other states, including Madison, Wisconsin, and Casper, Wyoming, and which held current contracts to construct at least four other post offices around the country.

Although the design incorporated an eclectic array of elements, such as Georgian windows and a main arcade with Italian Renaissance touches, the exterior of this largely brick structure has a Southwestern flavor. The building, formally dedicated on October 2, 1933, continued to house Modesto's main post office until 1967, when a larger mail facility was constructed. The structure continues to serve the postal needs of the neighborhood, functioning as the El Viejo Station of Modesto's new main post office.

[*National Register listing 02/10/83*]

Napa

1352 Second Street

REED AND CORLETT ASSOCIATED – 1933

A RARE CALIFORNIA EXAMPLE of Art Deco styling, the building was designed by local architect William H. Corlett. Notable details include the sculpted terra cotta cornice formed of alternating ram and cow heads and the large Art Deco eagles above each door panel. Now designated as "Franklin Station," the building has its main entrances placed on the east and west corners of the front facade. Despite the fact that the main workroom floor was divided into office spaces in the mid-1960s, the building retains its original 1930s plan and shape. [*National Register listing 01/11/85*]

Petaluma

120 Fourth Street

JAMES A. WETMORE AND LOUIS A. SIMON – 1933

THE PETALUMA POST OFFICE, essentially a symmetrical reinforced concrete structure with a red tile roof, is a mixture of architectural influences, such as Spanish Colonial Revival and Italianate-Mediterranean styling, accentuated with six bizarre terra cotta gargoyle-like downspouts that give it a modest Gothic touch and an Art Deco style eagle over the main entrance. The building, authorized under the Keyes-Elliott Act of 1926, was designed in 1932 and completed the following year.

[*National Register listing 01/11/85*]

San Francisco

Mission and Seventh Street

JAMES KNOX TAYLOR – 1905

ALTHOUGH DAMAGED and somewhat scorched by the Great San Francisco Earthquake, and the two-day firestorm that followed in April 1906, the post office and courthouse building was one of the few structures to remain standing in the business district. The city was isolated. Telegraph lines were down and mail deliveries seemed impossible, but postal employees worked heroically to restore service. Automobiles and

The San Francisco, California, main post office following the 1906 earthquake.

wagons were commandeered to collect and distribute mail. The appearance of the impressed vehicles, bearing hastily handpainted "U.S. Mail" signs, was greeted by appreciative shouts and cheers from the forlorn citizens housed in makeshift camps. Much of the mail collected during the first few days following the earthquake was written on rags, pieces of wrapping paper, sticks of wood, and scraps of newspaper. There were no postage stamps available, so postage was temporarily waived.

This post office is now the heaviest and largest building in the United States that is equipped with an earthquake isolation system. The 60,000 ton building was literally lifted from its foundation by hydraulic jacks, 256 steel columns were cut, and a friction pendulum system that allows the building to move with each quake was installed at the base of each column.

San Francisco

180 Steuart Street

GILBERT STANLEY UNDERWOOD – 1940

IN 1983 THE POSTAL SERVICE embarked in its first-of-its-kind approach to redevelop Rincon Annex in conjunction with a private developer. Completed in 1940, Rincon Annex was a three-story structure that contained approximately 270,000 square feet of space. Originally, the roofline did not feature a cornice or string course to mark its termination. This was excluded to facilitate future vertical expansion, which never occurred while the Postal Service occupied the building. Between 1940 and 1948, Anton Refeigier painted several massive and controversial murals on the lobby walls. These murals, which are devoted to California history, cover a 400-foot length.

Architecturally, the San Francisco facility is an exceptional surviving example of the Art Deco style. In redeveloping the property the Postal Service approached the project cautiously, due in large measure to the fact that the building was listed on the National Register of Historic Places, making it subject to preservation review by the San Francisco Redevelopment Agency. Postal officials also realized that the approved redesign would determine the parameters for use of the space and density levels, all of which had a major impact upon the property's profitability. Before offers were made to potential private sector investors, a great deal of effort was expended in planning spaces and market analysis.

The final redevelopment package, completed in August 1983, called for the renovation of the original building into office and retail space. It also included an agreement to construct 240,000 square feet of commercial space on an adjacent parking space, plus the addition of 260,000 square feet worth of towers for residential use. A 72,000-square-foot rooftop addition also was incorporated in the development plan to accommodate housing for low and moderate income families.

In November 1983, the Request for Proposals was issued based upon this redevelopment plan. The following June a development team was selected. This team, known as Rincon Center Associates, was given exclusive rights to negotiate the ground lease, which was signed the following April. Under the terms of the 65-year lease, the Postal Service receives a fixed rent adjusted every six years to reflect changes in the Consumer Price Index. In addition, the Postal Service receives a portion of the gross income from the rooftop housing. One of the major features of the redeveloped space was the addition of a five-story atrium into what was formerly the post office workroom. The atrium, which is accentuated by a stunning 85-foot water column, provides natural sunlight for the retail establishments which front onto it. The total mixed-use project was completed in 1989 at a cost of $200 million. This undertaking became the pattern for other such joint ventures between the Postal Service's Asset Development Division and private developers.

COLORADO

Denver

Eighteenth and Stout Streets

TRACY, SWARTWORT, AND LITCHFIELD – 1916

THE DENVER CHAMBER of Commerce began to pressure Congress for a new federal building in 1904. Part of the strategy included sending illustrations of Denver's outdated post office, along with views of the new post office at Pueblo, which was obviously much nicer and more efficient than Denver's outdated structure. Colorado's congressional delegation acted swiftly, securing an appropriation for a new federal building. The building site was purchased on January 3, 1908 for $486,879.62, but the pace of the project slowed significantly after that. The architects for the project, Tracy, Swartwort, and Litchfield of New York, was selected through a invitational design competition that included 12 firms. The white marble building was not completed until January 1916 at a cost of $1,990,132.77. Among the features of the building's interior is the inclusion of the names of the most famous Pony Express riders on the wall piers at both ends of the main lobby. The building, which is now shared by the U.S. court of appeals and the U.S. district court, was renamed in 1994 in honor of United States Supreme Court Justice Byron White. [*National Register listing 03/20/73*]

Frisco

510 Main Street

LOUIS WILDHACK – 1882

THE ORIGINAL PORTION of this building, a one-room cabin, was built in 1882 by Louis Wildhack, initially as a mining office; with later additions it served as a residence and general store/post office. The additions included a two-and-one-half-story frame section that was completed in the 1920s. The post office was moved into the building following Wildhack's appointment as postmaster in 1914, remaining there with one slight interruption until 1966, long after Wildhack's tenure as postmaster had ended.

At the height of Frisco's glory during the silver booms, the town had as many as 4 hotels and 31 saloons, but long after its heyday had ended, the town had still Wildhack's general store and post office, which and as a social hub of the community, serving as the town's principal meeting place for religious services, owing to the fact that in later years the town had no formal church. [*National Register listing 05/16/85*]

Grand Junction

400 Rood Avenue

OSCAR WENDEROTH AND JAMES A. WETMORE – 1918

IN ONE MONTH (April 1910) Colorado Congressman Edward Thomas Taylor initiated $425,000 worth of public building bills for his state. These "pork barrel" projects included authorizations for purchasing sites for post offices at Rocky Ford, Cripple Creek, Idaho Springs, Golden, Alamosa, Canon City, Salida, Durango, Telluride, Ouray, Montrose, Delta, Aspen, and Glenwood Springs. Each of these projects was capped at $15,000. Typically, Thomas added subsequent legislation that enabled Uncle Sam to build the offices on these sites, with each of these building bills typically carrying a $100,000 price tag. One of the biggest of his bills involved a $200,000 plan for the post office at Grand Junction.

The design for the federal building, originally planned as a two-story structure, was prepared under the supervision of Supervising Architect Oscar Wenderoth, but was redesigned during the administration of his successor, James Wetmore, in 1916 to include the addition of a third floor for the judicial occupants of the building. Construction of the building was carried out by the Dieter and Wenzel Construction Company of Wichita, Kansas. The company's original bid of $106,821 only covered the original plan. With the addition of the third floor, the total project required almost every penny of Representative Edward Thomas Taylor's original $250,000 appropriation.

In 1972 the Indiana limestone clad building was dedicated in honor of former Grand Junction Congressman Wayne N. Aspinall. Affectionately described as a "crusty Coloradan," Aspinall served as the Chairman of the House Interior Committee and was the author of over 1,000 pieces of legislation.

Manitou Springs

307 Canon Avenue

LOUIS A. SIMON – 1940

THE CONTRACT TO BUILD the post office at Manitou Springs, representing a common plan used throughout the 1930s and 1940s for many small town post offices, was awarded in December 1939, with construction starting the following month. The project was completed in November 1940. In this particular case the relatively common design was given special local significance through the use of the roughly cut native reddish-green sandstone for the exterior, a common local building material used in other structures in town. The roof is red tile and is capped by a wooden cupola. Interior highlights include seven-foot marble wainscoting that accents the main public lobby of this one-floor structure. The extensive use of marble in the interior reportedly makes this government-owned building an exceptional example of a small Depression-era Colorado post office. [*National Register listing 01/24/86*]

Trinidad

301 East Main Street

JAMES KNOX TAYLOR – 1910

FOR A SMALL COUNTY SEAT setting, the Trinidad post office is one of the finest examples of James Knox Taylor's Beaux-Arts style handiwork that can be seen just about anywhere in the country. Relying principally on the use of tan brickwork and sandstone portico with four Ionic columns, this one-story rectangular building with full basement possesses massive proportions, elegent symmetry, and fine masonry detailing.

[*National Register listing 01/22/86*]

HAWAII

Hilo

Kinoole and Waianuenue Street

HENRY O. WHITFIELD – 1917

THE HILO POST OFFICE was designed in 1915 by New York architect Henry O. Whitfield. Basically constructed of poured concrete, the initial portion of the building, with its main portico and four-story clerestory, was constructed between 1915 and 1917. Subsequent alterations included three-story wing additions, designed in 1936 and constructed in 1937 and 1938. [*National Register listing 10/01/74*]

Honolulu

Merchant and Bethel Streets

UNKNOWN – 1871

THE FIRST MISSIONARIES arrived in Hawaii in 1820. Correspondence from the Hawaiian Islands was haphazard in those early years as there was no organized postal system. Letters were dispatched through personal arrangements with ship captains, who agreed to carry them to their next port where they were deposited in the mail. On December 20, 1850, King Kamehameha III decreed the establishment of a post office in Honolulu, although the first actual post office building would have to wait until the reign of Kamehameha V. Designated as the "Kamehameha V Post Office" because it was constructed during his reign, this two-story structure is thought to be the oldest building in the United States constructed of concrete blocks and reinforced formed structural concrete. Initially the building was square, but an addition in 1900 gave it its present basic configuration.

Originally, the building was shared by the post office, the offices of the *Hawaiian Gazette*, and several other small businesses. In 1894 the post office took over the entire building. In 1922 the postal service moved to a new location, turning this structure over to Territory of Hawaii. Since then it has housed a number of different tenants, including a postal substation and a driver education program. Because of these various uses, the interior of the building does not reflect its original appearance. [*National Register listing 05/05/72*]

Honolulu

335 Merchant Street

YORK AND SAWYER – 1922

BY THE 1920s the postal service in Honolulu had outgrown its accommodations at the Kamehameha V post office, prompting the construction of this building, the first federal building constructed by the government after annexation. This symmetrical Spanish Colonial Revival style structure was built between 1921 and 1922, and then substantially altered between 1929 and 1930. The resulting structure is a three-story steel and poured concrete building, with six-story square towers, and an open arcade. [*National Register listing 01/27/75*]

Honolulu, Hawaii, post office.

Lihue

4441 Rice Street

LOUIS A. SIMON – 1939

A ONE-STORY REINFORCED concrete structure, the Lihue post office is basically an adaptation of the Depression-era post offices built on the mainland. Originally intended to be a typical "Starved-Classical" design, of the type common throughout the United States, local pressure prompted Supervising Architect Louis Simon to alter his approach, resulting in the construction of a building that better reflects the materials and climatic conditions common to Hawaii. Constructed of reinforced concrete on a site that was acquired in 1937, the Spanish Mission style building is said to have served as a prototype for the postal service's Schofield Barracks station, built in Honolulu a few years later. This post office also served as a model for other public and commercial buildings in the area. [*National Register listing 11/28/89x*]

Pearl Harbor

(U.S.S. Arizona and U.S.S. Oklahoma)

Pacific Ocean

UNITED STATES NAVY – 1941

SINCE THE TURN of the century, American warships have furnished postal facilities and the ships of the Pacific Fleet were providing such service to American seamen at Pearl Harbor in 1941. Preserved in a small cardboard box in the vault of the National Postal Museum in Washington, D.C., are several relics that serve as fascinating reminders of the Japanese attack on Pearl Harbor. The small box contained handstamps that were salvaged from the small post office aboard the battleship Oklahoma following the raid on U.S. military installations in Hawaii. On the morning of December 7, the Oklahoma was moored beside the U.S.S. Maryland on Battleship Row. When the aerial attacks began, the outward position of the Oklahoma helped to shield the Maryland. The Oklahoma, however, was left vulnerable, and it was struck by a series of bomb and torpedo blasts and ultimately capsized. The damage sustained was so severe that the ship sank on its way to California for salvage. Six marking devices were saved, including a registration handstamp marking device, dated "Dec. 6, 1941."

The Japanese attack was a serious blow to U.S. naval might in the Pacific. In all, 18 Navy vessels were sunk or damaged in the raid, including 8 battleships, 3 light cruisers, 3 destroyers, and 4 support ships. About 2,300 American servicemen lost their lives in the attack, and more than 1,100 others were wounded. The U.S.S. Arizona also had a shipboard post office.

IDAHO

Blackfoot

165 West Pacific Street

GILBERT STANLEY UNDERWOOD – 1936

THE ONLY ART DECO STYLE building constructed by the federal government in Idaho, the two-story Blackfoot post office and federal building principally consists of buff-colored brick with Indiana limestone and Arkansas fossil marble detailing. Exterior artistic highlights include such embellishments as a carved marble panel above the doors of the central entrance, which features a stylized eagle with outstretched wings, fluted brick pilasters, zigzag marble belt course, and fluted limestone cornice. Gilbert Stanley Underwood, a graduate of the Yale School of Architecture, served as the consulting architect for this project. The site for this federal building, one of six considered, was purchased in 1934 for $6,500. Construction, by J. O. Jordan and Sons of Boise, Idaho, which received a contract for the work based upon an accepted bid of $82,000, began in 1935 and was completed in 1936. An addition to the rear of the building was built in the mid-1970s. [*National Register listing 03/16/89*]

Bonner's Ferry

Off U.S. Route 95

EDWIN L. BONNER – AFTER 1876

THIS ONE-AND-ONE-HALF-STORY log building, covered with successive layers of siding over the years, was built by Edwin L. Bonner. Bonner also operated a rope ferry across the Kootenai River during the migration of miners and gold prospectors along the North Idaho Indian Trail to Wild Horse. Richard Fry operated the town's trading post and post office for about a quarter of a century, beginning shortly after 1876, in a structure that was said to have attracted "the usual gang of loafers" and that also became an important hub for the lead-and-silver mining operations in Idaho and British Columbia. Known as the "Bonner-Fry's Trading Post," the building was abandoned around 1892, when the establishments on the south side of the river began to prosper. The rope ferry operated by Edwin Bonner was later taken over as a county-operated enterprise in 1902, and was replaced by a highway bridge in 1906. [*National Register listing 09/07/84*]

Caldwell

823 Arthur Street

JAMES A. WETMORE – 1932

THE CALDWELL POST OFFICE was one of those buildings that got stuck in the limbo between the "pork barrel" spending sprees of the early 1900s and the fiscal realities of the 1920s and 1930s. The property for the post office was acquired in 1915, under a 1913 federal appropriation. Harold Peterson, an Omaha contractor, submitted the winning bid to build the post office, quoting a price of $76,719. Although Uncle Sam had owned the property since before World War I, construction was postponed until the Depression, when the nation began to use public works projects to boost the economies of local communities by providing jobs as well as money to purchase local building materials. According to Peterson, approximately one-half of the bid price was to be spent on local materials and labor. Although the principal beneficiary was the local community, Peterson estimated at the time the post office was completed in 1932 that additional materials had been purchased from vendors in 20 other states.

The original one-story brick structure is distinguished by slightly projecting central entry section and a triangular pediment that rises above the parapet. An addition, constructed in 1965 to the northwest side of the building, was slightly recessed from the original and is somewhat lower in height, giving the building an elongated appearance.

[*National Register listing 03/16/89*]

Kellogg

302 South Division Street

LOUIS A. SIMON – 1938

IDENTICAL TO NUMEROUS other post offices, such as the ones at St. Anthony, Idaho, and Helper, Utah, the post office at Kellogg is a standard symmetrically oriented one-story brick design void of distinguishing architectural embellishments, in the "Starved-Classical style." Carbon-copy projects of this kind were the result of using identical construction documents in order to save time and money. The post office at Kellogg was built by Benjamin H. Shelton of Colfax, Washington, at a cost of $51,413. The building, which was dedicated on June 25, 1938, is one of only six post offices in Idaho that contain Depression era murals. The other murals are at Burley, Buhl, Blackfoot, Preston, and St. Anthony. The five- by twelve-foot mural, entitled "Discovery," was painted in 1941 by California artist Fletcher Martin at a cost of $740. [*National Register listing 05/30/90*]

Paris

Main Street

LDS CHURCH – 1880

THE PARIS POST OFFICE was initially constructed by the Latter-day Saints (Mormon) Church as the local tithing office. This two-room 1880 structure, constructed of Smedley Milwaukee Brick on a rough stone foundation, also housed the Deseret Telegraph Company operator as well as the post office. After 1910 a local newspaper occupied the structure. Some subsequent alterations, notably the bricking in of two windows in the left-front elevation, are apparent in the structure.

[*National Register listing 11/18/82*]

St. Anthony

48 West First North

LOUIS A. SIMON – 1938

ALTHOUGH THIS IS A STANDARD small-town one-story single-purpose post office built during the Depression, the building had special significance to the community. Headlines in the local newspaper heralded the anxiously anticipated opening of the building, which was postponed for nearly two weeks because of delays in obtaining certain building materials. Not willing to continue to stave off the inevitable any longer, and sensing the public's growing exasperation over the delays, the unfinished building, constructed by Viesko and Hannaman of Salem, Oregon, was officially dedicated on January 17, 1938. Finishing touches on the structure required at least another week. Like the post office at Kellogg, this structure houses a Depression-era mural. The oil painting, entitled "The Fur Traders," was painted in 1939 by Elizabeth Lochrie, a prominent Montana artist.

[*National Register listing 03/16/89*]

Wickahoney

Stage Road between Mountain Home, Idaho, and Mountain City, Nevada

DOW DUNNING – 1895

THE PRESERVATION of this one-and-a-half-story rock post office and stagecoach station is primarily due to its desert location. This long-abandoned structure was built by homesteader Dow Dunning, who served as postmaster at Wickahoney from 1895 to 1911, and is one of the few surviving 20th-century stagecoach stations in Idaho. The building was constructed of stone in anticipation of many years of service as a way station for the Mountain Home and Mountain City stage route. Although the Wickahoney route provided important access to the mines in northern Idaho, it never achieved the level of importance that was anticipated.

[*National Register listing 05/27/82*]

MONTANA

Anaconda

218 Main Street

JAMES A. WETMORE – 1933

ANACONDA'S FEDERAL BUILDING is one of the community's most imposing structures. A two-story red-brick and sandstone structure, its main facade is dominated by a central portico that includes a colonnade with four massive fluted columns with Ionic capitals. Efforts to get a government-owned post office building began in 1914, but were shelved because of World War I. The small amount of federal construction done after the war further delayed attempts to build this post office. The onset of the Depression lead to greater expenditures for government-owned buildings, spending that ultimately lead to the construction of Anaconda's public building by John L. Soderberg Construction Company of Omaha, Nebraska. Constructed at a cost of about $120,000, the building was completed in the spring of 1933.

[*National Register listing 03/14/86*]

Billings

2602 First Avenue North

OSCAR WENDEROTH – 1914

THE SITE OF THE BILLINGS post office was purchased in 1909 for $9,000, but repeated attempts to acquire full funding for the construction were unsuccessful until 1913. Nine companies submitted construction bids for this project, which was awarded to J. H. Weiss of Omaha, Nebraska, with a winning bid of $109,748. The building was formally dedicated on Flag Day, June 14, 1914.

The exterior of this Second Renaissance Revival structure is principally buff-colored limestone. Two major additions and renovations took place in the 1930s and 1940s. The 1932 expansion amounted to approximately $143,000 worth of improvements, while the work carried out in 1940 cost about $200,000. [*National Register listing 03/14/86*]

Butte

400 North Main Street

JAMES KNOX TAYLOR – 1904

SIXTEEN DIFFERENT SITES for this building were considered before the government settled on the North Main Street location; a highly unpopular choice among the local community, but one that reflected the government's insistence on receiving clear title. The building was dedicated on December 8, 1904.

Considered an interpretation of Italian Renaissance styling, the exterior of this stunning building features a three-bay central entrance area with semicircular arched windows that span the area between the second and third floors, projecting out slightly from the structure's symmetrical sides for emphasis. The building is comprised of a granite-clad lower level, with red brick extensively used for the two upper floors of this combination post office and courthouse. Large terra cotta quoins accent the corners and highlight the window treatments of the top two levels. The exterior also features a 64-inch-tall terra cotta balustrade, with a central cartouche that serves to outline the perimeter above the third floor and conceals the attic level. A major addition, principally affecting the rear of the structure, was constructed in the 1930s, nearly doubling the original size of the building.

The court rooms of this federal building were the scenes of hundreds of bootlegging cases. One of the building's more notable judges, Judge C. M. Bourquin, was said to have been "one of the nation's most colorful judges, austere and caustic tongued, a terror to liquor defendants in dry days." Said to have believed in the motto that "This court may be in error, but never is in doubt," Judge Bourquin reportedly never sentenced a woman, refusing on the grounds that no female should be sent to jail until all male criminals were there. The main post office moved elsewhere in the 1960s.

[*National Register listing 11/15/79*]

Great Falls

215 First Avenue North

JAMES KNOX TAYLOR – 1912

THIS WAS THE ONLY Montana post office of the initial 38 towns incorporated under the Post Office Department's "Farm-to-Table" program. Inaugurated in August 1914, the program was an extension of Parcel Post. This program enabled farmers and urban dwellers to buy and sell produce and poultry directly between themselves, with the postal system acting as an impartial broker. Under the terms of this program, postmasters at designated towns received the names of interested farmers with produce to sell, and a printed list of current prices and descriptions of goods offered to be provided to potential city purchasers. The Post Office Department was proud of its role in this "direct dealing" scheme, which unfortunately lasted only a few years.

[*National Register listing 03/14/86*]

Missoula

200 East Broadway

JAMES KNOX TAYLOR – 1913

PUBLIC REACTION to the construction of the Missoula federal building in the 1910s was enthusiastic. Local newspapers characterized the three-story Second Renaissance Revival style building as "a handsome structure" and "an ornament to the city." This "ornament," originally constructed by Sound Construction and Engineering of Seattle, Washington, at a cost of about $160,000, was significantly enlarged in the late 1920s and 1930s through a series of additions, one of which was the construction of a greenhouse in 1938 that connected the main building with an annex. Postal operations were largely removed from the building in 1974. The Forest Service took over much of the vacated space, becoming the building's principal tenant in the 1970s.

NEVADA

Carson City

401 North Carson Street

MIFFLIN E. BELL, WILL FRERET, AND JAMES WINDRIM – 1891

THE FIRST FEDERAL BUILDING constructed in the State of Nevada, a Romanesque-style red-brick building with yellow-sandstone trim, which originally housed the post office, federal land office, weather bureau, and U.S. District Court, was designed by Mifflin Bell. The cornerstone for the Carson City federal building was laid on September 29, 1888, and the construction was completed by May 1891, during the administrations of Will Freret and James Windrim. Initially the clocktower featured four simultaneously operating seven-day clock facings in all four directions, but by the 1970s only the west-facing clock was operational. The State of Nevada took over ownership of the property when the post office was relocated in 1970.

[*National Register listing 02/09/79*]

Elko

275 Third Street

JAMES A. WETMORE – 1933

THIS TWO-STORY STRUCTURE, which achieves something of a Mediterranean-Revival styling thanks largely to its red-tile roof, was constructed mainly of buff-colored brick on a raised basement to serve the needs of the largest community in northwestern Nevada. Shortly after the post office was constructed, this prosperous cattle-raising community was described as being able to support "two small movie theaters, 50 saloons and gambling places and the oldest, most respectedly [sic] conducted red-light district in Nevada."

While it was not uncommon for the design of a proposed federal building to create a firestorm between the government and the local residents, in this particular case it was the site for the building that created the greatest upset. Initially, an acceptable piece of property was offered for $26,000, but the government was only willing to pay $15,000, anticipating that the local Chamber of Commerce would come up with the difference, which it would not do. Within a matter of weeks the government countered with an offer of $20,000 on another site, but this too was opposed by the local community. A third location was proposed by the community, but this was at first ignored by the government, which suggested placing the building at yet another site, somewhere no one would have wanted it. This hardball tactic seems to have done the trick, enabling the government to end the debate by accepting the third site, with the understanding that Uncle Sam would pay $15,000 and the local community would come up with the remaining $5,000. The subject just would not die, however. The controversy continued for weeks, threatening the building altogether. By May 1932, four months after this process had started, the local newspaper, *The Independent*, finally signaled an end to the location fight when it reported that, while the newspaper "has always felt that the site chosen for the federal building was not a proper one, an opinion that is shared by the majority of the people in this city. However, the site has been chosen ... and we gracefully admit defeat of the furtherance of a plan to have the federal building more centrally located."

Congress approved funding for the Elko post office in June 1932 and construction, carried out by Carl C. Madson Construction Company of Denver, began that summer. With all of the delays associated with the selection of the site, James A. Wetmore appears to have made up for lost time by reusing one of his earlier standard designs; yet, although Wetmore used these same proportions and exterior design articulations for this $140,000 post office elsewhere in the country, this basic design does not appear to have been duplicated anywhere else in the West.

[*National Register listing 02/28/90*]

Lovelock

390 Main Street

LOUIS A. SIMON – 1938

DURING THE DEPRESSION Louis A. Simon oversaw the design and construction of countless small-town post offices. This prospectively daunting construction schedule was simplified by a formula devised by the Treasury Department, which ensured that only minimum funds were spent on any one small project. The post office built at Lovelock represents the least amount spent on any post office, roughly $60,000. That amount of money bought a standard building designed to expedite construction and reduce costs. In this case, the standard "Starved-Classical" pattern consisted of a one-floor, buff-colored brick veneer, single-purpose post office that could be constructed in a short time, typically within as little as about ten months. This is one of four such post offices constructed in Nevada during the Depression. [*National Register listing 02/28/90*]

Reno

50 South Virginia Street

FREDERICK J. DELONGCHAMPS – 1934

THE ONLY EXAMPLE of an Art Deco style federal building in the State of Nevada, this three-story, light-green terra cotta building is notable, in part, for having been designed by a local resident, architect Frederick J. Delongchamps. Delongchamps, who began his architectural career in 1907 after studying in California, was a charter member of the American Institute of Architects. He served as the State Architect of Nevada from 1919 until 1926. Besides the post office at Reno, Delongchamps designed eight other government buildings in the state, including the county court house at Reno, which is diagonally across the street from this post office. The post office was built at a cost of $363,660 by the MacDonald Engineering Company of Chicago.

Delongchamps, who received the "Distinguished Nevadan Award" in 1966, died on February 11, 1969. His surviving buildings, including the Reno federal building, are a testament to his skills and creativity. Six years after Delongchamps' death, the city's main postal facility was moved to new quarters near the Reno airport, leaving only a postal station at this location.

[*National Register listing 02/28/90*]

Tonopah

201 Main Street

LOUIS A. SIMON – 1941

THIS ONE-STORY, buff-colored brick building is the only Depression-era building constructed by the federal government in Tonopah. Completed in 1941, it was the last federal post office constructed in Nevada prior to the start of World War II. Supervising Architect Louis A. Simon was responsible for the design, which was duplicated elsewhere in the western states.

This is an exceptional unaltered example of a small town, late Depression-era, single-purpose post office, devoid of significant detail. A central entry bay, with two equally sized flat arched window bays on either side, breaks the otherwise plain main facade. Above the front door, and fronting a transom window, is an ornate aluminum grille with a low-relief American eagle sculpted in the center. According to the request for eligibility for listing on the National Register of Historic Places, the building, which cost $95,000 to construct, "exhibits the modern or 'International' design influence in its flat facades and lack of explicitly articulated historical design elements, yet retains 'Classical' symmetry and proportion." Centered on the ridge of the building's copper-clad hipped roof is a square copper and glass cupola, capped by a weather vane.

[*National Register listing 02/28/90*]

Yerington

28 North Main Street

LOUIS A. SIMON – 1939

THE TOWN OF YERINGTON was originally known as "Pizen Switch," a name reflecting the liquor, referred to as poison but pronounced "pizen," that was served at a saloon called the "Switch." Believing that this was not really a proper name for the town, the residents changed it to "Greenfield," a pastoral name that mirrored the green fields that border the community. When the town celebrated the 1879 name change, the local newspaper, the *Lyon County Times,* proclaimed as follows: "Whiskey and hard cider flowed freely, but there were no fights. The music was furnished by a fiddle and two banjos. The place was re-christened 'Greenfield' and an organization formed to be known as the Committee of Vengeance, whose duty it shall be to murder and scalp any and every person who shall hereafter call it 'Pizen Switch.'" But even "Greenfield" was changed, altered to "Yerington" in the hopes of inducing railroad magnate H. M. Yerington to connect the community with his Carson and Colorado Railroad. This well-intentioned ploy did not succeed. All of these changes occurred in the span of 50 years.

In the more than a half-century since the government-owned Yerington post office was constructed, little has changed. This one-story red brick building, with its raised basement platform and copper-clad hipped roof, is an excellent example of an unaltered small-town post office of the type commonly built during the late 1930s. The building houses one of three New Deal era murals painted in Nevada during the Depression.

[*National Register listing 01/16/90*]

NEW MEXICO

Albuquerque

123 Fourth Street

JAMES KNOX TAYLOR – 1908

POST OFFICES ARE NOT always located on the best sites. In the early 1900s postal officials picked a site for Albuquerque's new post office based solely on the cost of the land, but the choice was unfortunate for other reasons. To prompt the Post Office Department to change their plan, according to the *Albuquerque Tribune,* resident Roy Stamm tried something a little unusual: "Taking the largest plat of Albuquerque [Stamm] could find, [he] red-inked every house of prostitution, each saloon, livery stable and corral; all blacksmith, wagon and paint shops, etc. The result was impressive—the proposed site looked almost like a little boat on a lake of red." This approach, combined with other local pressure, caused postal officials to have a change of heart. They picked this site on Fourth Street in a better part of town, where the post office remained for more than 50 years.

The design is said to resemble an oversized square Tuscan country house, with plain cream-colored stucco walls and flat-topped, hipped, red-tile roof. The original contractor for this project, which ended up costing twice what it was estimated to cost, was Anders Anson, who went bankrupt, delaying completition of the three-story project until 1908. An addition was made to the west end of the building 13 years later, and an even greater alteration was carried out in the 1930s, giving the building its current shape and size.

[*National Register listing 11/17/80*]

Clovis

Fourth and Mitchell Streets

JAMES A. WETMORE – 1931

NOW THE CARVER-CLOVIS Public Library, this two-story building, with its various shades of tan-colored textured brick used for the exterior walls and its hipped red-tile roof with large overhang eaves, reflects a Spanish-Colonial-Revival styling in keeping with its Southwest location. The building continued to serve as the post office until 1965, when it was purchased by the local school system, which used it as an educational service center until 1970. In 1974 it was acquired as the new home of the local library.

This building was built to budget, which in this case meant that it was able to be upgraded almost immediately. When the original construction bids came back under the anticipated budget, the walls were changed from stucco to brick and the foundation from cast concrete to sandstone.

[*National Register listing 12/27/84*]

Deming

201 West Spruce Street

LOUIS A. SIMON – 1937

THIS SINGLE-STORY, symmetrical, red-brick building, built at a cost of $62,400 by L. F. Dow & Company of Los Angeles, is Deming's first, and only, federally constructed structure. The building was formally dedicated on May 29, 1937. Among the dignitaries in attendance were Governor Clyde Tingley, Senator Dennis Chavez, and Postmaster General James Farley. Some residents apparently believed that they already knew how to treat Tingley and Chavez, but they were in a bit of a quandary about how to handle Jim Farley; the local newspaper observed:

> There has been much ado about what to do when PMG J. A. Farley arrives in Deming. Suggestions have been made that everyone should put on a lot of Hog!, be very formal and all that. We have a different idea. Unless we miss

> our guess, Mr. Farley is not apt to be too impressed by our formality, especially in view of the fact that most of us are just plain country boys and girls who do not keep very well versed in the practice of formality. What we want to say to him is that we are very happy to have him visit our community, and we want him to know he is more than welcome—so why not say that, in the simplest way "Howdy Jim. We're glad to have you with us."

The building Farley helped to dedicate was enlarged in 1967 to provide additional workroom and lobby space on the eastern side of the building, and additional office space was added to the western side. The alterations transformed the building from a single-purpose post office to a multipurpose federal building that could accommodate other government operations besides the postal service. The building is also noteworthy for the 5 by 12 foot New Deal public art mural, produced in 1938 under the auspices of the Federal Works Agency Section of Fine Arts by New Mexico muralist and landscape artist Kenneth Adams. [*National Register listing 02/23/90*]

Portales

116 West First Street

LOUIS A. SIMON – 1937

EFFORTS TO GET A NEW post office building at Portales, the county seat of Roosevelt County in east-central New Mexico, began to materialize in the early 1930s. The residents thought the idea of a new post office was ideal, and so did the local press, which expressed the view that "while the government is passing post offices 'round to aid in reemployment, Portales should show a united front in presenting its claim for such a building." A bill for fund appropriation was authored in 1934 and, in May, Senator Carl A. Hatch confirmed that a new post office building in Portales was well on its way to becoming a reality. In August 1935, Congressional approval was finally given to the project and the local newspaper proclaimed "Portales' long dream of a federal post office is to come true at last." At that point work progressed rapidly, so much so that the single-story red-brick building was dedicated on June 5, 1937. This was the only federal building constructed in Portales.

Some changes have occurred since the Depression, including a substantial expansion in 1966, with an extension to the rear portion of the building. Like many of its contemporaries, the Portales post office features a New Deal mural over the postmaster's door. In this case the 5- by 12-foot oil on canvas mural, entitled "Buffalo Range," was completed in 1938 by Theodore Van Soelen. Other post office paintings by Soelen appeared in federal buildings at Waureka, Oklahoma, and Livingston, Texas.

[*National Register listing 02/23/90*]

Early 1900s photograph of the post office in the Palace of the Governors at Santa Fe, New Mexico.

Santa Fe

Palace Avenue

UNKNOWN – 1610

CONSIDERED AMERICA'S oldest public building, the Palace of the Governors was the seat of government in New Mexico until 1901. Constructed of adobe in the early 1600s, this was the first structure erected in the city. The walls of this Spanish Colonial style building are about three feet thick. Between the 1880s and early 1900s the west end of the structure housed the Santa Fe post office. At that time restoration work was done on the "Palace" and its porch was restored to the simplicity of the original Spanish design.

Truth or Consequences

400 Main Street

LOUIS A. SIMON – 1940

THIS "STARVED-CLASSICAL" style post office was the first, and only, federal building constructed in Truth or Consequences, a town that up until 1950 was named "Hot Springs." The name-change, which was made in the hope of bringing more visitors to the town, was part of a promotional campaign associated with the tenth anniversary of a popular game show at that time. Unlike other buildings of this type, which were principally constructed of brick, this one-story post office is constructed of reinforced concrete "poured-in-place," a construction method that was not common in the West. The construction was carried out by Lundberg and Richter, an Oklahoma firm, at a cost of $85,000. [*National Register listing 02/23/90*]

OKLAHOMA

Cushing

628 East Main

UNKNOWN – ABOUT 1890

THIS WAS ONE OF THE FIRST post offices created following a land run in the Indian Territory [eastern Oklahoma]. Residents named their town in honor of Marshall Cushing, Postmaster General John Wanamaker's private secretary. The townsfolk never met Cushing, but they offered him a deal: "Give us a post office ... and it will bear your name." Cushing agreed. Unfortunately, not everyone liked the initial location. Some residents wanted it in one place, others wanted it someplace else. In a late night raid in 1902, one faction literally stole the building, and transported it on skids to their preferred location. The theft sharply divided the community, so much so that some folks refused to send or receive mail from the new site.

Guthrie

201 West Oklahoma

J. H. BILLINGS – 1906

A 10- BY 12-FOOT TENT with a daubed red "Post Office" sign was Guthrie's first post office. The tent was pitched by Dennis T. Flynn, the first postmaster, who had acquired two shingles from the local land office to mark off the government's plot. By the following morning, ten other tents were on the same site and the occupants all claimed the land. Flynn resolved the question of ownership and began setting up shop. Within a matter of days a proper post office was established, using an improvised 50-slot sorting case and a wooden plank for a countertop. Four clerks were hastily employed in advance of the arrival of the mail. No sooner did the first mail arrive than an anxious crowd descended upon the post office at 4 A.M. At first everything was total chaos, but order was finally restored, thanks to the arrival of soldiers from a nearby military post. Four lines were arranged to accommodate the 3,000 men calling for their mail. By nightfall the majority were still in line waiting to be served. The clerks were exhausted and could work no further. Those in line were told to camp in place until morning. That night Flynn and his clerks slept at the post office. Their wake-up call came before dawn with shouts of "O postmaster, you opened at four o'clock yesterday morning!" This building served as the post office in the early 1900s.

The Kingfisher, Oklahoma, post office is located on the site of the U.S. Land Office in 1889.

Kingfisher

Main and Roberts Streets

DIETER AND WENZIL COMPANY – 1913

BUILT ON THE "Government Acre," part of the 1889 land rush set aside for official use, Kingfisher's post office was constructed by Dieter and Wenzil of Joplin, Missouri, between October 1912 and September 1913, at a cost of $46,000. Among its most striking features are the large cornice brackets that were used to support the overhang of the red-tiled hipped roof. The two-story buff-colored stucco building, measuring 80 by 46 feet, continued to be used until 1976, when postal operations were moved to larger quarters. [*National Register listing 01/20/78*]

Oklahoma City

Robinson at Third

JAMES KNOX TAYLOR – 1912

INITIALLY KNOWN AS "Oklahoma Station," this community initially consisted of a railroad depot, telegraph office, watering tank, post office, and five houses. At that time the town's immediate population was about three-dozen people, but thousands lived in the surrounding countryside. Early in 1890 the post office was housed in a makeshift stockade, erected of secondhand logs. Despite its crude appearance, postmaster George A. Beidler hoisted the Stars and Stripes over his temporary post office, announcing that he was open for business. He was soon sorry that he had. The arrival of the first mail was like a magnet attracting a huge crowd, all clamoring for their mail at once. Beidler hastily organized his patrons into two lines, which steadily moved into and out of the post office for the next 13 hours.

In 1912 the permanent post office, a three-story Beaux-Arts style federal building, constructed principally of light gray limestone, was completed. A small alteration was made in 1919, followed by an out-of-character nine-story addition that was built in 1937 atop the 1919 revision.

[*National Register listing 08/30/74*]

OREGON

Corvallis

Jefferson and First Streets

JAMES A. WETMORE – 1932

DESIGNED IN 1930 and completed in 1932, the 32,967 square foot Corvallis post office, principally constructed of cream and buff-colored brick, stands out from neighboring structures, in part because six terra cotta gargoyles and a bas-relief terra cotta American eagle located on the parapet directly over the main entrance accentuate the building's otherwise plain facade. According to the Oregon State Historic Preservation Office, this particular style of architecture might perhaps best be described as "half modern."

Six buff-colored terra cotta gargoyles protect the Corvallis, Oregon, post office.

Eugene

520 Willamette Street

GILBERT STANLEY UNDERWOOD – 1939

CATEGORIZED AS A "Starved-Classical" post office with Art Deco tendencies, this federal building sits on a site the government acquired at a cost of $26,000. The plans for the structure were drawn up by the Office of the Supervising Architect, in consultation with Gilbert Stanley Underwood, a Yale School of Architecture graduate who consulted with the government's Public Buildings Administration on a number of federal projects, including the Seattle federal court house and the Los Angeles federal building. Construction of the federal building was carried out by an Oregon firm that bid $194,540. The two-story building, constructed of reinforced concrete, was occupied in July 1939.

[*National Register listing 08/14/85*]

Portland

511 Northwest Broadway

LEWIS P. HOBART – 1919

FUNDING FOR THE FEDERAL BUILDING at Portland was authorized in the early 1910s, thanks to the efforts of Oregon's U.S. Senators. When it appeared that work was not progressing fast enough, these same senators got to work again, threatening to take action in the Senate and calling on the secretary of the treasury for information as to why the Supervising Architect refused to carry out an Act of Congress by not constructing the building. The Treasury Department begged for forgiveness and asked that no such radical action be taken, attributing the delay to the fact that the building was to be designed by the winner of a competition among private architects.

The winner of the competition, San Francisco architect Lewis P. Hobart, envisioned an entirely new type of building; one that would serve strictly as an office building for the Post Office Department, not the type of monumental structures then generally in use. This idea struck a favorable chord with the local population, prompting the *Oregonian* to write on July 14, 1915, "Even before work is started on the new Post Office building at Portland, a new building of a type never before erected by the government, the Treasury Department is contemplating the erection of similar modern office buildings in some of the larger cities of the east, in lieu of the old Greek temple type that has been followed by government architects for years."

Delays, however, continued. By September 1915, with the prospects of winter setting in, residents began to despair. Hobart promised quick results and his plans were completed by December 1915, but because of manpower and material shortages during World War I, work on the structure was to take four more years. The Post Office Department was finally able to occupy the building in 1919. The resulting building is a tribute to Lewis P. Hobart, who is perhaps best known for the design of the Grace Cathedral in San

Francisco. Among his other designs are the University of California Hospital and the Fireman's Fund Insurance Building. Hobart died in 1954 at the age of 81.

[*National Register listing 04/18/79*]

TEXAS

Anderson

Near the intersection of Main Street and Highway 90

HENRY FANTHORP – 1835

ANDERSON IS NAMED IN HONOR of Kenneth Anderson, the vice president of the Republic of Texas, who died at the Fanthorp Inn in Anderson on July 3, 1845 and is buried in the Fanthorp cemetery across from the Inn.

The community's early postmasters served four governments over the years: the pre-Republic provisional government (1835-1836), the Republic of Texas (1836-1846), the Confederate States of America (1861-1865), and the United States.

Five governments have controlled the post office at Anderson, Texas.

The town's first post office was located in the Fanthorp Inn, an historic building that constitutes one of the oldest intact post offices in Texas. It was built by Henry Fanthorp, who arrived in Texas in 1832 and quickly amassed a small fortune from various business activities, including farming, marketing in corn, innkeeping, and service as the postmaster from 1835 through 1840. Fanthorp was one of the first postmasters appointed by the Republic's

provisional government. The post office did average business, with revenues reported to the Republic's postmaster general for 1839 amounting to $29. Fanthorp's stagecoach inn fared much better, largely because of its reputation for serving relatively decent food. However one boarder described the diet as:

> Morning coffee strong enough to bear up an iron wedge and fresh pork, fresh beef roasted and broiled and for dinner we have the same and for supper the same. Sometimes we had in addition a little chicken, turkey ... a few times a hard looking kind of apple pie and sweet potato pie. I wish I could describe them to you but it is impossible. For bread we have warm biscuits and corn bread. We have had a few times light bread. It is a great luxury. Butter we have had none on the table for the last week but that is of no consequence for when we did have it, it was so poor I could not eat it.

Such conditions aside, notable guests are said to have included Sam Houston, Ulysses S. Grant, Robert E. Lee, and Jefferson Davis. The inn, owned by the Fanthrop family for over 140 years, was acquired by the Texas Parks and Wildlife Department in 1977.

Austin

126 West 6th Street

THOUGHT TO BE ALFRED MULLETT – 1878

THIS BUILDING BEARS a strong general resemblance to the overall proportions and contours of the Cairo, Illinois, post office, except that it is clad in a different skin. The building is said to have been modeled after an Italian High Renaissance palace, a style which was highly unusual for 1870s Texas. The three-story symmetrical building is constructed principally of limestone, with two end pavilions connected by a two-story arcade, and an attic that is set back from the arcade and forms a terrace. The building, which was subsequently turned over to the University of Texas and is now known as "O'Henry Hall," was remodeled and restored in the early 1970s. [*National Register listing 08/25/70*]

Copperas Cove

1.6 miles southwest of Copperas Cove off U.S. 190

MARSDEN OGLETREE – 1878

WHILE THE LINTELS AND SILLS were finely finished, roughly dressed limestone, quarried locally and often laid to a thickness of as much as 19 inches, was otherwise generally used to construct the original post office at Copperas Cove. The building, constructed by Marsden Ogletree, one of the earliest settlers in the region and the town's first postmaster, is the only surviving structure from the original town. The building, which consists of two rooms with separate fireplaces, initially served as a dwelling and a relay station for a stagecoach route between Georgetown and Fort Gates. In later years the building housed the post office and a grocery store, and was also a private residence. The stage-stop and post office building, which stood vacant in the early 1950s and sustained some damage from vandals and general deterioration, was donated to the city of Copperas Cove in 1974. The building was restored during the 1970s as part of America's Bicentennial celebrations and now serves as the site of the "Martin I. Walker Historical Museum," a local museum commemorating the early history of the region. [*National Register listing 09/26/79*]

Dallas

Ervay and St. Paul Streets

JAMES A. WETMORE – 1930

JOHN NEELY BRYAN, the founder of Dallas, served as its first postmaster. The post office was in Bryan's rustic cabin from 1843 to 1846, now located on the grounds of the Dallas courthouse. Customers, however, were a problem, because there was not much mail. The monthly mail seldom consisted of more than two letters, and more often than not, one or both were for Bryan. Today, Dallas's post office is one of the busiest in the country. Bryan once reportedly said that "the town was named for my friend Dallas," and although historians are not certain, it is believed that Bryan meant George Mifflin Dallas, vice president under James Polk. It is possible that Bryan, a Tennessean, may have been acquainted with Dallas as a result of his association with Andrew Jackson.

Dallas's 1930s post office, a five-story structure with basement, is principally clad with rough and smooth Indiana limestone. Public reaction to some of the detailing was less than flattering. Negative comments appeared in the *Dallas Morning News*, directed at the design of the salmon-and-blue terra cotta spandrels that chronicle the movement of America's mail from the Pony Express to Air Mail Service, observing that the spandrels are "as startling as would be the discovery of a colored comic strip in the *Encyclopedia Britannica.*"

El Paso

219 Mills Avenue

ROWLAND GILCREST – 1916

CONSTRUCTED AT A TIME when the Mission styling of architecture was far more common in the Southwest, this building, which is said to have brought formal Beaux-Arts styling to West Texas, is considered to be one of the finest examples of this style in that portion of the state. This is a more imposing design than was commonly used for a city the size of El Paso, which in the 1910s had a population of about 35,000. The entrance portico to the two-story limestone and cast concrete El Paso post office is dominated by six impressive Ionic columns. With its massive, yet low, profile, the building's entrance portico is flanked by end pavilions that each contain central window sections that are framed by pairs of Doric pilasters. The exterior portico opens into a stunning high domed interior lobby that gives the building's principal public space a high degree of formality. The building was constructed under a

$350,000 appropriation, passed in 1911. Construction commenced the same year and was completed in 1916. Few changes have taken place since that time. Although the main city post office has moved to a more suburban setting, the 1916 building continued to be a practical location as a station in the old downtown section. [*National Register listing 07/19/84*]

Rio Grande City

423 East Main Street

HEINRICH PORTSCHELLER – 1886

KNOWN LOCALLY as the "Silverio de la Pena Drugstore and Post Office," this is considered to be the best preserved and most exquisite example of the type of buildings that were constructed by Heinrich Portscheller throughout the region during the second half of the 19th century. Most notable of this two-story buff-colored brick building's details are its finely wrought-iron balconies and its handsome proportions. Portscheller, a German immigrant, built sturdy masonry structures that reflect European influences. The original drugstore, initially operated by Silverio de la Pena until his death in 1894, remained in the building until 1914. That year the post office, which had been housed in the adjoining office areas of the building, occupied the entire structure, remaining at this location until 1950. In later years the site was used as a bookstore and a meeting place. [*National Register listing 09/02/80*]

Round Rock

Chisholm Trail and Emanuel Street

THOMAS C. OATTS – 1870

ALTHOUGH NOW PART of a private residence, the home of the first post office at Round Rock was in a one-story vernacular stone rubble building, constructed by the town's first postmaster, Thomas C. Oatts, who served as postmaster until the 1880s. The post office originally was located along on an old stagecoach route between Austin and Dallas that provided mail deliveries twice a week, and a feeder trail used by cattle drivers along the Chisholm Trail. Later, the town suffered a major blow when the International and Great Northern Railroad decided to bypass Round Rock in the 1870s, prompting many of the settlement's residents and most of its commercial activities to move further south to parallel the railway tracks. Restoration of many of the town's original buildings began in the 1940s. [*National Register listing 07/07/83*]

Stamford

Town Square

JAMES A. WETMORE – 1917

LOCATED IN THE MIDDLE of the town square on a spot that formerly had been the site of Stamford's first city hall, the current post office is a perfectly preserved one-story Beaux-Arts style building. The placement of the post office at this location was symbolic, reflecting the postal system's crucial role in the town's early prosperity. Constructed of buff brick, with concrete and wooden ornamentation, the building is dominated by a central portico supported by Tuscan columns. The structure is also noteworthy as an outstanding example of how this particular architectural style was interpreted in a small town setting.

[*National Register listing 09/24/86*]

Texarkana

500 North State Line

PERKINS, CHATTEN, AND HAMMOND – 1933

LIKE A TALE of two cities, half of the Texarkana post office is in Texas and the rest is in Arkansas. According to the Post Office Department in 1957, the post office in Texarkana is the only one of its kind in the United States. This post office served two states, two counties, and two cities, each with a separate and distinct government. The stamp and service windows, except for those used for general delivery, are in Arkansas. The lockboxes and carrier units are in Texas. Not to offend either state, the official address authorized for this post office has been "Texarkana, Arkansas-Texas."

Split almost in half, the Texarkana post office straddles both Texas and Arkansas.

Wichita Falls

120 North Main Street

JAMES KNOX TAYLOR – ABOUT 1911

LESS SOBER IN COMPOSITION than most of Supervising Architect James Knox Taylor's small post office designs, the two-story brick Wichita Falls facility used an embellished triple-arched entrance way and fanciful gatework to heighten the expression of the Beaux-Arts style. The playful oval treatments for the front mezzanine floor windows adds to the 1910 design.

UTAH

Cedar City

10 North Main

CANNON AND FETZER – 1934

REPRESENTING ONE OF the nation's finest surviving largely unaltered examples of a medium-sized "Starved-Classical" style federal building, the Cedar City post office is a two-story red brick building constructed on a raised granite basement platform. The main symmetrically arranged facade is divided into seven flat bays delineated by six fluted terra cotta columns with Ionic capitals. The main alterations were confined to the rear of the building, and include the expansion of the loading platform in the mid-1960s. [*National Register listing 11/27/89*]

Eureka

Main Street and Wallace Avenue

JAMES A. WETMORE – 1923

ALTHOUGH AT FIRST GLANCE the post office at Eureka, one of four postal facilities constructed in Utah during the 1920s and the first federally constructed post office in the city, appears to possess all of the characteristics of the "Starved-Classical" style, this building actually predates the Depression. As such, it represents a transitional style, one that bridges the Beaux-Arts and the New Deal era forms. Work on the site commenced during 1922 and the building was occupied by the summer of 1923. Architecturally, this one-story stucco building, which is devoid of any significant ornamentation except for its Spanish-tile coping, which gives it a somewhat faint Spanish Colonial flavor, lacks an identifiable style. Instead, it possesses classical symmetry and proportion, thereby reflecting the realization that form did not have to exceed function, especially in light of the post World War I economic climate. Of the four 1920s post offices constructed in Utah, only the Eureka post office has escaped extensive alterations. [*National Register listing 11/27/89*]

Helper

45 South Main Street

LOUIS A. SIMON – 1938

THE DESIGN OF THIS POST OFFICE is among the most basic of the "off-the-shelf" plans used for many small post offices during the Great Depression. The one-story red-brick post office at Helper was completed in 1938. Other post offices around the country are identical in appearance because they relied upon the exact same construction documents.

The design features a flat facade with five symmetrically arranged bays. The central entry bay, with its two wooden doors with single glass panels in each, reflects the simplicity of the overall design, as do the cast concrete window sills and lintels, the nine concrete steps, and the landing with its wrought-iron balusters.

Although the Helper post office is not architecturally very distinguished, it is well preserved and represents the materials and craftsmanship typical of federal construction projects during the Depression era. The National Preservation Act of 1986, which established the Register, calls for the retention of cultural properties worthy of preservation. The Postal Service takes an active role in inventorying and nominating properties under its control that qualify as historic or cultural sites. [*National Register listing 11/27/89*]

The post office at Helper, Utah, is a standard "Starved-Classical" structure.

Provo

88 West 100 North Street

LOUIS A. SIMON – 1940

THIS IS ONE OF THREE Depression-era post offices in Utah to be adorned with artwork paid for as part of the overall construction budget. The active and lively oil on canvas rendering of "Early and Modern Provo" was painted in 1942 by Everett C. Thorpe. Such lobby art was not sponsored by the federal government in an effort to provide employment for artists, but instead was awarded as federal commissions as a result of artistic competitions. The other Utah murals are in Beaver and Helper.

Rockville

State Route 15

EDWARD HUBER – 1870S

NOW PRIVATELY OWNED, the original rectangular red sandstone house, one of the community's earliest and finest homes, was constructed in 1864. A few years later a clapboard attachment with a shed-type roof was added to accommodate the post office and the offices of the Deseret Telegraph Company, which had almost 1,000 miles of telegraph lines that connected Mormon settlements in Utah, Arizona, Nevada, and Idaho. The clapboard section of the building continued to be used for decades. However in 1903 the telegraph service was discontinued in this section of Utah.

[*National Register listing 02/23/72*]

Salt Lake City

2155 South Highland Drive

LOUIS A. SIMON – 1940

ALTHOUGH MANY OLD post offices were later designated as "postal stations" after the main postal operations were relocated from those sites, this particular postal station was always intended to be just that. Known as the "Sugar House Station," this "Starved-Classical" style structure was the first such "station" specifically built in Utah prior to World War II. In 1938 the government appropriated $150,000 for this project. Two different sites were initially considered, one priced at $17,875, the other $29,900. The cheaper property was purchased in May 1938. W. J. Dean and Sons was awarded the contract to construct this station, which ultimately cost $85,976 to complete. Work on the facility commenced in 1939 and was completed in November 1940. The building, which received a two-story addition in 1962, continued to be used by the Postal Service until 1991.

[*National Register listing 02/18/94*]

This is America's oldest living post office, near Port Angeles, Washington.

WASHINGTON

Port Angeles

Directly South of Little River and Elwha

MOTHER NATURE – 1100

WILLIAM MCDONALD SERVED as the first postmaster in the Upper Elwha Valley, naming the post office in his honor and setting up shop in a huge hollow cedar stump on his property. To weatherproof his improvised post office McDonald added a simple roof. A few years later a small lean-to extension was added, but this burned in the 1890s. The stump continued to house the post office until about 1905, when the office was closed and mail service was transferred to Coventon. Today the badly disintegrated stump is only a fraction of its original size and shape, barely visible from the roadway. According to the Clallam County Historical Society, a survey of the stump was conducted about five years ago and the determination was made that there was not enough of it left to restore or relocate.

Port Townsend

1322 Washington Street

MIFFLIN E. BELL, WILL A. FRERET, JAMES H. WINDRIM,
AND WILLOUGHBY J. EDBROOKE – 1893

THE DESIGN AND construction of this post office is a primary example of the transience of the Treasury Department's Supervising Architects in the latter portion of the 19th century. Four Supervising Architects oversaw the project at one time or another, and each made changes to the building that reflected his own particular architectural tastes. The earliest drawings, completed in 1885, were prepared under the supervision of Mifflin E. Bell, whose term of office was from 1884 to 1886. Work began in April of 1887 under the supervision of Will A. Freret (1887-1888). Within a matter of months it was decided that the original building was simply too small. Subsequently, the drawings for the building were enlarged under the supervision of James H. Windrim, who served as Supervising Architect from 1889 to 1890. Windrim's replacement, Willoughby J. Edbrooke, who was the government's architect from 1891 to 1893, made the final inspection of the completed quarry-faced sandstone building. The imposing building, which is the oldest federally constructed post office in the state, originally dominated the bluff overlooking the Strait of Juan de Fuca, off Puget Sound. It is a distinctive Romanesque-style structure. [*National Register listing 05/30/91*]

Sedro Woolley

111 Woodworth Street

LOUIS A. SIMON – 1939

ONE OF SUPERVISING ARCHITECT Louis A. Simon's often used post office designs, this structure typifies his employment of standard elements, including the low-relief eagle sculpture over the main entrance of this simple, plain one-story structure constructed on a raised basement platform. Other examples of this type of "Starved-Classical" design can be found at Greybull, Wyoming, Kent, Washington, Clarkston, Washington, and Tillamook, Oregon. All of these post offices were completed between 1940 and 1941. [*National Register listing 08/07/91*]

Spokane

West 904 Riverside Avenue

JAMES KNOX TAYLOR – 1909

A GREAT DEAL OF CONTROVERSY surrounded the creation of the federal building at Spokane. The local community was enraged over the government's initial request that the site for the building should be donated, especially since property values were skyrocketing to a point where such a site was thought to be worth as much as $35,000 to $50,000. The government finally had to purchase the property for about $100,000.

The bickering continued, with disputes between the postmaster, Millard T. Hartson, and the Supervising Architect. Hartson was adamant that Taylor's design was inadequate. "We must have a five-story building; a three-story one will not accommodate the business," Hartson told the local newspaper, the *Spokesman-Review*, adding that "Mr. Taylor, the Supervising

Architect of the Treasury, positively refused to draw plans for a foundation of a five-story building unless it was settled that a five-story building was to be erected." Hartson had his way, but was no longer the postmaster when the five-story structure (including the basement and partial fourth floor) was completed in 1909. Extensions to the building were added during the Depression. [*National Register listing 12/08/83*]

Tacoma

1102 South A Street

JAMES KNOX TAYLOR – 1910

A THREE-STORY LIMESTONE structure, this Second Renaissance Revival style building served as a combination courthouse, customs house, and post office. The site for this building was acquired in 1903, but actual design and construction was significantly delayed because of the debate between the government and the American Institute of Architects over who was best capable of designing government buildings. The idea of conducting a design competition for this project stalled any work for more than five years. In the end the building was designed by the government's architect, James Knox Taylor, who chose to reuse architectural features that could also be found elsewhere in the state at the same time; including details for the federal buildings at Seattle (completed in 1909), Spokane (constructed in 1909), and Yakima (completed in 1912).

Among the greatest problems associated with the construction of the federal building at Tacoma was the public reaction to the use of "foreign" stone. Although the local community wanted the building to be faced in local Wilkerson sandstone, Taylor was adamant that Indiana limestone be used. This was seen as a great affront, one that was only diminished by the selection of a Spokane contractor to build the facility. [*National Register listing 05/30/91*]

Toppenish

14 Jefferson Avenue

LOUIS A. SIMON – 1938

TYPICAL OF NUMEROUS small-town post offices built during the Great Depression, this one-story red brick building was patterned after one of about a half-dozen standardized plans. Standardization of designs was essential during this time, so much so that the Treasury Department developed a set of "cabinet sketches" that provided standard floor plans for various sized offices nationwide. Wherever possible, the exterior details were changed to give these structures their individuality. In this particular case, the construction of the Toppenish post office, begun in 1937, was completed the following year. The facade is flat and essentially void of architectural detail; plain, but functional.

With respect to the number of federal projects initiated in Washington State, and in the nation for that matter, the Depression era was a particularly energetic period for post office construction. Nationwide, three times as many post offices were constructed between 1930 and 1939 as in the previous half century. In Washington state alone, 32 of the state's 44 federally constructed post offices were completed between 1933 and 1941. The rest were constructed between 1893 and 1918.

Waldron

Waldron Island

UNKNOWN – 1938

THIS IS AN ISOLATED SORT OF PLACE where one of the only ways to overcome loneliness is through the mail. The four-square-mile island has no phone service and all of its electricity is produced locally by generators. Its post office is one of the principal centers of the community and mail is a lifeline. According to the former postmaster, Alice Weaver: "The mail provides all connections—personal, business, reading material from the State library, periodicals and Parcel Post." Built of peeled logs, with oakum and grout filling the gaps, and a cedar-shake roof, Waldron's log cabin post office was constructed in 1938 as a general store and post office. The store portion of the place closed down during World War II.

This log post office in Waldron, Washington, is situated in one of the most remotely beautiful parts of the country.

WYOMING

Basin

402 West C Street

JAMES A. WETMORE – 1919

WHILE THE ARCHITECTURAL community generally disliked the buildings designed by the Office of the Supervising Architect, the director of that office in 1919, James A. Wetmore, praised the standardization made possible by the Treasury Department's "Classification System for Federal Buildings," a method of categorizing future building needs in accordance with the annual postal receipts of the community. Wetmore supported this concept, claiming that it was a way to "provide a rational system of uniformity and business economy in designing and constructing federal buildings, suitable in each instance to the public needs and without calling for waste in Government money." At a time when he was designing the Basin post office, Wetmore envisioned the possibility of creating a "master type of building for small communities," one that could perhaps be used in as many as 30 locations then under consideration, including Basin. Under the government's classification scheme, buildings with a post office having annual receipts of under $15,000 were to resemble an "ordinary class of building, such as any businessman would consider a reasonable investment in a small town." This one-story, buff-colored brick structure was built at a cost of $36,500 to serve a population of about 1,000.

Buffalo

193 South Main Street

JAMES A. WETMORE – 1928

THE PROPERTY FOR THE BUILDING was acquired in 1911, but because of World War I, the building was delayed. This was upsetting to the citizens of Buffalo, who were informed by the Treasury Department that the nation's resources were being diverted to the war effort and that they would just have to wait. Congressman Frank Mondell was specificially told that "unless this is done it will be impossible for the people of the United States to furnish the money which the Government must have to support our soldiers and sailors who are shedding their blood for us upon the battle fields." Mondell, who was a champion for the building, was promised that "this building will be progressed as rapidly as possible after the return of peace." However, it was ten long years after the 1918 Armistice before the construction was finally completed, due to the frugal mood of the country following the war.

This two-story buff-colored brick federal building was constructed on a raised basement by Charles Weiss and Sons of Des Moines, Iowa, and was dedicated on February 1, 1928. [*National Register listing 05/19/87*]

Douglas

129 North Third Street

OSCAR WENDEROTH – 1916

AMONG THE MOST STRIKING features of this two-story red brick post office are the broad overhanging eaves of its copper-clad hipped roof and its exceptionally fine brickwork, which includes a woven herringbone pattern with diamond-shaped inserts highlighting the sill line of the second floor windows. In many respects this building represents a bricklayer's dream come true. The site was acquired in 1909 and, although funds were allocated for the construction of the building in 1910, the work was delayed until 1914. The contractor, J. F. Jenkins Company of Ocala, Florida, completed the project in February 1916 for $60,850. [*National Register listing 05/19/87*]

Lander

177 North Third Street

JAMES KNOX TAYLOR – 1912

SENATOR CLARENCE D. CLARK took up the cause of getting a new post office for Lander in January 1908 and achieved fast results. The site for the building was purchased in April 1908, and the initial sketches were presented in September. The drawings bear an uncanny resemblance to the federal building at Cheyenne on a somewhat smaller scale. Final plans were submitted in April 1910, and construction bids were received and a selection made the following month, for a low bid of $99,343. In October the first of eight train car loads of materials began arriving from around the country, including Vermont granite, Pennsylvania structural steel, Oregon lumber, and Illinois terra cotta. The resulting Second Renaissance style three-story building, embellished with brick quoins which greatly exaggerate the horizontal importance of the main section of the facade, was dedicated in 1912.

[*National Register listing 05/19/87*]

Thermopolis

440 Arapahoe Street

JAMES A. WETMORE – 1933

A SMALL COMBINED post office and court house, the one-story brick and limestone federal building at Thermopolis was the city's first federally constructed post office. This structure was said to have only one equal in Wyoming, the massive court house and post office at Evanston completed in 1908. The main facade is distinguished by a five-bay limestone-clad central section flanked by two brick-faced end wings with limestone corner quoins. The five dormers on the red quarry-tile covered low-rise hipped roof gives the impression of a second-story, but this is an illusion that raises the importance of the attic area. [*National Register listing 05/19/87*]

Torrington

2145 Main Street

JAMES A. WETMORE – 1933

THE ONLY POST OFFICE in Wyoming that incorporates Art Deco embellishments, such as its bas-relief terra cotta American eagle over the main entrance, in an otherwise "Starved-Classical" shell, the one-story buff-colored brick post office at Torrington served a community of only about 1,800 residents in 1933 when it opened to the public. The town's small size almost doomed the project, because of a requirement that before a town would be authorized for this size post office it had to have receipts of $20,000 annually, which Torrington did not have. Congressional intervention apparently resolved this slight problem, and funds were appropriated in 1930. Construction, by Building Reconstruction, Inc., of Chicago, started in the spring of 1931 and resulted in the completion of what an article in the June 8th issue of the *Torrington Telegram* called the "greatest single accomplishment of the little town which sprang to life in 1889 in a dreary waste of sagebrush cactus, and marks the turning point to even greater development in the years to come." [*National Register listing 05/19/87*]

INFORMATION SOURCES

The following organizations and agencies can provide further information on subjects covered in *Great American Post Offices.* In addition, state historic preservation offices, state and local historical societies, and local post offices often have information concerning post office sites and architecture.

The National Postal Museum
Smithsonian Institution
Washington, D.C. 20560

Historian
United States Postal Service
475 L'Enfant Plaza, S.W.
Washington, D.C. 20260

Chief Archivist
Record Group 28
National Archives and Records Administration
Washington, D.C. 20408

National Register of Historic Places
Post Office Box 37127
Washington, D.C. 20013

National Trust for Historic Preservation
1785 Massachusetts Avenue, N.W.
Washington, D.C. 20036

Postal History Foundation
Post Office Box 40725
Tucson, Arizona 85717

FURTHER READING

Baker, J. David. *The Postal History of Indiana.* Louisville, Kentucky: L.H. Hartman. 1976.

Bauer, William H., James L. Ozment and John H. Willard. *Colorado Post Offices, 1859-1989.* Denver, Colorado: Colorado Railroad Museum. 1990.

Bauhman, Robert Williamson. *Kansas Post Offices, May 29, 1828-August 3, 1961.* Topeka, Kansas: Kansas Postal History Society. 1961.

Beckham, Sue Bridwell. *Depression Post Office Murals and Southern Culture: A Gentle Reconstruction.* Baton Rouge, Louisiana: Louisiana State University Press. 1989.

Blumenson, John J.-G. *Identifying American Architecture.* New York: W. W. Norton & Company. 1981.

Cheney, Roberta Carkeek. *Names on the Faces of Montana.* Missoula, Montana: Mountain Press Publishing Company. 1987.

Craig, Lois. *The Federal Presence: Architecture, Politics, and National Design.* Cambridge, Massachusetts: The MIT Press, 1984.

Crowther, Frank M. and Lawrence M. Merolla. *Post Offices of Delaware and the District of Columbia.* Hyannis, Massachusetts: H. J. W. Daugherty. 1978.

Dow, Sterling T. *Maine Postal History and Postmarks.* Lawrence, Massachusetts: Quarterman Publications. 1976.

Frazier, D. R. *Tennessee Post Offices and Postmaster Appointments, 1789-1984.* Dover, Tennessee: D. R. Frazier. 1984.

Gallagher, John S. *The Post Offices of Ohio.* Burtonsville, Maryland: The Depot. 1979.

Gallagher, John S. *The Post Offices of Utah.* Burtonsville, Maryland: The Depot. 1977.

Gallagher, John S. and Alan H. Patera. *Wyoming Post Offices, 1850-1980.* Burtonsville, Maryland: The Depot. 1980.

Harris, Robert P. *Nevada Postal History, 1861 to 1972.* Santa Cruz, California: Bonanza Press. 1973.

Helbock, Richard W. *Oklahoma Post Offices.* Lake Oswego, Oregon: La Posta Publications. 1987.

Helbock, Richard W. *Oregon Post Offices, 1847-1982.* Lake Oswego, Oregon: Raven Press. 1985.

Kay, John L. and Chester M. Smith, Jr. *New York Postal History: The Post Offices and First Postmasters from 1775 to 1980.* State College, Pennsylvania: American Philatelic Society. 1982.

Marling, Karal Ann. *Wall to Wall America: A Cultural History of Post Office Murals in the Great Depression.* Minneapolis, Minnesota: University of Minnesota Press. 1982.

McCarter, John G. *A Postal History Reference for the State of Kentucky.* Memphis, Tennessee: J. G. McCarter. 1985.

Merolla, Lawrence M. and Frank M. Crowther. *The Post Offices of Massachussets.* North Abington, Massachussetts: Massachussetts Postal Research Society. 1981.

Patera, Alan H. *The Post Offices of Connecticut.* Burtonsville, Maryland: The Depot. 1977.

Patera, Alan H. and John S. Gallagher. *The Post Offices of Minnesota.* Burtonsville, Maryland: The Depot. 1978.

Phillips, George H. *The Post Offices of South Dakota, 1861-1930.* Crete, Nebraksa: J-B Publishing Company. 1975.

Putnam, R. E. and G. E. Carlson. *Architectual and Building Trade Dictionary.* Chicago, Illinois: American Technical Society. 1974.

Ricks, Melvin B. *Directory of Alaska Post Offices and Postmasters.* Ketchikan, Alaska: Tongass Publishing Company. 1965.

Salley, Harold E. *History of California Post Offices, 1846-1976.* La Mesa, California: Postal History Associates. 1977.

Schmidt, Walter G. *An Encyclopedia of Texas Post Offices: Texas Post Offices Under Five Flags.* Chicago, Illinois: The Collectors' Club of Chicago. 1993.

Schultz, Robert G. *Missouri Post Offices, 1804-1981.* St. Louis, Missouri: St. Louis Branch of the American Philatelic Society. 1982.

Slawson, George Clarke, Arthur W. Bingham, and Sprague W. Drenan. *The Postal History of Vermont.* New York: Collectors Club. 1969.

Smith, Chester M. *The Postal History of Maryland.* Burtonsville, Maryland: The Depot. 1984.

Smith, Chester M. *The Postal History of New Hampshire.* Lake Grove, Oregon: The Depot. 1986.

Theobald, John. *Arizona Territory: Post Offices and Postmasters.* Phoenix, Arizona: Arizona Historical Foundation. 1961.

U.S. Government. *Reports of the Supervising Architect.* Government Printing Office. Washington, D.C. 1890s.

U.S. Government. *Annual Reports of the Postmaster General.* Government Printing Office. Washington, D.C. 1840s-1990s.

ILLUSTRATION CREDITS

Page x: Country store post office: National Postal Museum, Smithsonian Institution.

Page x: General Post Office, Washington, D.C.: National Postal Museum, Smithsonian Institution.

Page xiii: College Hill, Mississippi, post office: National Postal Museum,Smithsonian Institution.

Page 2: Interior of the New York post office: Joseph Cohen, United States Postal Service.

Page 4: Merchant's coffeehouse: Joseph Cohen, United States Postal Service.

Page 5: Post rider: National Postal Museum, Smithsonian Institution.

Page 7: Ladies reading letters: National Postal Museum, Smithsonian Institution.

Page 8: Roosevelt, Arizona: National Postal Museum, Smithsonian Institution.

Page 9: Cheyenne, Wyoming: National Postal Museum, Smithsonian Institution.

Page 10: Oklahoma City: National Postal Museum, Smithsonian Institution.

Page 11: Ransacking Charleston's post office: National Postal Museum, Smithsonian Institution.

Page 13: Invitation to the opening of the New York City post office, 1845: Joseph Cohen, United States Postal Service.

Page 14: Interior of the New York City post office: Joseph Cohen, United States Postal Service.

Page 15: Philadelphia's Merchant's Exchange: National Postal Museum, Smithsonian Institution.

Page 16: Chicago post office: National Postal Museum, Smithsonian Institution.

Page 17: Railroad terminals: National Postal Museum, Smithsonian Institution.

Page 18: Ladies window: Joseph Cohen, United States Postal Service.

Page 20: Lafayette, Indiana: National Postal Museum, Smithsonian Institution.

Page 21: 1890s Illinois post office: National Postal Museum, Smithsonian Institution.

Page 22: Marta, Texas, post office: National Postal Museum, Smithsonian Institution.

Page 23: Interior of post office: National Postal Museum, Smithsonian Institution.

Page 24: Exterior view of post office: National Postal Museum, Smithsonian Institution.

Page 31: Female postmaster: National Postal Museum, Smithsonian Institution.

Page 32: Rural letter carrier in Virginia: National Postal Museum, Smithsonian Institution.

Page 45: Rural letter carrier in Michigan: National Postal Museum, Smithsonian Institution.

Page 46: Interior of post office: National Postal Museum, Smithsonian Institution.

Page 52: Princeton, New Jersey, post office: Postmaster, Princeton, New Jersey.

Page 57: Supervising Architect's renderings: National Postal Museum, Smithsonian Institution.

Page 58: Alfred Mullett rendering of Boston post office: National Postal Museum, Smithsonian Institution.

Page 59: Springfield, Missouri, post office: Postmaster, Springfield, Missouri.

Page 60: William Martin Aiken's rendering of Paterson post office: National Postal Museum, Smithsonian Institution.

Page 62: Galena, Illinois, post office: Postmaster, Galena, Illinois.

Page 63: Washington, D.C., post office: National Postal Museum, Smithsonian Institution.

Page 64: Alfred Mullett rendering of Charleston, South Carolina, federal building: National Postal Museum, Smithsonian Institution.

Page 65: Second Empire post offices: National Postal Museum, Smithsonian Institution.

Page 67: Alfred Mullett rendering of the Chicago post office: National Postal Museum, Smithsonian Institution.

Page 70: Supervising Architect's renderings: National Postal Museum, Smithsonian Institution.

Page 71: Port Townsend, Washington, federal building: Greg L. Emerick and Jim Espensen, United States Postal Service.

Page 72: Mifflin Bell rendering of Aberdeen, Mississippi, post office: National Postal Museum, Smithsonian Institution.

Page 72: Workroom floor, St. Louis: National Postal Museum, Smithsonian Institution.

Page 73: Bridgeport, Connecticut, federal building: National Postal Museum, Smithsonian Institution.

Page 73: Rochester, New York, federal building: national Postal Museum, Smithsonian Institution.

Page 74: James Knox Taylor rendering of Waterloo, Iowa, post office: National Postal Museum, Smithsonian Institution.

Page 76: San Francisco postal station: National Postal Museum, Smithsonian Institution.

Page 78: Georgetown, South Carolina, post office: Postmaster, Georgetown, South Carolina, United States Postal Service.

Page 79: James Knox Taylor rendering of Los Angeles federal building: National Postal Museum, Smithsonian Institution.

Page 80: Supervising Architect's renderings: National Postal Museum, Smithsonian Institution.

Page 84: National Postal Museum building: National Postal Museum, Smithsonian Institution.

Page 85: Postal Savings cartoon: National Postal Museum, Smithsonian Institution.

Page 89: Parcel Post cartoon: National Postal Museum, Smithsonian Institution.

Page 91: Parcel Post shoppers: National Postal Museum, Smithsonian Institution.

Page 94: Wakefield, Rhode Island, post office: William P. Harrington, United States Postal Service.

Page 95: Ellenville, New York, post office: Martin A. Crossey, United States Postal Service.

Page 96: Princeton, New Jersey, post office lobby mural: Victor M. Zuczek, United States Postal Service.

Page 98: General mail facility, Houston, Texas: National Postal Museum, Smithsonian Institution.

Page 101: Pacific Grove, California, letter carrier Ralph Kent: courtesy Genevieve Noyes.

Page 102: Chicago post office: Rosetta Johnson, United States Postal Service.

Page 105: Letter carrier badge: courtesy Genevieve Noyes.

Page 106: Exterior of Memphis, Tennessee, post office: James Bruns.

Page 108: Boston federal building: Postmaster, Boston, Massachusetts, United States Postal Service.

Page 110: Hartford post office frieze: Ewin P. Sanchez, Jr., United States Postal Service.

Page 115: Concord, New Hampshire, post office: National Postal Museum, Smithsonian Institution.

Page 116: Littleton, New Hampshire, post office: Bob Uisnovckas, United States Postal Service.

Page 117: Mifflin Bell rendering of Manchester, New Hampshire, post office: National Postal Museum, Smithsonian Institution.

Page 119: Pawtucket, Rhode Island, post office: National Postal Museum, Smithsonian Institution.

Page 119: Providence, Rhode Island, post office: National Postal Museum, Smithsonian Institution.

Page 123: Views of Plymouth, Vermont, post office: National Postal Museum, Smithsonian Institution.

Page 124: Kenton, Delaware, post office: Robert M. Biger.

Page 129: Post Office Department headquarters, Washington, D.C.: National Postal Museum, Smithsonian Institution.

Page 130: Postal Service headquarters, Washington, D.C.: United States Postal Service.

Page 131: James Knox Taylor rendering of Annapolis, Maryland, post office: national Postal Museum. Smithsonian Institution.

Page 133: Westminster, Maryland, post office: Postmaster, Westminster, Maryland, United States Postal Service.

Page 134: Jersey City, New Jersey, post office: Frank Baronne, United States Postal Service.

Page 136: Albany, New York, post office: National Postal Museum, Smithsonian Institution.

Page 138: New York City General Post Office: Joseph Cohen, United States Postal Service.

Page 140: Poughkeepsie, New York, post office: Al Nowak/On Line Studios, Inc.

Page 141: Dillsburg, Pennsylvania, post office screenline: National Postal Museum, Smithsonian Institution.

Page 144: Bristol, Virginia, post office: Roger Mangus, United States Postal Service.

Page 145: James Store, Virginia, post office: Herb Barnes, *Daily Press/Times*

Page 146: Richmond, Virginia, federal building: National Postal Museum, Smithsonian Institution.

Page 147: Elkhorn, West Virginia, post office: Joan Semonco, United States Postal Service.

Page 147: Fairmont, West Virginia, post office: Debbie Sanford, United States Postal Service.

Page 148: Headsville, West Virginia, post office: National Postal Museum, Smithsonian Institution.

Page 150: Magnolia Springs, Alabama, post office: Kaye Manders, United States Postal Service.

Page 152: Clopton, Alabama, post office: Betty S. Deloney, United States Postal Service.

Page 153: Fairfield, Alabama, post office: Less C. Burkart, United States Postal Service.

Page 155: Little Rock, Arkansas, federal building: National Postal Museum, Smithsonian Institution.

Page 156: Key West, Florida, post office: National Postal Museum, Smithsonian Institution.

Page 158: Miami Beach, Florida, post office: Michael R. Miles, United States Postal Service.

Page 159: Ochopp, Florida, post office: National Postal Museum, Smithsonian Institution.

Page 162: Savanna, Georgia, federal building: Sandy Moore, United States Postal Service.

Page 164: Covington, Kentucky, post office: Robert Winters, United States Postal Service.

Page 167: New Orleans, Louisiana, federal building: National Postal Museum, Smithsonian Institution.

Page 169: Aberdeen, Mississippi, post office: F.S. McKnight Collection, Evans Memorial Library, Aberdeen, Mississippi.

Page 171: Vicksburg, Mississippi, federal building: Mississippi River Commission, Lower Mississippi Valley Division.

Page 173: Alfred Mullett's rendering of the Raleigh, North Carolina, federal building:National Postal Museum, Smithsonian Institution.

Page 175: Charleston Exchange Building: Davis W. Wild, United States Postal Service.

Page 179: Jellico, Tennessee, post office: Ha Ree Odon, United States Postal Service.

Page 180: Memphis, Tennessee, federal building: National Postal Museum, Smithsonian Institution.

Page 181: Nashville, Tennessee, federal building: National Postal Museum, Smithsonian Institution.

Page 182: Alfred Mullett's rendering of Cairo, Illinois, federal building: National Postal Museum, Smithsonian Institution.

Page 188: William Potter's rendering of Evanville, Indiana, federal building: National Postal Museum, Smithsonian Institution.

Page 191: Atchison, Kansas, post office: Wayne L. Gibson, United States Postal Service.

Page 194: Weskan, Kansas, post office: Mary L. Glad, United States Postal Service.

Page 197: William Aiken's rendering of Saginaw, Michigan, federal building:National Postal Museum, Smithsonian Institution.

Page 199: Minneapolis, Minnesota, post office: Jim Ahlgren, United States Postal Service.

Page 202: Berger, Missouri, post office: National Postal Museum, Smithsonian Institution.

Page 202: Louisiana, Missouri, post office: National Postal Museum, Smithsonian Institution.

Page 203: Notch, Missouri, post office: National Postal Museum, Smithsonian Institution.

Page 204: St. Louis, Missouri, federal building: National Postal Museum, Smithsonian Institution.

Page 209: Cleveland, Ohio, federal building: National Postal Museum, Smithsonian Institution.

Page 211: Toledo, Ohio, post Office: National Postal Museum, Smithsonian Institution.

Page 216: Craig, Alaska, post office in a jar: National Postal Museum, Smithsonian Institution.

Page 221: Yuma, Arizona, post office: Postmaster, Yuma, Arizona, United States Postal Service.

Page 224: Modesto, California, post office: National Postal Museum, Smithsonian Institution.

Page 225: San Francisco, California, federal building: National Postal Museum, Smithsonian Institution.

Page 230: Honolulu, Hawaii, post office: National Postal Museum, Smithsonian Institution.

Page 243: Palace of the Governors, Santa Fe, New Mexico: National Postal Museum, Smithsonian Institution.

Page 245: Kingfisher, Oklahoma, post office: National Postal Museum, Smithsonian Institution.

Page 246: Corvallis, Oregon, post office: John Herrington, United States Postal Service.

Page 248: Fanthorp Inn, Anderson, Texas: Terry A. Edwards, United States Postal Service.

Page 252: Texarkana, Texas, federal building: National Postal Museum, Smithsonian Institution.

Page 254: Helper, Utah, post office: Walter L. Borla, United States Postal Service.

Page 256: Cedar stump post office: National Postal Museum, Smithsonian Institution.

Page 259: Waldron, Washington, post office: Richard Brommett.

INDEX